The publisher and the University of California Press Foundation gratefully acknowledge the generous support of the George Gund Foundation Imprint in African American Studies.

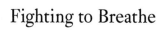

Fighting to Breathe

CALIFORNIA SERIES IN PUBLIC ANTHROPOLOGY

The California Series in Public Anthropology emphasizes the anthropologist's role as an engaged intellectual. It continues anthropology's commitment to being an ethnographic witness, to describing, in human terms, how life is lived beyond the borders of many readers' experiences. But it also adds a commitment, through ethnography, to reframing the terms of public debate—transforming received, accepted understandings of social issues with new insights, new framings.

Series Editor: Ieva Jusionyte (Harvard University)
Founding Editor: Robert Borofsky (Hawaii Pacific University)
Advisory Board: Catherine Besteman (Colby College),
Philippe Bourgois (UCLA), Jason De León (UCLA),
Laurence Ralph (Princeton University), and
Nancy Scheper-Hughes (UC Berkeley)

Fighting to Breathe

*Race, Toxicity, and the Rise of
Youth Activism in Baltimore*

Nicole Fabricant

UNIVERSITY OF CALIFORNIA PRESS

University of California Press
Oakland, California

© 2023 by Nicole Fabricant

Library of Congress Cataloging-in-Publication Data

Names: Fabricant, Nicole, author.
Title: Fighting to breathe : race, toxicity, and the rise of youth activism in Baltimore / Nicole
   Fabricant.
Other titles: California series in public anthropology ; 54.
Description: Oakland, California : University of California Press, [2023] | Series: California
   series in public anthropology ; [vol 54] | Includes bibliographical references and index.
Identifiers: LCCN 2022022528 (print) | LCCN 2022022529 (ebook) | ISBN 9780520379312 (cloth) |
   ISBN 9780520379329 (paperback) | ISBN 9780520976627 (epub)
Subjects: LCSH: Air—Pollution—Social aspects—Maryland—Baltimore. | Youth
   movements—Maryland—Baltimore—21st century.
Classification: LCC TD883.5.M32 B35 2023 (print) | LCC TD883.5.M32 (ebook) |
   DDC 363.739/2097526—dc23/eng/20220812
LC record available at https://lccn.loc.gov/2022022528
LC ebook record available at https://lccn.loc.gov/2022022529

31 30 29 28 27 26 25 24 23 22
10 9 8 7 6 5 4 3 2 1

I dedicate this book to two freedom fighters:
Michael Fabricant (my father) and
Marleny Soleto de Arauz (my mother-in-law).

CONTENTS

Conclusion
153

ILLUSTRATIONS

CHARACTERS

In place of real names I have used pseudonyms throughout the book, except for Destiny Watford, Marvin Hayes, Gary Liss, Brenda Platt, and other public (often political) figures.

Jimmy Brown: Grew up in Cherry Hill public housing and joined Free Your Voice (FYV) through our 2016–2017 participatory action class at Benjamin Franklin High School (BFHS).

Cheryl Casciani: Baltimore City Board of School Commissioners member who visited Curtis Bay with Destiny on a toxic tour.

Ricardo Chavez: A Latinx organizer from The Worker Justice Center.

Councilwoman Mary Pat Clarke: Baltimore City Council member representing District 14. Frequent Baltimore City Council member and sometime president from 1975 until 2020. Also a champion of zero waste.

Elizabeth Doran: Physicians for Social Responsibility. She was part of the original Dream Team and has more recently led toxic tours of Curtis Bay for Towson University students.

Rosalyn Drey and **Leanna Jackson**: FYV students who cowrote and performed a rap at the Board of Education meeting.

Damion Floyd and **Juan Gonzalez**: The sole members of the first cohort of Baltimore Compost Collective youth workers.

Crystal Green: FYV student, later a United Workers (UW) organizer and South Baltimore Land Trust organizer.

Marvin Hayes: Director of the Baltimore Compost Collective and a youth advocate and mentor.

Nicole Hughes: Towson University anthropology student and mentor for BFHS cohort 2018–2019.

Angela Johnson: Head of the Environmental Science Program at BFHS.

Terrel Jones: FYV student who experienced multiple housing displacements and homelessness.

Gary Liss: Hired by Free Your Voice youth as a private consultant to create a zero-waste plan for Baltimore City.

Stephanie Logan: Towson University anthropology student and mentor for BFHS cohort 2018–2019.

Dario Lopez: Started organizing with Free Your Voice at fourteen. Grew up in Lakeland and first-generation Central American.

Jeanette Love: Intern for Neighborhood Design Center as well as an artist and activist in general.

Henry Lowry: Steelworker, union member, and supporter of the trash-to-energy incinerator.

Maureen McDonald: Architect at Neighborhood Design Center who cotaught our participatory action class 2016–2017 and 2017–2018.

Luis Mendoza: FYV student who was arrested at sit-in.

Daniel Murphy: Worker Justice Center organizer responsible for South Baltimore region.

Brenda Platt: Director of Composting for Community Project at the Institute for Local Self-Reliance (ILSR).

Councilman Ed Reisinger: Baltimore City Council member representing District 6 and zero-waste champion.

Mia Sanchez: A Free Your Voice organizer and artist who painted a portrait of Harriet Tubman along with the word *Lead* on the stage at the land trust lot.

Mayor Brandon Scott: Baltimore City mayor and member of the Democratic party elected in 2020. Formerly, he was president of the Baltimore City Council.

Janette Simpson: Professor in Fiber Department at Maryland Institute College of Art and a member of the Dream Team.

Kenneth Smith: Free Your Voice student in 2018–2019 cohort and later a Free Your Voice organizer.

Daisy Thompson: Started with Chesapeake Center for Youth Development; later The Worker Justice Center organizer and executive director of South Baltimore Land Trust.

David Upton: Youth composter for Baltimore Compost Collective (2019–2022).

Angela Warren: Designed a solar plan for Food Machinery and Chemical Corporation (FMC), which was the proposed site for the nation's largest trash-to-energy incinerator.

Destiny Watford: Free Your Voice student; later The Worker Justice Center organizer and a South Baltimore Land Trust organizer.

Mayor Jack Young: Democratic interim mayor for Baltimore City from 2019 to 2020. He was president of the City Council when former mayor Catherine Pugh was indicted for a children's book fraud and forced to resign from office.

FOREWORD

James Baldwin once said, "If I love you, I have to make you conscious of the things you don't see." And then there was my grandmother, who would often say, when I was growing up, "When you know better, do better."

We currently have over one hundred thousand people dying prematurely from air pollution across the country each year, which is more than those dying from drug overdoses, car crashes, or gun violence. Over one million children in the United States have lead poisoning, slowly draining them of the possibilities of an extended, and high-quality life. The same communities that house these children endure dangerously high levels of air pollution and other toxins. Relatedly, in our nation we have twenty-five million adults and seven million children suffering from asthma. Latinx and African American children are disproportionately rushed to hospital emergency rooms due to asthma complications, and in these neighborhoods, residents are now more likely to die from COVID-19 than those who live in areas with lower rates of air pollution.

For decades, broken systems driven by systemic racism and significant disinvestments have placed our most vulnerable communities living amidst toxic pollution, shortening our lives and weakening the economic foundations that are critical for healthy and sustainable communities. Yet we have too many leaders, including politicians, choosing to not notice the public health and environmental crises in Black, Brown and working class communities. When our leaders fail to see, it can be easy for us to do the same, making it all the more important to document the exceptions.

In the Curtis Bay community of Baltimore, Maryland, and thousands of others like it there is a rallying cry: "I can't breathe." This call for justice is an illumination of the grave injustices that continue to play out in vulnerable communities across our country. It is also a battle cry, calling allies to the frontlines to force positive change in communities that have often been the dumping grounds for toxic pollution. This book, *Fighting to Breathe*, is so much more than the documentation of some things that happened on the South Baltimore Peninsula from 2011 to 2021. It is a blueprint for how we begin the long journey from "surviving" to "thriving."

To achieve this goal, we must put power back into the hands of the people. Nicole Fabricant, like the authors of the "Principles of Environmental Justice," formulated at the 1991 National People of Color Environmental Leadership Summit, reminds us that community members of all ages can and, more importantly, *need* to be equal partners in development work from start to finish. She reminds us, too, that environmental justice is a human right.

Residents in communities like Curtis Bay are shifting paradigms by reclaiming their power and demanding that authentic collaborative partnerships honor their voices, knowledge, and experiences. The information shared in this book will prepare new generations of leaders with the skills necessary to navigate twenty-first-century policies and develop a set of winning solutions. The strategies for change developed and implemented by students at Benjamin Franklin High School and the South Baltimore Community Land Trust reinforce the fact that youth in partnership with community activists have the innovation and ingenuity to create transformational change. These remind us that art and culture build bridges by educating onlookers, facilitating dialogues, and enabling the collective envisioning of something better. In so doing, they create opportunities for neighborhoods to determine their futures for themselves.

Beyoncé (Giselle Knowles-Carter)—North American singer and songwriter—aptly once shared, "You have the power to change perception, to inspire and empower, and to show people how to embrace their complications, and see the flaws, and the true beauty and strength that's inside all of us." This anthology of stories, actions, and strategies not only helps us to reconnect with our own humanity, but it also breathes life into all those who are fighting against environmental injustices, pointing us, once again, toward the north star of justice. My sincere hope is that the residents of Curtis Bay in Baltimore, Maryland, who have been "fighting to breathe" for nearly a century—and everyone else living the injustices of environmental racism—no longer find themselves in a sacrifice zone, where residents are literally dying for a breath of fresh air, a drink of clean water, and land free from toxic pollution.

Mustafa Santiago Ali
CEO and Founder of Revitalization Strategies
Vice President at the National Wildlife Federation (NWF)
Chief of Programs, Union of Concerned Scientists (UCS)

PREFACE

In New York City in 2014, Eric Garner was put into a prohibited choke hold by a police officer while other officers pinned him to the ground. In the minutes before his body went limp—documented in footage filmed by a bystander—the unarmed Garner can be heard gasping "I can't breathe" eleven times. Thus originated one of the most popular rallying cries of the Black Lives Matter movement. According to journalists for the *New York Times*, by June 29, 2020, Garner was one of at least seventy people who "died in law enforcement custody after saying [these] same words" (Baker et al. 2020). "I can't breathe" is now used around the world and in multiple languages at protests of and in shows of solidarity against police violence. But "I can't breathe" has an even deeper history. For generations, systemic racism has informed decisions about where to build oil and gas refineries and garbage infrastructure (including landfills and incinerators) and where to dump chemicals (including factory waste). In these cases, perpetrators have been unethical factory owners, racist real estate brokers, and NIMBY-focused urban planners.[1] Without choke holds, and without the knees of White cops on Black necks, they make it so that people of color must fight to breathe.

Sociologists Lindsey Dillon and Julie Sze described breathing as "typically unnoticed, unconsidered, unseen—an invisible other—that becomes visible in particular moments for particular groups" (Dillon and Sze 2016). Likewise, generations of Black and Brown men, women, and children who have organized against the contamination of their airways, as well as their soil and waterways, are "typically unnoticed." Environmental activists of color fighting to save their communities were, and continue to be, overshadowed by White-led campaigns that were less threatening to corporate profitability, and perhaps more comfortable (though here you must ask, for whom?) to "Save the Planet" and "Save the Animals." This book, with its focus on high school students of color who organized, protested, performed, demanded accountability, and designed solutions, asks you to notice, to consider, and to see breathing. More specifically, it asks you to learn to see the fight for "the right to breathe" in all of its complexities and including all of its participants. *Fighting to Breathe*, the title of this book, therefore, refers not only to the added work of inhaling and exhaling air pollutants in too many neighborhoods of color, but to the community-led activism that aims to end environmental racism in those same neighborhoods.

ACKNOWLEDGMENTS

"Who are you from?" Eric Jackson (servant director of Black Yield Institute in Cherry Hill) asked his students while leading a political education course in the Winter of 2020. This book is a product of who I am from.

Before acknowledging my most recent interlocutors, I honor and recognize my roots, and the roots of my political activism. Betsy and Michael Fabricant modeled a life of integrity, a life dedicated to the most disenfranchised. They built The Elizabeth Coalition to House the Homeless in Elizabeth, New Jersey. Summers they packed my brother and me up and headed to upstate New York where they were supervisors at Vacation Camp for the Blind. I grew up bridging these two worlds.

My father and mother are my greatest sources of inspiration. They carried me on their backs to demonstrations as my father fought local politicians in Elizabeth, New Jersey. They showed me how to give unconditionally and modeled the art of relationship building and organizing from a young age. My father's passion for justice is a fire that burns in his belly, and he passed that fire on to me.

Growing up in Elizabeth, New Jersey, shaped my understanding, from the start, of environmental injustice: My parents told me that when I was two, I used to pick up trash and announce to everyone within earshot that it belonged in the trash can. "What's that smell?" they remember me asking; "It smells like eggs." Not unlike the children on the South Baltimore Peninsula who identify the BRESCO trash incinerator as a "cloud maker," I interpreted the pollution around me as breakfast. Kids have a way of making sense of toxic worlds.

Predominantly first-generation Latinx and working-class Elizabeth also taught me to feel my race (white) and my class (middle). My parents sent me to public schools that gave me tools to navigate structural inequality and taught me to form allegiances and build solidarity in the face of difference. All of my childhood friends' parents migrated to the United States from Latin America. All came to work manual labor jobs inside factories and give their children opportunities for upward mobility. My first encounters with the violence and brutality of low-wage labor happened inside the homes of these adults, the parents of my dearest friends. By the age of five, I knew what economic struggle looked, smelled, and tasted like, especially for first-generation migrants and their families. Perhaps listening to the stories my friends' parents shared, hearing about their hardships in Elizabeth, made me want to become an anthropologist. By the time I was seventeen, I wanted to tell stories that were rarely, if ever, told.

I found public school in Elizabeth challenging. I recall rote learning, standardized testing, and disinvested teachers. But all of this changed when I arrived to a small liberal arts college in Western Massachusetts that would challenge me intellectually and give me the space and freedom to explore my academic passions. Mount Holyoke College (MHC) helped me find my voice. I had many mentors at MHC who shaped my desire to be an ethnographer and my passion for activism. It was there (at a predominantly white, upper-middle-class college) that I felt alone, and so I escaped to the grassy green fields of Holyoke to work with first-generation Puerto Rican farmers. It was there, with my hands in the dirt, learning about agroecology and surrounded by the sounds of merengue, salsa, and the Spanish language that I felt a sense of community. Mount

Holyoke gave me the classes I yearned for as a high school student. My mentor, Preston Smith (professor of politics), helped me to connect what I was learning in college to growing up in Elizabeth. He introduced me to community-based learning as a sophomore and taught me how to connect urban inequality and politics to the hands-on praxis of farming. Preston introduced me to radical urban studies scholars and marxist political scientists like Adolph Reed, and he encouraged me to theorize with and alongside urban farmers. I am forever grateful for what he taught me inside and outside the classroom. He, among many others at Mount Holyoke including Lynn Morgan and Andrew Lass helped to foster my political passions away from the classroom. I return to this undergraduate experience because it lit something inside of me, sparked a desire to learn even more.

While graduate school at Northwestern University was grueling, my mentors there transformed me into an intellectual. I knew I always wanted to have an office surrounded by books. At first, as a child, I thought I wanted to be a rabbi, but then realized that I was an atheist, so I settled for academia. Micaela di Leonardo gave me the tools to think and to write as a marxist. Mary Weismantel guided me through hundreds of books on gender and sexuality and Latin American social movements. Both provided a tremendous amount of support and encouraged me, just as my undergraduate advisors had, when my instincts were to escape the educational institution by integrating myself into the world of the Landless Peasant Movement (Movimiento Sin Tierra, or MST) in Bolivia. While graduate school was challenging, I have these two powerful Marxist feminists to thank for all they did in preparing me to be a fierce political economist. My daily discussions with Latin American historian and friend Josef Barton, also at Northwestern University, continually reminded me to "trace people's stories." He made me a sharper ethnographer. Josef Barton provided a tremendous amount of emotional labor and support as well.

When I got to Baltimore, post-PhD, I found a community of activist-intellectuals who pushed me to think harder and to become a better organizer. Destiny Watford and Michael Murphy pulled me into the Free Your Voice Energy Answers campaign in the early days, and I am so thankful that they took a chance on me that day in my office. Destiny was afraid that I was going to try to transform her into an anthropologist. Little did she know we would eventually be working together to free the tools of anthropology from the academy, teaching ethnographic research methods to Curtis Bay youth in the hopes that they would do more than write conference papers and peer-reviewed articles. I am so grateful for my community of freedom fighters: Daisy Thompson, Crystal Jones, Terrel Jones, Jimmy Brown, and so many other youth who have inspired me to not just teach about just transitions and "worlds otherwise" but to pull my students into movements fighting for housing justice and zero waste. None of what we did in the classroom as Free Your Voice would have been possible without Angela Johnson, who turned her environmental science class over to us in 2015. She has long been committed to liberatory education in which organizers and academics together build classroom curriculum. Thank you to Ms. Johnson and to Principal Christopher Battaglia at Benjamin Franklin High School! Thanks go out to all who have supported our classroom, including Marvin Hayes (who ignited in all of us "compost fever"!) and Brenda Platt (of the Local Institute for Self-Reliance), Dorcas Gilmore (who taught us about the importance of cooperatives and solidarity economics), and Aiden Faust (our favorite archivist from UB who helped us locate articles and build out our community-based archive). Kyle Pompey—a Baltimore-based photographer—has been documenting our movement as an organic photo-journalist since 2016. He taught and continues to teach Free Your Voice students how to use the camera, how to edit images, and how to build narratives within and through photography. We are forever grateful for his gifts to South Baltimore.

Through the work of organizing and teaching at Towson University, I found like-minded intellectuals and scholars who were meeting monthly as part of the Baltimore School. The Baltimore School is a school of thought rooted in discussions about inequality in Baltimore (focused foremost on the issues of race, sexuality, gender identity, and socioeconomic and immigration status) in relationship to political economy. Many of my ideas about "toxic entanglements" and how toxicity works alongside denial of services and predatory lending practices were strengthened by rich conversations with my interlocutors in the Baltimore School. Some of these comrades include John Duda, Kate Khatib, Lawrence Brown, Ailish Hopper, Nicole King, Lester Spence, Robbie Shilliam, Sarah Fouts, Christy Thornton, and Stuart Schrader. I love thinking alongside each one of you.

My two dear comrades in struggle who helped strengthen the book deserve their own acknowledgment: Nicole King and Lawrence Brown. Nicole King (associate professor of American studies, UMBC) started me down this path, as she had done oral history work in Fairfield, Wagner's Point, and Curtis Bay before I even arrived to Baltimore. We became fast friends and her public history course and research projects have become a model for how to do this kind of work *in and for* communities. Lawrence Brown (an equity scientist and Afrofuturist) has been a dear friend and interlocutor since our days organizing at Tent City around issues of homelessness in Baltimore. His book *The Black Butterfly: The Harmful Politics of Race and Space in America* (2019, Johns Hopkins University Press) is a vital resource for learning to think about our historically segregated city and how to build a truly just and equitable Baltimore. We will continue to think, teach, write, and organize together.

While The Worker Justice Center was my political home when I moved to Baltimore in 2011, due to the conflicts that arose pre-COVID-19 pandemic, I chose to throw myself into farm work at Black Yield Institute (an organization working to address food apartheid in Cherry Hill, Baltimore) in 2019 to the present. Eric Jackson (servant director of Black Yield) became a dear comrade. And he was the one friend who showed up to give me a hug when I was emotionally beaten down by the conflicts tearing The Worker Justice Center apart. He cared for and nurtured me when I felt I could no longer fight and assured me that my quest for accountability was honorable. I remember sitting at The Cherry Hill Urban Community Garden in tears over the things I had seen and heard; he listened and found the words I needed to keep fighting.

I owe a lot of thanks to Towson University for rolling the dice on me. My colleagues Matthew Durington and Samuel Collins chose me in 2010 (barely out of graduate school) when they knew I would bring my passions to Towson University. They knew how radical I was and never tempered my politics. On the contrary, they have both found resources and financial support for me to build meaningful relationships and partnerships throughout Baltimore. My co-conspirators Elyshia Aseltine, Heather Hax, and Jessica Shiller share my never-ending commitments to justice. Thanks, sisters!

Dean Terry Cooney was a tremendous source of support for this project and many others including my trips to West Virginia with students. Dean Chulos and Provost Melanie L. Perreaux both provided financial support for the project. Thank you.

Towson University has allowed me to push the boundaries as a teacher and educator. I look for and often mentor first-generation college students. I have taken these students everywhere with me, from Kayford Mountain in southwest Virginia to witness mountaintop removal coal mining, to southwestern Pennsylvania to hear from members of communities inside the belly of the beast that is natural gas fracking, to South Baltimore where we craft curriculum with high school students, and to the Cherry Hill Urban Community Garden. I am thankful for the ways they have challenged me, posed hard questions, and forced me to rethink my intellectual pursuits. I think of them in generations and cohorts. The first generation includes David Reische, Xitlali Ceballos, Antonio Hernandez, Kelly Mitchell, Natalie Demyan, and De Carlo Brown. The second generation includes Morgan Bengel, Cameron Rines, Corey Naden, Bilphena Yahwon, and Breya Johnson. The third generation includes Sabrina Thomas and Melissa Holler. And the last generation of Freedom Tigers includes Jasmine Allen, Alejandra Mora, Alyson Hatfield, Michaela Logan, Rachael Wallace, and Kierra

Suydam. This last generation became a tight-knit community of powerful women, supporting one another through the COVID-19 pandemic. Myeasha Taylor (Farm Manager for Black Yield) taught us the art of farming. We all turned ourselves over to the Cherry Hill Urban Community Garden, to building, and to feeding the community. You have kept me going during these difficult times! Keep the flame!

I owe a special thanks to my dear *Bolivianista* friends and co-thinkers Bret Gustafson, and Pamela Calla. You have sharpened my thinking on Bolivian social movements and supported my transition from Bolivia to Baltimore-based struggles for justice.

Kate Marshall (my editor at University of California Press) reached out to me as she was following my work with Free Your Voice on social media. I did not think there was a book in this project, but she persisted and continued to encourage me to move forward. She helped clarify what was important about this story and sat on benches to brainstorm with me at more than one AAA meeting. Thank you, Kate, for your commitments to radical scholarship! Enrique Ochoa-Kaup, who answered a million questions about maps, images, and layout: thank you, too.

I would be remiss not to thank my amazing friend and editor Dawn Pankonien. When I felt there was no book here and was ready to give up on the project, she breathed new life into this project. Her tremendous editorial skills during the wee hours of the night tightened the narrative and sharpened the characters. She stimulated me to get up at 4 a.m. during the Covid-19 pandemic to edit marked-up chapters and tighten my writing. This book is in large part what it is because of her tremendous commitment to this project. Thank you for understanding me and the story I wanted to tell.

Thank you to Mustafa Santiago Ali—a personal friend and mentor—for writing the foreword to this book. I continue to learn from him, grow through his wisdom, and occasionally convince him to come to Curtis Bay.

When I moved to Bolivia in 1999, I got to know Marleny Soleto de Arauz (my mother-in-law), who quickly became another of my personal heroes. Marleny opened her doors to the poor and needy. She cooked in a large pot and shared her food with anyone in the community who needed nourishment. She lived her politics through her hospitality and her cooking, as well as through countless other acts of kindness. Later, she would direct much of her kindness toward me when she came to share my home in Baltimore in 2011 and helped my husband (her son) and me raise our children. Marleny accompanied me during grueling days of organizing and activism, sharing with me the labor of feeding, caring for, and entertaining my two babies, and, in so doing, she made it possible for them to grow up in movement spaces just as I once had. Even while she was sick, toward the end of her life, Marleny continued to give, helping Free Your Voice students and other activists with the hard manual labor of clearing land for the South Baltimore Community Land Trust lot, and always feeding organizers with her delicious baked goods. She died unexpectedly as I was writing this book, and her absence left a hole in our world. This book is a product of Marleny's spirit of generosity and her daily acts of care, what many social scientists call "kin work." May her spirit live on from generation to generation.

My husband, Luis Arauz, and my two children, Amelia and Ariel "Ari" Arauz, have supported me and nourished me through the writing of this book. They have cooked dinners together, danced around the house, sang songs to me, and made me laugh when there was such darkness in the world. My kids have grown up in this movement (when Ari was two years old, he shouted on his way to preschool, "What do we want? Justice! When do we want it? Now!"). I am thankful for all the Baltimore activists who have adopted my family as fictive kin and inspired us to continue to fight for justice.

May we fight so that our families and all of Baltimore's children can live in an equitable and sustainable city.

Introduction

On the South Baltimore Peninsula, where this book is set, breathing is complicated. There, toxic emissions are among the highest in the nation. Take, for example, the case of Curtis Bay, one of six neighborhoods located on the peninsula. From 2005 to 2009, the Curtis Bay zip code (21226) ranked among the top ten zip codes in the country for the quantity of air toxins released, and it ranked first in the country for toxic air pollution from stationary sources with 20.6 to 21.6 million pounds of air pollutants released into the atmosphere each year (Environmental Integrity Project 2012). Even after hospitalization rates for asthma in Curtis Bay fell in 2016 (due largely to legislation that enforced pollution controls for the coal-fired power plants in the area), the neighborhood continued to have one of the highest rates of respiratory illness in the state. In 2012–2013, the Environmental Integrity Project (EIP) research team noted that as a result of the cumulative effects of stationary toxic industries, Curtis Bay–Brooklyn was one of the highest-risk areas in the nation for respiratory problems. As a whole, Baltimore City is in bad shape, too. In 2013, the asthma hospitalization rate in Baltimore was 2.3 times higher than Maryland's average. Asthma emergency room visits in Baltimore were 2.5 times the state average (Environmental Integrity Project 2012).

Fighting to Breathe focuses primarily on high school students who, along with their teachers and allies, chose to fight the individuals and organizations responsible for the levels of toxicity that underlie these statistics. For more than a decade, the students worked to eradicate inequities in land use and waste management, two intersecting systems that have exacerbated uneven development and the race- and class-based health disparities that persist in Baltimore today. The goals of the students were not simply to understand systems of inequality but to envision, design, and create development alternatives that would improve the lives of poor Black and Brown people. Their proposals for and then actions toward new, better, more just urban development were intended to meet human needs rather than industry needs.

Baltimore development policy and implementation to date have produced a devastating palimpsest: more than a century of unjust housing, environmental, and other state laws perpetuate the exploitation of some but not all lands for industrial production. While factories are condensed into specific neighborhoods, their owners are empowered by a layering over of pro-industry policies, adopting practices that maximize their profits while threatening the respiratory systems of the humans—employees as well as neighbors—who share airways with those factories. Most of the time, this adversely impacts poor people of color.

What follows is an ethnographic account of the racialized, environmental violence affecting residents living in neighborhoods of Cherry Hill, Mount Winans, Wesport, Lakeland, Brooklyn, and Curtis Bay.[1] All are located on the South Baltimore Peninsula. All are home to residents who are poor and mostly of color. All are engulfed by industry.[2] As factories and incinerators crowded in during the past century, these six neighborhoods experienced systematic divestments in education, health care, housing, recreational space, and transportation infrastructure.

In this book, I identify environmental toxicity as yet another form of state-sanctioned violence, one that wreaks havoc upon lands as well as bodies and in so doing affects all aspects of human daily life. Undoing the systems that produce and reproduce harm in poor and Black and Brown communities is daunting. Like the criminal justice system that too often provides police with impunity for brutality and even murder, market-driven logics make it difficult to hold industrial polluters, for example, accountable for their toxic impacts and consequent high rates of illness and death.

The US Environmental Protection Agency (USEPA) defines environmental justice as: "The fair treatment and meaningful involvement of all people regardless of race, color, national origin, or income with respect to the development, implementation, and enforcement of environmental laws, regulations, and policies. Fair treatment means that no population, due to policy or economic disempowerment, forced to bear a disproportionate share of negative human health or environmental impacts of pollution or environmental consequences resulting from industrial, municipal, and commercial operations" (Pellow 2018). Environmental toxicity, in contrast to environmental justice, refers to historic patterns of pollution, exposure, contamination, and chemical explosions.[3] This violence is not accidental but rather deeply embedded in historically established systems and structures that perpetuate market-mandated exploitation of natural resources, including human beings.[4] They perpetuate, too, the deregulation of environmental protections by local, state, and federal officials. At the time of my research, disentangling systems of toxicity from the health risks they posed was part of the daily labor of youth organizers on the South Baltimore Peninsula.

Baltimore is a city of contradictions. While slavery flourished in Baltimore, the city was also home to one of the most powerful local civil rights movements in the United States (King, Drabinski, and Davis 2019). And though located south of the Mason-Dixon line, "sometime after World War II the Southern-ness of Baltimore began," in the words of *Evening Sun* reporter Carl Schoettler in 1977, "thinning out like the quality of rye whiskey" (in Rasmussen 2010). The debate over whether Baltimore is of the South or of the North has been hashed and rehashed

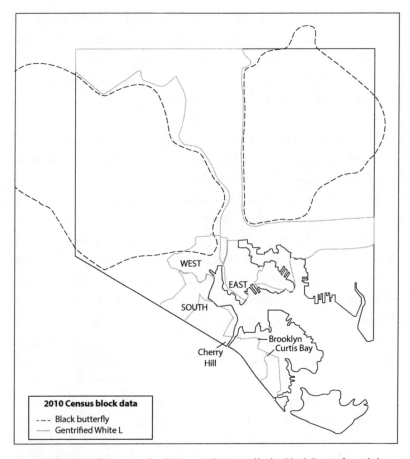

Map 1. This map illustrates what Lawrence Brown calls the Black Butterfly and the White L. *Credit:* Paporn Thebpanya.

since the end of the Civil War, with many Baltimoreans today concluding that the city is a liminal and in-between place. The deep race and class inequalities revealed by Baltimore's geographic landscape, however, are anything but liminal. Equity scientist and public health scholar Lawrence Brown made famous the notions of a "White L" and a "Black Butterfly" in the city (see Map 1). In his words: "Because of 105 years of racist policies and practices, Baltimore's hyper-segregated neighborhoods experience radically different realities. Due to this dynamic, the white neighborhoods on the map that form the shape of an 'L' accumulate structured advantages, while Black neighborhoods, shaped in the form of a butterfly, accumulate structured disadvantages. Baltimore's hyper-segregation is the root cause of racial inequity, crime, health inequities/disparities, and civil unrest" (Brown 2016b). Following Brown's observations, many scholars and journalists have gone so far as to describe the White L and Black Butterfly as two separate Baltimores: one of hyper-investment and capital accumulation and the other of hyper-*dis*investment and decay (Fernández-Kelly 2015; Spence 2015, 2018; Crenson 2017; King et al. 2019; Fabricant 2019).

Interestingly, South Baltimore, including the South Baltimore Peninsula, does not fit the White L and Black Butterfly typology. Instead, it is situated much farther south than even the tip of the gentrified White L (see Map 2) south of the Under Armour–Sagamore Port Covington Development and south of the Hanover Street Bridge. The South Baltimore Peninsula is deindustrialized and populated by poor and working-class people, some of whom are descendants of Eastern European and Appalachian labor migrants, while others are the descendants of Black labor migrants, many of whom arrived during the Great Migration, including just after World War II.[5]

Laura Pulido wrote in her analysis of Flint, Michigan, that some people like to claim racism is not relevant for thinking about environmental injustices because White people are also hurt by pollution, and White bodies can also become toxic sinks for industrial pollution (2016, 2018). But this line of logic refuses to acknowledge how racism functions to shape valuation processes in development and other urban planning. In 2021, the residential sectors of the South Baltimore Peninsula, like much of Flint, were considered, by politicians and potential investors alike, to be worth very little (for investment, for desirable residences) and thereby disposable. This was by virtue of their being occupied by people who were predominantly poor and of color, though the talk was of values and not of race and class. In the case of the peninsula, like

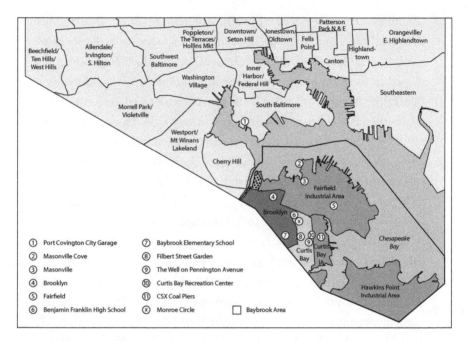

Map 2. South Baltimore and the geographic areas considered part of the South Baltimore Peninsula. *Credit:* Paporn Thebpanya.

that of Flint, unchecked racism and classism, which shaped how leaders saw lands (as disposable) resulted in urban planning decisions to use the region for dumping waste and industry infrastructure plus other polluting facilities that no one else wanted. What happens when waste and heavy industry are condensed in a singular neighborhood, or side of a city, or say, a peninsula is, perhaps, predictable. But I am using this book to ensure it is made visible.

Most of us are connected to neighborhoods-turned-dumping-grounds and/or industrial zones like the peninsula through our waste cycles. Every time we throw something away, it is either buried or burned, and more often than not, there is someone living next door to wherever the burying or burning takes place. On the peninsula, just as in other marginalized sectors of our cities and towns, the smell of garbage and the sounds of the heavy trucks provide multisensorial reminders to residents that their neighborhoods do not matter—at least not to the politicians and industry heads who continue to divest from and/or rezone their neighborhoods. And maybe not to us, either. How we consume and what we throw away make it difficult for young children (and their parents and grandparents) to breathe, lead healthy lives, grow, and thrive. Not only should we care about communities that have disproportionately high rates of asthma, communities whose residents of all ages must fight to breathe, therefore, but perhaps we should feel implicated in their toxicity. Not so that we become defensive of our consumption practices, to be clear, but so that we choose to make new, better political decisions fast. A systematic shift to cleaner air and better regulation of heavy industry, to fair housing and to a zero-waste system that is sustainable (and just) requires participation from all of us—on the peninsula, in its sister and brother neighborhoods, and everywhere else, too.

RECLAIMING TOXIC LAND
FOR ALTERNATIVE DEVELOPMENT

Public health scholars working in environmental justice communities have gathered an abundance of quantitative data about how air contamination causes respiratory illnesses, cardiovascular complications, birth defects, and more.[6] However, there remains a lack of qualitative data to describe the lived human experiences and quality of life resulting from air contamination—especially for young people (Environmental Integrity Project 2012; Thurston 2017; Wu et al. 2020). Relatedly, there is very little documentation of how the cumulative impacts of layers of environmental injustices motivate youth to engage in political struggle—the project of this book.

In that this book documents hundreds of years of environmental racism, it is a tragic book. But this is also a hopeful book. This is a book that tries to put the public health data into conversation with "the people," and especially, young people, by examining the ways in which those who are living amid industrial toxicity are surviving, thriving, pushing back against toxic assault, and creating new and innovative solutions to the contamination around them.

Marxist geographer David Harvey wrote that "the right to the city rises up from the streets, out from the neighborhoods, as a cry for help and sustenance by oppressed people in desperate times" (2008). Harvey argued, "To claim the right to the city in the sense I mean it here is to claim some kind of shaping power over the process of urbanization, over the ways in which our cities are made and re-made and to do so in a fundamentally radical way" (2008). "From their very inception," Harvey continued: "cities have arisen through the geographical and social concentrations of a surplus product. Urbanization has always been, therefore, a class phenomen[on] of some sort, since surpluses have been extracted from somewhere and from somebody (usually an oppressed peasantry) while the control over the disbursement of the surplus typically lies in a few hands" (2008).

In the aftermath of the 2015 and 2020 anti-police violence uprisings in Baltimore following the killings of Freddie Gray in Baltimore and George Floyd in Minneapolis, respectively, many new and creative movements surfaced to address how oppressed groups can assert their "right to the city."[7] The foci of these groups ranged from educational justice to food sovereignty to housing equity and beyond. On the Peninsula, residents and grassroots activists built power and solidarity for housing and environmental justice, most visibly.

Even before this, however, in the year 2011, the high school students at the center of this book came together around these same issues. They did so in an after-school program they named "Free Your Voice," prompted by the slogan "A Voice Is All You Need" from an Amazon Alexa commercial featuring Chance The Rapper. The students you will meet in the book are many. Destiny Watford, a fierce young woman who questioned why her community became a dumping ground, threw herself into activism while still in high school.[8] She later attended Towson University, and eventually, won the Goldman Environmental Prize.[9] Crystal Green—a close friend of Watford's—started organizing with Destiny Watford in the halls of Benjamin Franklin High School (BFHS) and evolved into a seasoned leader fighting for housing justice and a champion zero-waste organizer. Crystal grew up in Curtis Bay, moved away to college, and then came home to train another generation of young organizers. Terrel Jones—a shy and awkward high school student—moved from home to home and lacked the confidence to speak at the initial group meetings. His experiences of housing displacement marked his emotional and physical insecurity; he often looked away from his interlocutors while speaking. Yet Free Your Voice gave him both a sense of belonging and newfound confidence as an organizer. Daniel Murphy—a Peace Corps volunteer turned social worker—was the teacher and organizer for The Worker Justice Center who was instrumental in bringing this original group of students together, helping them to find the tools to question the political and economic systems at work in their community. He is described by the youth as both mentor and friend. Terrel Jones, Luis Mendoza, Leanna Jackson, and Rosalyn Drey are the other students who made up the first cohort of Free Your Voice. They were young activists who began their social and political activism by organizing against a proposal to build the nation's largest trash-to-energy incinerator in their backyards. The students refused to accept one more polluting industry in an already overburdened and toxic geographic space. Their campaign, initiated as an environmental justice movement, grew as they began to ask larger questions about who owns the lands in their community and who makes decisions about what to do on those lands. The students developed political agendas, acquired leadership and media literacy skills, and fought not only to reclaim lands but to redefine development strategies for human needs, which they saw as a redress for the long history of structural and social wrongs in the region.

From 2013 to 2021, a second cohort of Free Your Voice students, this time even more closely aligned with adult activists, continued the fight for environmental justice on the South Baltimore Peninsula. Following up on the success of the "Stop the Incinerator" campaign, they sought "fair development," understood to be a more racially equitable form of development, one that prioritizes people and human needs over profits and demands building healthy communities from the bottom up—with poor people and people of color central to decision-making processes.[10] In fair development, public investments maximize all individuals' access to education, jobs, health care, and long-term and sustainable housing.

The young people featured in this book who comprise the second cohort of Free Your Voice activists, again, are many. Jimmy Brown grew up in public housing in Cherry Hill, a mostly poor, majority-Black South Baltimore neighborhood. He joined the Participatory Action Research class of 2016–2017 at Benjamin Franklin High. Dario Lopez started organizing at fourteen. He grew up as a first-generation US resident from Central America in the Latinx neighborhood of Lakeland. One winter, Dario's parents were forced to choose between paying the mortgage and paying the electricity bills, a choice that left the family without electricity for four months and required the children, like their parents, to sleep in their clothes each night. This hard reality along with the rest of his family's financial struggles motivated Dario to join Free Your Voice and to get interested in alternative development in Curtis Bay.

Throughout this book, I show the ways in which the students of Free Your Voice, both in the first and the second cohort, built relationships and trust with their peers and colleagues and later with their neighbors by asking questions collectively, engaging in research, assembling teams of experts, and generating meaningful data. The qualitative and quantitative data they collected became an arm of their environmental justice movements (rather than fodder for peer-reviewed papers that are hidden behind paywalls or shared at exclusive professional conferences). The students transformed their findings into powerful weapons, generating maps to be held high at protests and raps and reports used to educate city officials and/or inform a much broader network of community members about the human consequences of living in a toxic environment.

ORGANIZATION OF THE NARRATIVE

Fighting to Breathe is a story of toxic entanglements and increasing housing and land precarity on the South Baltimore Peninsula. By toxic entanglements I refer to the interconnectedness of political actors, including city officials, and large scale (corporate) business and property owners from the private sector who find it in each other's best interest to work together and make decisions that compromise the health and well-being of the rest of us. Toxic entanglement is an idea that calls to mind public-private partnerships, with tentacles that envelop industries, wrapping themselves around products, services, jobs, infrastructure, and so on such that community residents are left with no choice but to depend upon polluting industries for daily survival. The end result of these toxic entanglements is organized abandonment along with mislocated accountability—as the students' narratives will demonstrate.

In chapter 1, I describe the distinct periods of industrial development on the South Baltimore Peninsula, starting with guano production in the 1800s, moving into the canning industry in the early 1900s, to the expansion of oil and WWII-era shipbuilding. From guano to the canning industry, I explore how white ethnic workers were made expendable through low-wage labor regimes. Their bodies became vessels for absorbing benzene, gasoline, and plumes from oil blasts. While political figures implemented racially restrictive covenants and residential zoning predominantly in East and West Baltimore in the early 1900s, the era of oil and gas in the twentieth century brought total disregard for the Black, Brown, and poor white persons who lived on the peninsula. Explosions and fires frequently threatened homes, humans, and livelihoods. This chapter ends with a look at the relocation plans of the families who lived engulfed by industry—an early example of organizing and resistance in the community that set the stage for contemporary activism on the peninsula.

In chapter 2, I detail the birth of the Free Your Voice program inside the halls of Benjamin Franklin High in the late 2000s.[11] The chapter describes the transformation of youth from disinterested to engaged citizens who became a vital part of the broader collective fighting for environmental and housing justice in Curtis Bay. Initially by sharing stories of their often traumatic experiences and learning to trust one another, and later through systematic study of the failed and failing institutions and structures that organized their (and all of our) lives, including waste management, housing, and policing and criminal justice, the youth became the experts. They assumed roles as teachers and leaders in their communities, working to educate their families, friends, and neighbors about injustices and, relatedly, about environmental hazards and pollution.

In chapter 3, I look at the Stop the Incinerator Campaign, led by local students in collaboration with other community members, which marked the beginning of the Free Your Voice students' fair development work on the South Baltimore Peninsula. The political and corporate forces advocating for the placement of the incinerator on the peninsula were formidable. The project was proposed in 2011 by then governor of Maryland, Martin O'Malley, who joined former Baltimore Mayor Stephanie Rawlings-Blake in arguing that the project would keep trash out of landfills and create construction jobs and other permanent employment for Baltimore residents. But the rhetoric surrounding this plan obscured the environmental consequences of the waste-to-energy incinerator: the thousands of pounds of lead, mercury, and fine particulate matter as well as the carbon dioxide that would be released into an already over-polluted region of the city. While the high school students were victorious in their efforts to halt the construction of the incinerator, they learned, as a result of the campaign, that escaping one would-be industrial mega-polluter was not enough. To control future development of the region, community members needed to own the land.

In chapter 4, I tell the story of community land trust work on the South Baltimore Peninsula. Large-scale redevelopment has become a solution to urban decay, so that public subsidies now finance private development for the entrepreneurial class. Rarely do residents of poor Brown and Black communities—those most likely to be displaced when development spurs gentrification—get a say in these practices. Fair development movements empower poor people and people of color to fight back. On the South Baltimore Peninsula starting in 2015, fair development included the creation of community land trusts or (CLTs) which provided equitable models of alternative housing for the poor and a vision for reclaiming community green spaces.

In chapter 5, I trace the evolution of the Zero Waste campaign from the Free Your Voice classroom at Benjamin Franklin High to the streets of Baltimore, where a broader coalition of experts and allies, along with the students, not only promoted waste reduction measures such as composting but also brought in an outside consultant and produced a practical guide to zero waste for Baltimore City officials. Fair development, they concluded, requires more than equitable land ownership. It requires starving the incinerators by reducing and ideally eliminating the waste streams that flow into them. While the Zero Waste campaign led to much infighting and no clear victory, there are many lessons to be learned, which I recount here.

By way of a conclusion, I reflect on how activist scholars can become better accomplices in movements that are often fraught with contradictions and internal dilemmas.[12] My hope is that some of these insights from inside the movement might help academics—and activists—to better engage with community members with (and for) whom they work. Specifically, I provide insights into multiracial coalition-building, the kind that is designed by poor and Black and Brown organizers—young as well as old—who are often from the communities in which they organize. Questions of how poor people of color can lead grassroots movements and inform state and national policy are of particular importance now as we face multiple and intersecting crises in the United States. Perhaps most important is how youth education and social reproduction can contribute to building more sustainable and just futures in a moment of radical ecological, climactic, and public health crises.[13]

In the postscript, I reflect on broader trends and possibilities in community organizing today. Many activists across Baltimore talk about a "nonprofit industrial complex" in communities like Sandtown-Winchester and "white savior" solutions to Black poverty and inequality. Often, white-led organizations are described as swooping into the Peninsula and/or Curtis Bay with "outsider knowledge and resources" (Cole 2012; Cobb 2015; King 2020), failing to understand culturally relevant and appropriate alternatives. Struggles around power dynamics, whiteness, and access to grants and capital are sources of tension, fracturing The Worker Justice Center. The story of internal struggles and external projects of land trusts and green industries continues to unfold; the next stage of the campaign and alternative forms of economic development and politics are still being written.

The challenges of organizing amid a public health crisis are especially vexing. How to find needed resources for economic development programs without compromising the integrity of one's work, how to address growing educational inequalities born of the necessity for remote learning, and how to persist despite safety requirements that put fundamental training and movement building on hold are just a few of these. Though other issues have also become urgent at this moment, ensuring access to long-term and affordable housing, good jobs that provide health care, and breathable, *nontoxic* air to residents in communities that have been failed again and again by developers—past as well as present, public as well as private—are vital to our survival.

AUTHOR'S NOTE

I have always been an organizer. I went to graduate school to become an academic, but my heart has always been in organizing. My earliest memories of movement organizing were with my father in Elizabeth, New Jersey—a working class Latinx city where I grew up and went to public schools. I remember my father yelling ferociously at our mayor to house the homeless. I was maybe five at the time, and this experience lit a fire inside of me. Carrying me on his back, feeding me as we marched, and passing me on to my mother as he was arrested. I watched and listened to this passionate orator as a child, and I learned from him as an organizer and a freedom fighter. My parents' social relationships in Elizabeth were deeply rooted in our community, and in organizing work with the homeless. The Coalition to House the Homeless was an institution they built with raw and blistered hands, empty pockets, and unflinching determination to provide shelter for those who arrived from Latin America, the Caribbean, and Africa without familial support. I grew up in the "spaces" of organizing as a child—I remember late-night meetings and soup kitchens where large ladles banged against huge metal pots and hundreds of plastic bowls were filled in mechanistic fashion. I remember community events where performance and theater were part of our everyday joys, moving us to heartfelt tears and, also, to laughter. I remember living in hospitality houses and being enveloped by this deep and meaningful community of justice. This is what my father (along with my mother) sowed, watered, and harvested throughout the early years of my life.

My summers were spent in upstate New York where my parents worked as supervisors at Vacation Camp for the Blind. This, too, was a space filled by intimate relationships and community, where I watched as a young child. My babysitters, from the South Bronx, from Spanish Harlem, from East New York, raised me during those summers. They shared stories of struggle with me, but also nurtured me with song, dance, and comedy routines. Camp became a safe haven for me, away from the truck traffic and the intense smells of pollution in Elizabeth. I remember learning how to read braille, how to sign to deaf campers, and suddenly how to live outside of myself. I learned how to turn myself over to folks with severe special needs. We helped to feed, bath, and dress special-needs campers. I grew into a junior counselor, a counselor, and eventually a supervisor. I took with me from camp a political education and a whole lot to think about.

While graduate school was about getting through readings, writings, and eventually long-term research projects on time, I was organizing there too. In my early years as a graduate student, I was part of the graduate student–organized anti-war movement, and in my latter years, I organized with Unite Here Chicago for just and fair treatment of hotel workers. These were my safe spaces, filled with "my people." They were my solace away from elite university spaces where I felt suffocated by ideas that were difficult to connect to real people's real lives on the ground. My dissertation work in Bolivia turned into something other than what I had proposed as soon as I got into "the field," as they say, becoming a quest to organize with the Landless Peasant Movement (MST) in Latin America. At one point my advisor asked, "Are you coming back to finish your dissertation? Or will you simply become a part of the movement?" I did finish the dissertation. But to "become a part of the movement" has always defined my life. Which is to say I always felt a deeper sense of belonging to social movements than to any academic community.

When I moved to Baltimore in the summer of 2010, I was asked to become a part of the Environmental Justice Movement shortly thereafter by Destiny Watford and Daniel Murphy. They found me at Towson University and invited me to join what students and organizers called the Dream Team (a group of public health experts, teachers, educators, and environmental lawyers) for the Free Your Voice Energy Answers Campaign in 2012. I started by folding myself into daily organizing work, chauffeuring students to events and protests, and supporting their work whenever I saw opportunities to amplify their voices. The work evolved over the years, and in 2015, Destiny, Daniel, Terrel, and I launched the first iteration of a collaborative project inside Benjamin Franklin High. Benjamin Franklin was (and is) the local community school, pulling youth from all six of the neighborhoods on the South Baltimore Peninsula. It was also a failing school (with test scores and graduation rates below city averages) in the first decade of the 2000s. After a "community needs assessment" in 2010 school leaders and an area nonprofit, United Way of Central Maryland, worked to transform Ben Franklin into a community school with all sorts of sociostructural supports including a day care facility, a team of mental health experts, and college readiness programs for students.

The project we launched was a year-long, in-school, Participatory Action Research (PAR) class.[14] During the class, high school youth would learn ethnographic methodologies and then utilize them to examine environmental inequities. Free Your Voice, Towson University, and Benjamin Franklin High were the predominant collaborators. Collectively, we shaped popular education curricula and activities for the students, and we pushed the boundaries of educational bureaucracy. Angela Johnson (head of Environmental Science at Benjamin Franklin High School) was a force to be reckoned with. She supported and pushed forward the collaboration (and she picked kids up from their homes on weekends to bring them to housing and zero-waste events). We built trust in one another, and in the program we were designing, and eventually (in 2018), we got Towson University to offer three college credits to high school students participating in the yearlong project.

After ten years of organizing and teaching, I am now a member of the South Baltimore Community Land Trust, a member of the Zero Waste Coalition and a teacher, friend, and an organizer with Free Your Voice. My understanding of the daily challenges, tensions, and struggles comes from inside of the movement, not from the perspective of a scholar studying movements. While many researchers mostly see the "public face" of the movements they study, my positionality as an activist has given me entrée into the unseen of movement organizing. I have witnessed internal conflicts of organizations as well as the everyday forms of abuses and violence that community members, and also organizers, face. This book reflects my ten-year commitment to social and racial justice organizing in Baltimore, just as it reflects the limitations that come with my racial and socioeconomic positionality. My position as a white, middle-class college professor living in North Baltimore meant that I could leave Curtis Bay each day, travel north, and teach undergraduates in spaces of privilege and accumulated wealth. In recent years (corresponding to the last chapters of this book), my frustration over this duality has motivated me to channel some of my activist efforts toward my own institution. Along with my other activism, I now work to organize students, faculty, and staff at Towson to pressure the university, and all University of Maryland system schools, to divert food waste from our waste stream and support community-controlled and community-owned composting.

My mobility also defined the organization of the book itself. My ability to move between worlds shaped how I see and understand organizing work as central to rethinking, redefining, and reengaging the racialized and uneven geography of Baltimore. Rather than romanticizing resistance, however, I want to capture the complexity and the daily struggles of working to build a model of fair development despite the internal tensions, crises, and eventual break of South Baltimore from The Worker Justice Center. Being an organizer with the South Baltimore Community Land Trust enabled me to document the processes while participating in them. And I learned that it is in the murky gray spaces of organizing, or even while working through internal conflicts and challenges, that great learning often occurs. And with this learning, I realized, stronger leaders can emerge instead of formed, and even more resilient inter-racial, intersectional coalitions can be built.

What I am trying to state here is that this is not a traditional ethnography in which a researcher conducts "participant observation" and interviews his/her "informants." My activist fieldwork was marked by "observant participation," a concept intended to emphasize a researcher's role as an active participant in the process under study (Stuesse 2016). As this book makes clear, my participation took a variety of forms in a variety of settings: daily land trust activity in Curtis Bay, teaching high school students about participatory action methods, spending countless hours in the Filbert Street Garden, joining toxic tours with allies and students, planning campaigns, participating in civil disobedience and marches, organizing workshops, and serving as a member of The Worker Justice Center and Free Your Voice committees. Further, I was part of collectives around accountability and transparency when (internal to The Worker Justice Center) injustices surfaced. These activities gave me access to thousands of informal one-on-ones, group meetings, and small-group discussions. I also conducted approximately seventy one-on-one interviews with members of The Worker Justice Center, allies who have supported and participated in the Fair Development Round-table, the Affordable Housing Trust Fund campaign, and the Zero Waste campaign.

Through my activist-ethnographer lens, I saw how the ideas, the creativity, and even the malleability of the proposals for citywide campaigns were formed and given life at the grassroots. It was the youth and their allies who built the movement to stop incineration, and it was they, again, who envisioned what a zero-waste future could look like. Their stories can offer other neighborhoods inspiration and, even more concretely, tools to fight the complex and interlocking alliances of capitalist extraction—the toxic entanglements.

What follows is more than a narrative of historic injustice and grass-roots, community-based organizing as a response. This is a story about how young kids of color on the South Baltimore Peninsula moved from numbness and paralysis to questioning, moved from seeing broken parts of a failed system to envisioning alternatives to our (increasingly global) political economic system. This is a story about how to build a cohesive, representative, and perhaps even radical political agenda where youth of color are front and center. And this is a story about how to innovate culturally relevant and bottom-up solutions that stem from our economic, ecological, and public health crises. But this is also a story about the messiness of organizing and the daily frictions and tensions (if unaddressed) that can halt these radical solutions. I invite you to think with me, at the end of this book, about how to address the daily raced, classed, gendered, and generational frictions in organizing so that we can build our environmental- and racial-justice movements stronger, and so we can build the kinds of communities in which we all want to live.

CHAPTER ONE

Failed Development on Baltimore's Toxic Periphery

A History

On a Monday morning in September 2017, workers at the Solvay USA Inc. chemical plant in the Fairfield industrial area of the South Baltimore Peninsula were transferring chlorosulfonic acid, a chemical used in soaps, detergents, and other consumer goods, "from a tanker to a trailer"—this according to the Baltimore City fire chief, Roman Clark—when something went terribly wrong (Burnett 2017; Mirabella 2017).[1] As a result, area officials scrambled to warn nearby workers and residents to shelter in place. The mandate started immediately and lasted for several hours. Later, students from the nearby Benjamin Franklin High School (BFHS) would recall feeling "terrified" after they were told that chlorosulfonic acid could be lethal and that they had to remain in lockdown with windows tightly sealed until the US Centers for Disease Control (CDC) deemed it safe for them to leave the school (Campbell and Dance 2017).

In the days following the event, reporters—no doubt borrowing from officials—used words such as *spill* (Burnett 2017) and *leak* in their headlines, words that suggested that what happened at the Solvay plant was accidental. *Baltimore Sun* business reporter Lorraine Mirabella wrote that "a cloud of chlorosulfonic acid *escaped* into the air" (my emphasis, Mirabella 2017), as if the cloud, rather than plant officials, was to blame.

However, it is inaccurate to dismiss what happened at the Solvay plant that day as a mere accident. The chlorosulfonic acid released into the air by well-meaning plant employees trying to do their jobs was, in fact, part of a decades-long history of such events, a history riddled with unjust urban development practices and other uneven patterns of land use in Baltimore more generally.

Think again of the terrified high school students, sheltering in place and waiting for word from the CDC. Adolescents breathing in lethal acids is indicative of the variety of ways in which people of all ages, as well as the land, in Baltimore's southern peninsula are treated as disposable. The Solvay disaster that day wasn't a fluke; it was part of a historic process by which South Baltimore became a dumping ground for the rest of the city: a home for factories, for refuse, and for members of the Black and white ethnic working class—all of which were unwanted (by city officials, investors, and other wielders of capital) in the city proper. In this chapter, I trace Baltimore's long history of industrial development, dating back to the guano trade, in order to show the residual effects of these industries. I focus on the cumulative externalities (i.e., on the costs to "third-party participants") of those industries that make living and breathing difficult for the residents of Baltimore's industrial peninsula. Finally, I describe the youth activism, ignited by this history of failed development. I introduce readers to a population of high school students, students who feared for their well-being during the Solvay plant spill and who demanded better, more just, and less toxic development ventures, students who wrested power from transnational corporations and who, in so doing, returned ownership of the means of production to their community.

Toxicity can refer to the extent to which substances can harm us and other organisms. Substances, such as guano (the excrement of seabirds and bats used as fertilizer), petroleum, and chlorosulfonic acid, for example, cause varying degrees of damage to humans and to the natural world. However, *toxicity* can also denote the extent to which our political and economic leaders have deemed Black, Brown, and poor white "bodies"—along with their neighborhoods—disposable. Baltimore's toxic periphery reflects back to us a toxicity that is chemical as well as political-economic and social.

The lands of the South Baltimore Peninsula were first commodified for the guano trade, before becoming home to the more generalized fertilizer and chemical trades in the early twentieth century. Still later, the peninsula was filled with heavily industrialized and toxic brownfield sites. These were eventually abandoned, after which their very rot and decay became attractive to a new generation of waste infrastructure "capitalists" (those who profit as owners, directors, CEOs, and managers of waste facilities). The transition from brownfield sites to waste infrastructure sites occurred over the course of one hundred years, while the racial-ethnic makeup in Brooklyn–Curtis Bay (on the peninsula) also shifted. Overwhelmingly Eastern European in the early twentieth century, Brooklyn–Curtis Bay was nearly 50 percent Black and Brown at the end of the twentieth century.

The tale I tell here is of Brooklyn–Curtis Bay, (Old) Fairfield, and Wagner's Point. These Baltimore neighborhoods are located on a thirteen-hundred-acre peninsula (that justs into the Patapsco River at the southernmost tip of the city) known as the South Baltimore Peninsula, "the industrial peninsula," or sometimes simply "the peninsula." The region was once described as "the prettiest, healthiest, and most delightfully located suburb south of Baltimore" (King 2014). It was filled with lush farmland, unpolluted and rich in succulent seafood that could be harvested by anyone willing to walk to the water's edge. In the middle of the nineteenth century, the peninsula (still a suburb) was filled with farms and "pleasure resorts." From that time to the present, the history of the region is a history not only of the (largely German and Polish) white ethnic families that settled there, beginning in the 1880s, and of the Black families that arrived soon after, who migrated from the US South and were pushed to the outskirts of Baltimore by a lack of housing for Blacks inside the city limits, but it is also a history of toxicity. It is a history of hiding contagious human beings at the periphery. Even before industry arrived to the peninsula, a pest hospital in Curtis Bay established peripheral lands as a kind of "dumping ground" for sick and diseased bodies.[2] It is a history of replacing lush hinterlands with factories and other "fruits" of urban industrial development ventures (see Map 3). From the late nineteenth century to the mid-twentieth century, fertilizer industries, petroleum-product tank farms, asphalt storage sites, railroad tracks, multinational chemical companies, an auto terminal, and a municipal-and-county wastewater treatment plant encroached upon these neighborhoods (Diamond 1998).

In 1845, the Crisp family, whose members were major landholders at the time, sold twenty acres of the peninsula to the City of Baltimore for the construction of a Marine Hospital. And though this was originally intended to treat sick immigrants and returning sailors, following the 1871 smallpox epidemic, city officials repurposed the hospital, transforming it into a pest house as well as a cemetery, designating it as a space where contagious bodies could be isolated and, if necessary, disposed of. The creation of the pest house initiated a tug of war over the region, with politicians and investors fighting over whether the peninsula should be residential or industrial, pleasurable or toxic.

The Crips family (whose members founded the Fairfield Improvement Company in 1878), along with a group of prominent businessmen including lawyers and financiers interested in real estate ventures (and who founded the Patapsco Land Company) had big ideas for turning the peninsula into a thriving metropolis, one that would be filled with homes, businesses, and residences (Diamond 1998). Another prominent Baltimore family, the Penningtons, imagined instead a region of industry (the Penningtons took over the Patapsco Land Company, also in 1878). With access to members of the most powerful social circles in the city, the Penningtons and their associates advertised "the Point" as a place that was safe for investment and ideal for industry. In fact, Fairfield already housed three thriving industries: Baltimore Chrome Works, Barn Fertilizer Works, and Monumental Chemical (Patapsco Land Company 1874).

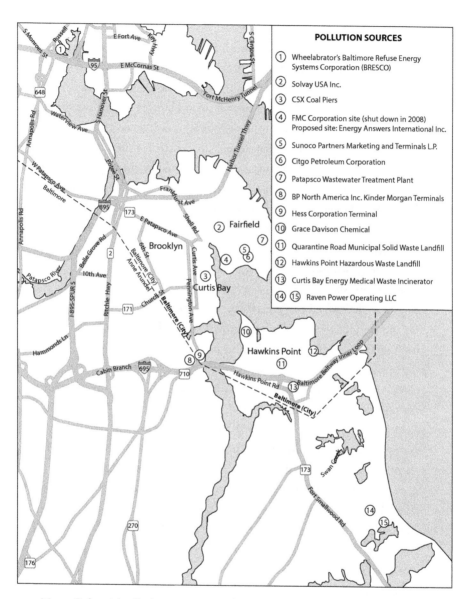

POLLUTION SOURCES

1. Wheelabrator's Baltimore Refuse Energy Systems Corporation (BRESCO)
2. Solvay USA Inc.
3. CSX Coal Piers
4. FMC Corporation site (shut down in 2008) Proposed site: Energy Answers International Inc.
5. Sunoco Partners Marketing and Terminals L.P.
6. Citgo Petroleum Corporation
7. Patapsco Wastewater Treatment Plant
8. BP North America Inc. Kinder Morgan Terminals
9. Hess Corporation Terminal
10. Grace Davison Chemical
11. Quarantine Road Municipal Solid Waste Landfill
12. Hawkins Point Hazardous Waste Landfill
13. Curtis Bay Energy Medical Waste Incinerator
14. 15. Raven Power Operating LLC

Map 3. Industrial pollution sources around Baltimore. *Credit:* Paporn Thebpanya.

In 1871, the fight over whether the peninsula should be (primarily) industrial or residential evolved, coming to a head when city officials sent laborer William Hemsetter to the site of the former pest house (since burned) in order to care for a poor Italian immigrant by the name of Mary Sansone, who had the misfortune of being, at the time, Baltimore's only resident known to have leprosy (a bacterial infection that can affect a sufferer's eyes, skin, respiratory tract, and nervous system). The very presence of Sansone on the peninsula threatened future development of the area. Her sickly body communicated contagion to would-be buyers, thus diminishing real estate values and thereby creating a major problem for the investors envisioning a residential peninsula.

Sansone, born to Italian immigrants in 1868, presumably contracted leprosy when she traveled to Guyana as a teenager. It was only years later, after she moved to Pennsylvania, married, and became pregnant, that she noticed two mysterious brown spots above her elbow (Wiggins and Einik 2009:2). According to hospital papers, Sansone's illness progressed rapidly from there, as spots began to cover her feet and ankles, then her arms, legs, and face. After tending to her for six years, Sansone's husband brought her to downtown Baltimore for treatment, where physicians at Johns Hopkins Medical Center diagnosed her with leprosy. Doctors tried unsuccessfully to have Sansone relocated outside of Maryland. City officials decided, instead, to quarantine her on the peninsula. Though leprosy was not particularly contagious, experts believed that moving "Sansone the Leper" out of the city's most populated and well-to-do city center would calm the people of Baltimore (Ahmann 2018a, 2018b).

Almost immediately, The Fairfield Improvement Company filed a lawsuit against the city, arguing that Sansone's presence would cause "irreparable injury" to their property. Faced with the threat of contagion, individuals would not buy up plots on the professedly "pristine" peninsula: "Fairfield Beautiful Fairfield. South of Patapsco River . . . beautifully laid out," one advertisement proclaimed (Patapsco Land

Company 1874). Though their protestation was a bit ironic, given that the same speculators who were singing its praises had sold land on the peninsula to the City of Baltimore just decades prior for the establishment of a hospital, the speculators now stressed that the public fear would put their investments at considerable risk. In December of 1897, a judge ruled in their favor and issued an order enjoining the city from moving Sansone to the peninsula. Officials weighed the risks to health against the risks to commerce and decided against quarantine (in favor of commerce). This marks the only time an individual was prevented from quarantining in Baltimore, and as American Studies scholar Nicole King argues, this was one of the first examples of the hinterlands battling the city over questionable land uses (2014). Far more often, officials found it both useful and easy to push illness to the urban margins (King 2014; Ahmann 2018a, 2018b).

Though the Crisps and the Fairfield Improvement Company won their case, and the city could not use the hinterlands for pest houses anymore, the South Baltimore Peninsula had by then assumed a reputation for toxicity, and the fate of the region was set. More toxicity—not in the form of human bodies but chemical substances—followed, as industry would continue to encroach upon the peninsula, spreading toxicity like a cancer to the soils, the waterways, and the airways, affecting playgrounds as well as private homes. People's desires for more consumptive and leisurely lives sparked a quest for oil. Eventually railroads would crisscross the once lush fields, as energy conglomerates used large swaths of the peninsula to store crude oil that was to be transported across the United States. But let's start with guano.

GUANO ARRIVES TO THE PRISTINE
FARMLANDS OF THE PENINSULA

The agrarian character of the formerly "pristine" lands on the peninsula began to change in the late 1800s. Nicole King quotes journalists for the *Baltimore Sun* reporting, "Once dotted with [beautiful shorelines]—summer houses of city folks, waterfront resorts and beer gardens of the horse and buggy days . . .—these early industries changed the whole face of the territory" (quoted in King 2014: 431). King adds, "The metropolis was consuming the hinterlands and a new spatial story was emerging" (431). This "new spatial story" taking shape on the peninsula was one of toxic underdevelopment that entrapped poor whites and poor Blacks in a geographic region well on its way to becoming engulfed by fertilizer and, later, other chemical industries.

Already at the social and cultural margins of Baltimore, the economic underdevelopment of the peninsula and the march toward increasingly noxious industries proceeded with "guanomania" in the late 1800s. Guano fertilizer from Peru and the Navassa Islands in the Caribbean was a prized commodity, particularly around the Chesapeake Bay where nearly a century of cotton and tobacco farming had drained the soil of its nutrients. As pressure on the land increased along with population growth, the option to leave lands fallow (so they could replenish their fertility naturally) became less and less feasible. Guano provided a ready alternative, despite its being so hazardous that merchants, captains, and ship owners, aware of its dangers, viewed it as a cargo of last resort.

During transport, a yellowish dust covered the ships that carried guano, and the poisonous odor dried out the noses and irritated the eyes of workers who loaded and unloaded the fertilizer. Yet conditions were even worse on Navassa Island in the Caribbean, where Black laborers mined the guano with picks and shovels in the sweltering tropical climate. It was backbreaking work, and reportedly, it drove some workers to suicide to escape the harsh conditions (Fesperman 1998, 1999; Lesher 2008; James 2012). From 1864 to the early 1891, the Navassa Phosphate Company, based in Fairfield, sent Black laborers—often prisoners from Baltimore—and white supervisors from Baltimore down to Navassa to work in conditions that are easily understood as a perpetuation of slave labor decades after slavery was outlawed.

In addition to suffering the harshness of daily mining tasks and weather conditions, guano miners suffered from work-related health conditions. Some guano miners developed lung damage from inhaling guano dust, while all struggled to breathe amid the suffocating fumes guano mining produces. The dangerous fumes that contaminated the Black bodies of the workers who traveled in and out of the peninsula's port was a form of slow violence. Evincing their desperation, the undernourished workers, treated with extreme brutality, responded with another form of violence: they rebelled in 1889, killing five of their white supervisors. Jobs on the peninsula at the Raising Plant, Baltimore Chrome, and Monumental Acid, all part of the guano industry, were also harsh. Workers described their hands being burned with chemicals and told of unregulated equipment that resulted in injuries to many laborers. With the dangerous work came substandard housing (Olson 1997).

In 1893, there were 221 people living in Fairfield, which was the first of the peninsula's neighborhoods to be industrialized. By 1893, there were 2,100 workers employed at nine factories in Fairfield (Diamond 1998: 27). From the beginning, most workers at the fertilizer factories, including the Navassa Phosphate Company, were Black men who had migrated from rural parts of the state due to job shortages. Historian Sherry Olson described the homes built in Fairfield to house the influx of newly arrived workers as "shanties built by industry or tolerated on the industrial land adjoining the fertilizer and chemical factories" (1997: 276). It was nearly impossible during this period for Black individuals to buy land—or even for white developers with plans to build houses for Black individuals to buy land. The only option for would-be home-owners who were Black was secondhand housing, and any expansion of this housing supply depended on Black families moving out to other parts of the city. Additionally, the houses in Fairfield were kept in poor repair, as the City neglected this geographic area just as they did other regions of the city that were all or almost all Black.

Guano also left an epigenetic imprint on the peninsula and on the lands, the bodies, and even the housing structures of the peninsula. Chemicals and heavy metals haunt bodies in the same way that chemicals and fertilizers haunt the biosphere, leaving layers of benzenes, asbestos, fluoride, lead, chromium, and polychlorinated biphenyls (PCBs). "Past environments serve as ghosts inside of us" wrote historian and environmental justice scholar Michelle Murphy (2016 in Vasudevan 2019: 784). Just as chemicals cause historical or intergenerational "trauma" to lands, which results in their premature withering and rotting from ongoing overexposure, chemicals can contribute to historical or intergenerational, bodily trauma.[3] Toxins can alter gene expressions causing physiological changes, not only in exposed adults but in future generations, through an epigenetic imprint or biological "memory" of trauma (Vasudevan 2019). One end result is the possibility of chronic illnesses and early death for the descendants of the descendants of those unjustly exposed, as laborers or as neighbors to the toxins of heavy industry.

The rise of the guano industry, while seeming to provide work for a new population of Black men on the South Baltimore Peninsula, thus exacerbated race- and class-based inequalities that persist today. The substandard housing, substandard schooling, severe health risks, and lack of critical citywide services that accompanied the industry were part of an economics of underdevelopment, locking guano workers into poverty for generations to come. Again, it is inaccurate to think of the toxicity of guano on the peninsula only as the literal toxicity of the fertilizer wafting in the air, though this is important. The social and political economic hierarchies that were amplified by the guano industry were every bit as toxic. Just as Mary Sansone's quarantine on the peninsula marked the area as a dumping ground, the presence of guano factories was the impetus for ever more noxious forms of development on the peninsula. The industries that followed (fertilizer, oil, petrochemical, and coal) further the poisoning of bodies and soils.

ZONING FOR NUISANCE INDUSTRIES AND DUMPING
THE PATAPSCO SEWAGE TREATMENT PLANT
ON THE PENINSULA

The entire South Baltimore Peninsula was zoned "nuisance" by city officials in the early twentieth century, opening the floodgates for more chemical and petrochemical industries to move into the area. The guano import/export trade and the fertilizer industries that followed led to the zoning of the entire area as heavy M-3 zoning (meaning that the Fairfield neighborhood was zoned heavy industry) with residential zoning only a few blocks away. As a result, the peninsula became a kind of regulation-less utopia for industrial expansion. M-3 heavy zoning policies gave free rein to corporate heads looking to use lands, use cheap labor, and even "dump" waste and chemicals out of sight and out of mind. Zoning such as this is what professor of urban planning Yale Rabin (1990) called "expulsive zoning."[4] In the case of the South Baltimore Peninsula, zoning was used not only to exclude the nuisance industries from middle- and upper-class neighborhoods in Baltimore but also to expel lower-class residents from areas designed for heavy industrial uses. Thus, middle- and upper-class residents got what they wanted (distance from toxicity), while industrial heads got what they wanted (an abundance of lands). Not consulted and invisible, except when being relocated, were the poor Black and white ethnic, immigrant residents already at home on the peninsula.

The City first annexed the neighborhoods of Curtis Bay, Fairfield, and Wagner's Point, on the southern half of the peninsula, in 1918 without asking residents whether they wanted their neighborhoods to be annexed, and then, in 1923, city officials zoned these neighborhoods for the heaviest industrial usage (Diamond 1998). When residents in the region began calling for basic services, the prior zoning allowed city officials to pretend these residents didn't exist: these neighborhoods were for industry, not people, the zoning laws said. Urban studies researchers have labeled this strategy as "benign neglect" or "organized abandonment" (Gilmore 2008; Kotlowitz 2009; Rugh and Massey 2010; Heynen 2016). Regardless of labeling, the outcome was that people on the peninsula were rendered invisible. Yet the irony is that despite their invisibility, these residents shared a deep sense of community that made them quite visible to one another.

COMMUNITY IN OLD FAIRFIELD AND WAGNER'S POINT

Despite the peninsula's reputation as "Baltimore's forgotten corner" (King 2014; King and Rich 2021), residents maintained tight-knit social networks and a strong sense of community. This was most evident in the predominantly Black neighborhood of Fairfield, the residents of which endured racism and hardships for generations. Early Fairfield had a mythic reputation for being a rare, mixed-race community in which members of all races got along. Longtime resident and community leader Jennie Fincher moved to Fairfield from Virginia with her family in 1914. In an interview in 1993, Mrs. Fincher claimed that Fairfield was one of the first truly integrated communities in the city of Baltimore (*Baltimore Sun* June 26, 1941, quoted in King 2014).[5] More recently, Nicole King citing a 1911 Baltimore Sun article, wrote, "The Blacks call the whites by their first names and the whites, fraternally, greet the Black people in the same spirit. They eat together and live together. Fairfield makes its own laws, settles its own disputes, cleans up its own bloody sawdust and ignores civilization" (2014: 445). Many residents did not want to leave the area despite being surrounded by industry. This was, in part, because of the deep sense of community they felt. Similar to the social networks and community-based survival strategies that anthropologist Carol Stack described (1975) in her ethnography of "the Flats" (a low-income neighborhood in Northern California in the 1970s), Baltimore City officials' neglect of the peninsula necessitated that residents form especially strong kin and fictive kin relationships to survive; this interdependence fomented strong senses of connection among them: to each other, and to place. Residents of Fairfield recounted baseball games, festivals, and parties that brought together generations of neighborhood residents. They mentioned, too, the central importance of the Black church as a hub of social and spiritual life in the community (King 2014).

Wagner's Point, just next to Old Fairfield, began as a company town built by Martin Wagner who profited from mostly Polish immigrant workers he contracted for his oyster- and fruit-packing plant, who set up homes and infrastructure in Wagner's Point. In 1896 Martin Wagner moved from Canton to Anne Arundel County to be closer to the produce farmers of the Eastern Shore, who shipped him their produce in small boats. Wagner bought a fifty-acre tract and set up an "integrated" operation, with his workers not only packing and canning oysters and fruits but also manufacturing the tin cans and the wooden boxes in which the products were contained and then shipped. He later built one hundred East Baltimore–style row houses for his employees who, again, were primarily Polish immigrants (Matthews 1999b; Klein 2000). Wagner contracted laborers to build a public school, drug store, bakery, shoe store, and restaurant, in addition to a well-stocked grocery and provision store from which goods were sold at city prices (King 2014).

While city officials ignored them, residents remembered spending their weekends watching semipro baseball games and dancing in a waterfront pavilion while drinking beer. (The latter was possible only because Wagner's Point was not annexed to the city until 1918.)[6] Senior citizens interviewed in the 1990s who spent time in Wagner's Point in the 1950s, recalled it as a charming and whimsical place—a Polish enclave in the middle of the Point that seemed to have everything it needed (Ahmann 2018a).

In 1913, Wagner's cannery burned down, and as a result, over four hundred workers lost their jobs. Also as a result, Martin Wagner began to sell his lands, piece by piece, to oil companies. While the Ellis Oil

Company was already in the region at this time, others were eager to join: in 1914, Prudential Oil Corporation established a refinery in the middle of the peninsula, approximately equidistant from Wagner's Point and Old Fairfield. The Texas Oil Company of Delaware and today what is better known as Texaco arrived on the peninsula before World War II and is, still today, located along the southeast waterfront where its huge tanks loom over the vacant land that remains on Wagner's Point (Klein 2000).

THE POLITICAL ECOLOGY OF ENERGY NEEDS: COAL AND BIG OIL ENGULF THE PENINSULA

Coal and big oil were making their indelible marks on the peninsula just as the railroad industry was intruding farther and farther onto the peninsula. Baltimore & Ohio (B&O) opened a railroad line to the community in 1882, constructing a vast switching yard only a half mile from Fairfield and Wagner's Point, thereby luring even more factories to the area (Kelly 2019). By 1918, B&O facilities designed and completed an open-air coal pier to unload cars of coal coming from Northern Appalachia into vessels on the South Baltimore Peninsula. This coal pier was the first major bulk cargo facility built in the United States, utilizing high-capacity belt conveyors and traveling ship loaders. By the 1950s, the peninsula was hemmed in by railroad tracks carrying coal from Appalachia to Baltimore.[7] And though rebuilt in 1960, the coal pier continues to operate as of this writing in 2022.

Coal dust contains impurities that include trace heavy metals selenium, chromium, arsenic, mercury, and lead.[8] Dust flies off the piles of coal being loaded and unloaded on CSX Chesapeake Coal terminal pier. There are days that the coal pile at the Curtis Bay coal pier is so high it looks like it would dwarf a four story building. Coal dust discharged into the water off the side of the pier where levels of metal are not always monitored by the EPA affect waterways and the fish species that live in the water (Wheeler 2013). Contaminated water floods lands, leaving coal dust impurities in the soils in which farmers grow foods destined for local tables and atop which animals graze. And contaminated water seeps into the groundwater that residents drink.

Coal dust accumulates inside the lungs of residents of the peninsula in the same way that it seeps into the soils. Some coal dust particles are microscopic, less than 2.5 microns across, enabling the particles to penetrate deep inside the lungs of those who breathe them in. Inhalation of coal dust has been linked to respiratory illnesses like chronic obstructive pulmonary disease and emphysema and elevated risks of cancers (Morfeld et al. 2002; Stayner and Graber 2011).

Coal wages a long and slow war on the lands, waterways, and human bodies it contaminates; some have even referred to coal as a "silent killer" (Braben et al. 1994; US Department of Health and Human Services 1995; Lockwood 2012; Ferber 2013; Wheeler 2013; Rakumakoe 2017; Geiling 2018; El Morabet 2019). In contrast, fossil fuels, particularly oil, can result in rapid, almost instantaneous contamination, given possibilities for oil spills, leaks, and even explosions. Oil-related spills and explosions on the peninsula happened quite frequently in the early twentieth century. Take, for example, the following event on July 19, 1920. In the afternoon on this day, lightning struck two tanks (owned by the New York based United States Asphalt Refining Company) which, combined, contained fifty thousand barrels of petroleum. According to the *Baltimore Sun*, one tank "exploded with a roar that could be heard for miles and with a force that hurled the top of the tank into the street more than 200 feet away" (King 2013). After burning for many hours, the tanks boiled over and released burning oil into the streets, lighting tanks of the Texas Oil Company on fire and burning through the streets of Wagner's Point. Twelve houses along Wagner's Point's Third Street were destroyed as a result. A reporter for the *Baltimore Sun* reported: "Before the torrents of blazing oil, hundreds of residents fled from their homes screaming in terror. In their arms some carried babies, others carried household effects, while still others, wild-eyed and panic stricken, fled coatless and hatless in a frantic effort to escape the blazing flood" (Forgo 2020). The headquarters of the East Brooklyn Volunteer Fire Company and the laboratory of the United States Asphalt Refining Company were also destroyed in the fire that day, along with rail cars and automobiles. While six alarms were sounded and eighteen fire engines were sent to fight the blaze, water cannot be applied directly to burning oil, which made this an especially difficult fire to contain. Firemen dug trenches to redirect the burning oil, wet down surrounding areas, and pumped oil out of tanks into the streets. Firemen and volunteers took three days to put out the fire. While there were no reports of deaths or serious injury that day, nineteen homes were destroyed, and thirty-nine others were left uninhabitable (Forgo 2020). The oil tank explosion of 1920 was an early sign that living in close proximity to oil and chemical companies can have dire consequences.

BOOMS OF THE WORLD WAR II ERA, BUSTS FOR BLACK LABORERS

If ever there was a heyday for the South Baltimore Peninsula, it was the World War II era, which brought unionized jobs and new waves of would-be shipbuilders and other workers—from Appalachia and the US South, especially—to Fairfield (Figures 1 and 2). Scholars have described the "hustle and bustle" of shipbuilding on the peninsula in the 1940s (Olson 1997; Stockett 1997; Durr 2003; Pietela 2010; Rudacille 2010; Crenson 2017). Between 1941 and 1945, workers at the Fairfield shipyard built a total of 384 Liberty ships, more than any other shipyard in the nation (Jones 2019). The yard also churned out 94 Victory ships— the larger, faster cousin to the Liberty ships—and 45 Landing Ship-Tanks (known as LSTs), making it one of America's most productive wartime shipyards (Jones 2019). Work on ships was plentiful. And one rarely saw images of the harsh physical labor required of the shipyard workers (Durr 2003).

The Fairfield shipyard was located on the south side of the Patapsco River in what is called the Baltimore Harbor, and it had the most employees of any of the Bethlehem Shipbuilding Company owned shipyards (Abel 2019).[9] An estimated twenty-five thousand Black workers, mostly men, were hired for jobs during the city's war industry, six thousand in the shipyards alone (Abel 2019). Many of the workers obtained these positions by responding to recruiters from Bethlehem Steel, who, believing them to be most malleable, preferred contracting out-of-town Black workers for their shipyards, blast furnaces, and rolling mills (Pietila 2010, 78).

Although the expansion of semiskilled positions offered newcomers job advancements, Black workers were excluded from leadership roles and supervisory positions. As historian Marilynn Johnson wrote, "Foreman, leaderman, and other supervisory positions were dominated by old-timers and other white male workers" (1996, 63). Management-operated apprenticeship programs, too, were often closed to Black applicants (Rubin, Swift, and Northrup 1974: 42). Companies that included Kaiser and Dry Dock shipyards along with Newport News Shipbuilding Company instead channeled Blacks laborers to semi-skilled positions such as welding, burning, and ship fitting (Rubin et al. 1974: 63), while the trade unions refused to include Black laborers in their bargaining (Archibald 1947).

While all laborers were exposed to toxic substances in the shipyards, Black workers held the toughest jobs and therefore endured the most dangerous conditions. Before the toxicity of asbestos became as well known as it is today, ships often were laden with the fibrous material from bow to stern. Paradoxically, asbestos products were utilized on ships for safety reasons, yet it was likely asbestos that posed the greatest threat to workers. Court dockets from the World War II era and extending into the 1960s and early 1970s, especially those in New York

Figure 1. A worker resting during lunch hour at the Bethlehem-Fairfield Shipyards. *Credit:* Library of Congress, Public Domain Prints & Photographs Division, Farm Security Administration/Office of War Information Black-and-White Negatives. Photo by Arthur S. Siegel.

and California, are full of examples of former shipyard workers who contracted asbestos-related diseases and could trace their exposures back to one or more shipyards. Workers even with a moderate level of cumulative asbestos exposure were almost four times more likely to die from mesothelioma as members of the general population, while those

Figure 2. Workers building the SS *Frederick Douglass* at the Bethlehem-Fairfield Shipyards. *Credit:* Library of Congress, Public Domain Prints & Photographs Division, Farm Security Administration/Office of War Information Black-and-White Negatives. Photo by Roger Smith.

with a high level of exposure were over seven times more likely to die of mesothelioma (Carbone 2012). This physical toxicity of asbestos compounded the racism of the Jim Crow shipyards. Just as the toxic substances were trapped inside bodies, workers were entangled in everyday forms of racism, at work and at home.

SUBPAR AND ENVIRONMENTALLY TOXIC
HOUSING FOR BLACK DEFENSE WORKERS

As jobs drew workers to the Bethlehem Fairfield shipyards, demand for housing rose. Rather than creating additional permanent housing, however, the federal government set up a huge trailer park on the peninsula, with five hundred government owned and eighty privately owned trailers situated close to sites of work (Olson 1997).

This was just one in a series of unfair housing practices victimizing Black residents in and around Baltimore—and the United States. Following the war, factories and plants that had been taken over by the US government were returned to original business owners, and the South Baltimore Peninsula was reshaped by the construction of even more toxic plants, many owned by the new-to-the-region fertilizer and chemical companies (King 2014). Amid these changes, Fairfield Homes, containing some three hundred units of mostly two-story row homes and intended to house white families, was constructed, opening to occupants on March 1, 1942. At this time, the preexisting residential community of Fairfield, now referred to as "Old Fairfield," government officials transformed the site into public housing; its residents were overwhelmingly Black and poor (Fesperman 1999; McCraven 1997).

The new Fairfield Homes remained an all-white development until after the City purchased it in 1953. Community groups fiercely opposed the purchase, and residents of Fairfield Homes asked the City to keep the project building segregated (Diamond 1998). But as early as October 1, 1954, the first Black family moved into Fairfield Homes. Within one month of this date, 40 percent of the occupants were Black. Just a few years later, 100 percent of occupants were Black. As white residents were replaced by Black residents, the City divested in the housing project, leaving it to decay.[10]

Directly adjacent to Fairfield were all-white Curtis Bay and Brooklyn neighborhoods, often described as a single neighborhood using the moniker Brooklyn-Curtis Bay. Following the war, Brooklyn Homes, which was an all-white public housing project in Brooklyn, was a breeding ground for white supremacist groups like the United Klans of America and the National States' Rights Party, which opposed desegregation of housing (Williams 2004). In the O'Donnell Heights Homes, located in what is considered Southeast Baltimore, in December of 1966, white occupants organized against integration and used the phrase "human trash" to describe Black residents, along with a discourse that emphasized pathology, linking Black bodies to disease and contamination with their metaphors. A small group of white tenants who opposed desegregation in 1967 posted a flyer imploring White residents to beware of the "perils" of Black integration. Titled, "Negroes and O'Donnell Heights," it read: "The people you have elected to office are rewarding you with their garbage. They are about to take O'Donnell Heights and turn it into a City Dump by sending you the city's trash ... the Negro. [...] The city is going to the dogs (the Negroes) so McKeldin and D'Alessandro want you to share their misery. They live far, far, from the blacks but they believe that the blacks are good enough for the hillbillies and the slobs. Are they?"[11] The back of this pamphlet proclaimed, "People of O'Donnell Heights and surrounding areas: Listen and stand up for yourselves, Negroes in your neighborhood mean CRIME! Murder, rape and robbery upon you and your family." (Williams 2004: 116–17).

While hate followed urban Black residents as they moved—and were moved—within the peninsula, terrified and terrifyingly racist white residents campaigned and proclaimed and defaced and perpetuated physical violence. City officials assisted the white antagonists by keeping neighborhoods on the peninsula segregated through de jure means, isolating Black residents in housing projects like Fairfield Homes, and denying basic services and infrastructure. Very quickly, however, city officials began to envision new endeavors for the peninsula.

WASTELANDING IN THE 1980S AND 1990S

The peninsula through the 1980s and 1990s was characterized by deindustrialization and economic decline, along with an expansion of garbage industries (though "Big garbage"), which first arrived to the peninsula in the 1960s. The City's divestment in Fairfield and Wagner's Point transformed these neighborhoods into postindustrial wastelands.

Wastelanding, a term coined by Traci Brynne Voyles (2015) to describe the process by which lands of certain (poor and/or of-color) people are rendered pollutable, aptly describes the process by which Baltimore City officials, in cahoots with private industries, both devalued and revalued peninsula lands, thereby transforming them into a literal dumping ground. From 1943 to 1983, the metropolitan areas of Baltimore experienced a "garbage crisis," during which the City built new waste incinerators to burn hundreds of thousands of tons of garbage daily. By the 1960s, the rising pile of rubble alongside downtown urban renewal sites disrupted private developer schemes and the city began relocating waste management to South Baltimore.[12] In 1983, contractors for the City built the Baltimore Refuse Energy Systems Company Incinerator (or Wheelabrator BRESCO), Wheelabrator Baltimore is a waste-to-energy incinerator located in the Westport neighbohrood of Baltimore, often simply referred to as BRESCO. BRESCO, a 2,500-ton/day wasteto-energy incinerator designed to burn suburban trash, remained out of sight from most Baltimoreans and is still in use today (Cumming 2021). BRESCO was paid for by city bonds passed for "clean technology" (Cumming 2021).

Alongside the incinerator in Hawkins Point, Baltimore officials created what is today the largest landfill site in Baltimore. In the words of Energy Justice researcher Dante Swinton, "The landfill actually came online at the same time as the incinerator. The city wanted to lower its cost of waste disposal, they wanted to send it outside of the city's boundaries. . . . So, the incinerator came on, the landfill came on, and . . . half the weight that goes there [the landfill] is incinerator ash. The Quarantine landfill, still seventeen million taxpayer dollars away from completion, is about 82 percent full and on track to reach capacity in 2026" (in Dance 2019). Anything that cannot be burned at BRESCO is dumped in this massive landfill, where garbage sits for years, turned over by bulldozers, so it can slowly decompose.

Add to these the construction of the largest medical waste incinerator, which was established in 1991 in Curtis Bay. It was originally called Medical Waste Associates, Phoenix Services, Curtis Bay Energy, but is today called Curtis Bay Medical Waste Service, and it spews all sorts of toxins into the air. Medical waste incineration produces mercury and dioxin pollution; mercury can lead to immune system failure and lung and kidney damage; while dioxin, a known carcinogenic that is able, too, to disrupt hormones and reduce fertility, is one of the most toxic chemicals known to mankind (Rice et al. 2014; Campanale et al. 2020; ATSDR 2020). There was a need for a facility to dispose of the medical waste which is now shipped throughout the United States.

Along with dreams of profits tied to wastelanding, Baltimore officials also dreamed of building an "Industrial Ecological Park" on the peninsula, specifically in Fairfield. The city demolished Fairfield Homes in 1997 (see Figure 3). Fairfield Homes was one of the many all-Black housing projects that fell into a state of decay and neglect, surrounded by toxic brownfield sites that private chemical companies feared would leave them vulnerable to residents' suits over health concerns tied to contamination (Matthews 1999a). The response to decay, rot, and blight is usually "redevelopment," which is code for demolition and usually, following demolition, some form of renovation to provoke gentrification. Redevelopment also sometimes means privatization, as cities sell out to industry. For example, there was a push in the 1990s to turn the Fairfield Homes into the Industrial Ecological Park I mentioned above. This was to be part of a broader empowerment zone initiative.[13] The effort never came to fruition, but city officials arranged for residents living in the communities "engulfed by industry" (Diamond 1998; Bloom 2002; King 2014) to

Figure 3. Last house standing in Fairfield. *Credit:* South Baltimore Land Trust.

receive legal assistance. This soon materialized into a "buyout" of homes in Wagner's Point. Residents were "awarded" relocation packages from the city that included anywhere from $35,000 to $62,000 (Bloom 2002).

Despite all the development and "redevelopment" dreaming by city officials aligned with the private sector, resilient groups of laborers and community residents not only continued to live alongside toxicity but also worked, traveled to school, and fought hard to remain in their homes. They even found ways to hold some industries accountable for damage, and they have organized and proposed alternatives to current toxic practices that have bubbled up from the grassroots.

Students who crouched in the halls of Benjamin Franklin High that day of the Solvay plant chemical spill weren't just dealing with an isolated accident; this was about the cumulative impact of industry over time and how their bodies, lands, and waterways became a dumping ground for the city's overdevelopment. The toxic emissions on the South Baltimore Peninsula are among the highest in the nation and this is not an accident but rather quite intentional; it was environmental injustice by design.

THE STUDENTS RESPOND

Destiny Watford and her high school friends first heard about plans to build the nation's largest trash-to-energy incinerator in their neighborhood in 2011. They raised their hands to indicate who did and did not have asthma and found that more than half of them did.[14] This jarring new awareness moved them to action.

Soon, Destiny and other BFHS students began to study the political ecology of disinvestment. The students challenged themselves to think about "healthy" or "sustainable" investments that did not extract capital, or underpaid labor from poor people of color and working-class and impoverished whites. As the students moved beyond historical texts and secondary source materials, they met urban developers, participatory design architects, zero-waste innovators, and cooperative economic businessmen and women. They dreamed of new land-use patterns, new forms of socioeconomic relationships, and long-term stable and affordable housing. They crafted their own proposals for "equitable development." Some might call it utopian, but the youth described their project as economically and ecologically sound development steeped in local knowledge and local cultural frames.

Many of the Benjamin Franklin High School students saw vivid connections between the past and the present. They wanted to reconnect with residents who once lived in Fairfield Homes and those who were relocated from Wagner's Point in order to understand what these communities looked and felt like and how people supported one another. What remained visible to the students was the crumbling infrastructure, contaminated brownfield sites, and postindustrial wastelands spewing smoke from garbage incinerators. Yet the excavated stories and artifacts of "lost communities" (King 2014) that residents told helped youth in the 2000s piece together vibrant and colorful patchwork of communal resilience, social support networks, and even basic services that they built without the help of the city (Bradley and King 2012). These were the rich forms of autonomy and "self-reliance" of the communities that lived, breathed, and survived alongside toxic industries.

The South Baltimore Peninsula became a living classroom for youth to teach others about toxicity; they led toxic tours of their neighborhoods, tested soils for lead and heavy metals, and even conducted coal dust sampling. Meeting multiple times per week as a part of an after-school program they named Free Your Voice, the youth would demand more than buyouts around issues of safety. They realized that not only were they engulfed by industry, not only did they have to fight to clean up that industry, but they also had to rethink and redesign economic development in their community. Among other things, together they developed a multi-scalar approach to development that emanated from the South Baltimore Peninsula as a kind of experiment for change, redefining and reenvisioning development for the city and state as they did so. The South Baltimore Peninsula became a politicized incubator for a citywide movement to push for an end to incineration, for fair development and the building of community land trusts, and for zero-waste initiatives.

CHAPTER TWO

Free Your Voice

An Origin Story

From the main road leading into Curtis Bay, famously called Shell Road after the oil company, a row of CSX rail cars, piled high with black coal and covered in a fog of coal dust, form a kind of assembly line of hyper-mechanized production. While CSX trains slow to a crawl, smoke billows from incinerators in the gray-blue Baltimore skyline, and billboards exclaim "Don't Die of an Overdose." The signage renders visible the local and increasingly national opioid addiction crisis and is an attempt to scare users into seeking help from medical practitioners. The irony is that on the South Baltimore Peninsula, many more people die of every-day lung and respiratory illnesses tied to toxic industries than from addiction to illegal drugs (Baltimore City Health Department 2017b).

To get to Benjamin Franklin High School, one must turn from Shell Road onto Patapsco Road (the main drag of this postindustrial wasteland), where rows of broken-down houses come into view. Looking closely, one can see paint chips that have flaked from the houses accumulating alongside and underneath porches. Toys are strewn about lawns, and American flags stand tall and proud.

At the Curtis Bay Recreation Center, where children gather for after-school learning, employees worry about the layers of coal dust lining the windowsills. A massive, open-air coal pier—the largest

47

Figure 4. Massive CSX coal pier. *Credit:* Photo by Kyle Pompey.

coal export pier on the East Coast—sits across the street, less than five
meters from the Rec Center windows (Figure 4).[1] In front of the coal
pier is a children's park, a desolate playground with old hypodermic
needles and empty bottles strewn about. Graffiti in dark bold colors sig-
nifies those who have laid claim to this "turf." A pool that once was part
of this recreational scene is a dry basin, cracked by exposure to the sun.
Directly behind the pool are the Hazel Street homes, which remain
abandoned and boarded up after a fire devastated the block of row
homes in 2017. Over thickly boarded-up doorways and windows dangle
signs listing code violations. Garbage piles outside the front porches
of these boarded homes tell onlookers that there is still life amid this
"blight"—that the humans are still here, despite the inhospitality of
it all. The coal infrastructure, the empty and cracked pool, and the
boarded-up homes are less than a mile from both the elementary and
the high school in this neighborhood. What area kids see, and what
they breathe, is toxic.

From Patapsco, one turns onto Fairhaven Avenue en route to Benjamin Franklin High, passing Fred and Margie's on the way. It is a small, bar-in-the-front, restaurant-at-the-back type of place where industrial workers, construction workers, and truck drivers (many of whom drive the massive semis that release PM$_{2.5}$ into the air of this community) gather after their shifts to grab beers and/or a bite. Margie greets customers with a smile that is difficult to read. She is in her mid-fifties, a thick woman with a sharp, working-class Baltimore accent, and she has lived in Curtis Bay most of her life. She owns the restaurant, and she is the restaurant's only server, juggling multiple orders along with the work of managing the establishment on a normal business day.

In front of Fred and Margie's is Cambria Street. Lined by small row homes, it is a narrow, one-way street, like most in this area. Signs reading "No Trespassing," "Beware of Dog," "Private Property," give textual form to residents' fears. Some of the homes are boarded up and vacant; others have front yards overgrown by grass and brush. Someone has placed a sticker that reads "No sex trafficking" on the stop sign near the high school.

Benjamin Franklin High, located on Cambria Street, is just south of Fred and Margie's. The sign above the school door reads, "Benjamin Franklin at Masonville Cove," and "Bayhawks," with green and yellow painted stripes streaming down the sides of the brick building. An American flag flies from an especially tall flagpole out front. The house across from the school has a wooden treehouse in the yard that can be seen from the campus. There, for more than a year, a noose hung from the tree along with a sign that threatened the lynching of all trespassers.[2]

FREE YOUR VOICE PROGRAM DESCRIPTION

Inside Benjamin Franklin High School, the Free Your Voice program, which was, at first an after-school activity and later part of the regular school day, has students come together to study the social and environmental problems that "personally" affect them, problems that are also historic and political, economic, and horrifically unjust, even if they are more palatable to us today than, say, hangings indexed by a noose in the neighbors' yard.

The students who participate in Free Your Voice were aware that the problems they study have affected and continue to affect not only themselves but their friends and neighbors on the peninsula, too. And they learn, through each other and alongside their instructors, that they can effect major changes. Take, for example, the problem of breathing on the peninsula. In 2011, when Free Your Voice first took shape, students talked about watching brothers or sisters sleep at night to make sure they were breathing. And whenever Marvin Hayes (Director of the Baltimore Compost Collective, BCC) asked Benjamin Franklin students in a classroom setting, "How many of you experience asthma or have someone in your family who has respiratory problems?" nearly 90 percent of the students would raise their hands.[3] Baltimore City has the highest rate of acute asthma events in Maryland. Asthma hospitalization rates are impacted by a multitude of factors, including health insurance and the availability of asthma inhalers; poor housing conditions, including mold, mice, and cockroaches; emotional stress; and indoor and outdoor air pollution, all of which can trigger asthma attacks (Environmental Integrity Project 2012). And in fact, Baltimore's lowest-income zip codes, including neighborhoods in East and West Baltimore, have the highest asthma hospitalization rates, while the wealthiest zip codes, in Roland Park and Mount Washington, have the lowest. The problem "was bigger than just us," student Crystal recalled realizing: "We related to the issues because we all had asthma. . . . You would've thought it was a kind of asthma campaign at the beginning. . . . My brother had [asthma], so that hit me really hard. Like, oh my god, my brother was having asthma attacks almost every day around that time. To me, that was personal. That's why I felt I stayed [in the Free Your Voice program]. Because it directly related to family, friends, people I knew with these problems." Another student, Destiny, was as passionate and energetic as Crystal. She was also deeply sensitive, and she eventually grew into an aggressive advocate for social and environmental justice in her community. Destiny, too, recalled how asthma played a role in helping her connect her personal life to bigger, structural questions within her community:

> My sister's best friend at the time . . . her younger brother died from an asthma attack! He died. We were all . . . even my mom . . . so worried about him. She was crying at our house. It was so, so much. Watching it. Seeing these things and you can't really do anything about it. People's lives are . . . in jeopardy all the time. . . . I knew I wanted to play some part or role in [the fight for environmental justice]. I remember early on I was learning about human rights and trying to figure out what rights meant to us, really thinking about our neighborhood, if our rights are being violated, and we've never thought about it in that way. I mean, we were just shook about just how many human rights violations we were living without even realizing it. What made it easier, at least for me, and I think other folks too, was that coming at it from this human rights perspective, and seeing that we don't even have the right to breathe clean air in our neighborhood, it was an easier way for us to understand and be motivated to learn . . . and do the research.

For students in Free Your Voice, questions of environmental health and the right to breathe necessitated investigation into the underlying causes of asthma and other respiratory problems. "We related to one another initially because of our staggered breathing. We all had the fear of not being able to breathe, which lived deep inside of us," Crystal explained. Shared vulnerability became a bridge to building solidaristic relationships and collectivism and, ultimately, the activism to change things. But let's go back to 2010, one year before Free Your Voice was founded, for just a moment.

In 2010, former Peace Corps volunteer turned organizer for The Worker Justice Center Daniel Murphy was tasked with organizing a human rights committee on the South Baltimore Peninsula.[4] As one part of his organizing efforts, he introduced an after-school program at Benjamin Franklin High School that borrowed its pedagogy from Brazilian education activist and author Paulo Freire. The program, which became known as Free Your Voice, created space for students to gather, share personal stories, and eventually, discuss and respond to the structural problems of poverty and inequality in their community. Borrowing Freire's notion of "problem-posing education," the program provided students with opportunities to teach the teacher rather than to memorize and be taught (these latter are components of what Freire called the "banking system of education," a system that maintains oppression, according to Freire, by viewing students as containers into which information can be fit, rather than as knowledge makers in their own right). In problem-posing education, Freire asserted: "The students—no longer docile listeners—are now critical co-investigators in dialogue with the teacher. The teacher presents the material to the students for their consideration, and re-considers her earlier considerations as the students express their own. The role of the problem-posing educator is to create, together with the students, the conditions under which knowledge at the level of the *doxa* is superseded by true knowledge, at the level of the *logos*" (Freire [1970] 2018: 81). Many of the questions the students posed, and around which that would later organize their research, came directly from their experiences growing up poor.

But because trauma defined everyday experiences for so many of the youth who participated in the Free Your Voice program, the project was, initially, about getting the students to share their vulnerabilities. "How can we create a safe space where students did not feel judged and could share freely?" asked Murphy. Additionally: how can a teacher or organizer create a space where youth can share trauma and come to share in their senses of vulnerability? Murphy described fostering rapport by doing what students wanted to do, and without time limits, as key. "There weren't any restrictions for relationship building. We would play board games and other stuff that they liked to do. It wasn't just about the intellectual and political work but the work of getting to know one another and trust one another. You know there wasn't a lot of limits in terms of our time, but there wasn't anything preset about it because it wasn't about a schedule we established. It was very organic. My goal was for that to be happening all day and night." After playing board games or hanging out together, the students found it easier to open up to one another in other ways, too. They began to share stories about their lives. In student Terrel Jones's words:

> We are all kids who go through so much struggle in our lives. Some being great. Some being small. It's still a struggle. And no matter how big a problem is . . . it puts a lot of stress on an individual person. Hearing other people's struggles made me realize I was not alone. It makes you think that there are other people going through similar kinds of things. They live in the same circumstances that I do, and you suddenly feel less alone in the world.

Murphy and other adult leaders involved in Free Your Voice worked with students to leverage their confidence. This meant focusing on what students were good at, what they felt were their "inner passions," and then showing them that these were relevant—the latter Murphy described as "out of the box thinking":

> It might not seem obvious that whatever skill [students] have is related [to opposing a proposal to build an incinerator next door, for example] . . . but chances are it is, in some way. Art, music, culinary skills, y'know, whatever. Something. Everyone's got something. It's how you build those little bridges so people see that's where our power comes from. But . . . that's not the culture we're in, to use those things for some kind of collective purpose.

Related to getting students to open up to one another while also acquiring shared values, "repetition is key," Murphy believed, along with the act of making things in collaboration. "Making hundreds of sunflowers and cutting them out [for a protest or a march]. That became a backdrop for having really good conversations," he explained.

> Y'know, people making stuff, you see the accomplishment at the end. It's beautiful when you make these giant sunflowers made up of smaller sunflowers. In the process, you're talking about a lot of stuff. Some of it was related to the issues [of environmental justice], but a lot of it isn't. All that

stuff . . . that to me is more fruitful for organizing [students, community members, really, anyone].

Murphy described repetitive actions as "embodied learning":

> It's embodied. It feels good when you do it, so you wanna do more of it. It's functional, as well, in generating something you need. But, yeah, anyway, the repetition . . . I think we tried to find things that would build in a need to sustain activity over a long period of time. If it's purely discussion based, the stamina for discussions can be very low, and there's no need to sustain the discussion past the five-minute mark when you run out of steam. But if you're sustaining a conversation over making wooden blocks to look like vacants, That takes days, if not hours. Then, you're able to sustain a conversation throughout all those days unless the making stuff is so demanding you can't talk at the same time. That was always a balance: to find the right amount of making things. . . . Y'know, we didn't want to be a sunflower-making group for the sake of it, obviously. There's nothing wrong with that, but . . . that is not what we wanted to become.

Once the students in Free Your Voice learned to trust one another, they wanted to understand what produced the traumas they lived, the ones they were describing to each other. "What are the problems we experience together?" they asked. And "how can we solve these problems?"

In order to focus these questions still further, Murphy utilized what is known as the Socratic method, described by political science professor Rob Reich (Sanford 2003) as follows: "In the Socratic method, the classroom experience is a shared dialogue between teacher and students in which both are responsible for pushing the dialogue forward through questioning. The 'teacher,' or leader of the dialogue, asks probing questions in an effort to expose the values and beliefs which frame and support the thoughts and statements of the participants in the inquiry. The students ask questions as well, both of the teacher and each other." As an organizer and educator, Murphy wanted to hear what youth were thinking, how they were making sense of their own situations and connecting these to inequities in the community:

For example, we started conversations about . . . whatever . . . not in any specific way . . . a conversation about the community. But then I would ask: can things change? Can we affect some sort of change in this community? I assumed the answer wasn't going to be a resounding yes. I thought maybe it would be suspicious like a lot of "I don't knows." I had faith that there would be enough tension there to dig deeper. Productive tension is good. Then, if there was, my job was to grab onto that tension, listen carefully, and push it a little further. If there was a statement of "they would never let this happen," then that's an amazing gift to the conversation because you can guess who is "they." . . . Not slamming down on them, but in a genuinely curious way. Like, who do you think of when you say "they"? If anything. And if you don't, do you want to think about that? Let's explore who the "they" are. . . . That led to researching actors.

I think this is what [student] Terrel refers to a lot. A lot of our initial conversations was me playing devil's advocate and asking a lot of questions. For Terrel, being asked to share stuff that he has never been asked to think about before by another person and especially by a traditional teacher held him accountable. But no one who seems to be coming to you and saying, do you want to try to do something? Then, actually fostering a process like that is critical for youth, especially for poor youth. So the Socratic method worked in pushing many of these youth further.

The constant questions guided youth to become student investigators of their community and their environment, never accepting simple answers or solutions and always digging a bit deeper to the structural (or root) causes of a problem.

Murphy worked alongside the students while they reviewed relevant literature, visited archives (online and offline) and city code enforcement databases, interviewed community residents, and mapped sections of the peninsula where they lived. These methods allowed the students to explore, collectively, the histories of several of the toxic industries present on the peninsula. The students read *The Environmental History of Fairfield and Wagner's Point* by Philip Diamond (1998). They also built a website (https://stoptheincinerator.wordpress.com/) about the history of uneven geographical development and subsequent environmental injustices in their community. As they grew into their roles, the students developed key facilitation skills, where they would lead and then train the next generation of youth wanting to engage in this kind of work. The audience for student research, according to students in the program, as well as Murphy, was other high school youth, but it was also much broader—broader even than the neighborhood of Curtis Bay or the entire South Baltimore Peninsula. The audience "was always the outside world," said Murphy.

THE PROBLEM TREE, THE POWER CUBE, AND ETHNOGRAPHY

One exercise utilized by Murphy and the students is known in education and social justice circles as "The Problem Tree." This collaborative, qualitative exercise invites participants to envision the roots of a problem (again, in fitting with Freire's model of "problem-posing education") as connected through a trunk to branches of a tree, which are connected to the leaves, which sprout from them. As decolonial thinker and indigenous activist Eve Tuck explains, "The Leaves represent the overt, most evident symptoms of the problem. The Trunk represents the immediate causes of the leaves. What informs the overt symptoms of the problem? The Roots represent the deep social, economic, and political structures and attitudes that feed the trunk" (2008). Intensely pedagogical and theoretical, this exercise is at the same time accessible, easily reproducible, and malleable. Free Your Voice youth used it to prompt early-stage, participatory inquiry before choosing research questions and designing research projects. Students often asked, "What are the roots of the problem?" In other words: How can we map the structures that feed the leaves of the tree—the symptoms of the problem?

Often the students found, as a result of their research, that the roots of the problems they studied were linked to the economy, which produces and perpetuates unjust hierarchical orders (across race, class, gender, ethnicity, citizenship, and place) and related, uneven distribution of resources, unfair zoning policies and land-use patterns, and more. In

2012, when students organized against the politicians and investors who proposed building an incinerator next door to them (chapter 3), students labeled the roots of their "problem tree" as the human rights violations perpetrated for more than a century by toxic industries located on the peninsula. The branches of the tree they sketched represented the socioeconomic and health consequences of incineration (which threatened to become the newest polluter on the peninsula).

The problem tree challenged Free Your Voice students to understand the root causes of poverty, something many of the youth found difficult to do initially. Instead, they found themselves blaming "behaviors," and blaming individuals for choosing the wrong behaviors (including prostitution, drugs, and gang activity). "This place is a dumping ground because community residents don't know how to take care of it" was something that the students uttered in various ways in the early days of Free Your Voice. According to the Worker Justice Center organizers, blaming one another for the problems of poverty is an internalized form of oppression. Speaking of "behaviors" as roots of the problems of poverty rather than as something stemming from still deeper injustices is part of a process in which victims are blamed while the individuals who benefit from (and usually work to sustain) historically emplaced structural injustices go unnoticed—and/or are sometimes even heralded as the good guys.

According to American Studies scholar Julie Sze, what is perhaps the most difficult part of organizing work is getting activists to see and understand that race, class, gender, immigration/refugee status, indigenous land claims, and territorial sovereignty are all interconnected (Sze 2020: 5). Academics refer to this as intersectionality. Murphy's problem was not only how to get high school students to see the contexts underlying the behaviors they so readily recognized as problematic, but also, how to get them to see that, in his words, "race, poverty, [and] inequality are linked in a toxic brew." The problem tree exercise helped students to see beyond individual behaviors and individual deficiencies to conceptualize the ways in which a deep history of uneven geographical development and uneven distribution of resources rooted in racism and classism created many of the problems in their community.

Another popular education tool used by Murphy and the Free Your Voice students was the power cube designed by political sociologist John Gaventa. This framework for analyzing spaces, places, and forms of power and their interrelationships encourages students to analyze power at distinct scales (local, national, global) while learning to distinguish among distinct forms of power (such as closed, invited, claimed/ created). Though visually presented as a cube with six sides, each side contains nine smaller cubes, like a Rubik's cube (Gaventa 2006). The power cube shows how power operates and how individuals in civil society can/cannot make claims on space (Gaventa 2006; Luttrell et al. 2007). Starting in 2013, the power cube became an especially important exercise for Free Your Voice students, helping them to recognize power and to trace decision-making at local, city, regional, and state levels as these related to incineration. With practice, students became adept at identifying who made the decisions affecting their community, and they were able to conclude that it was the mayor, city council, and transnational corporations.

Also during power cube exercises, conversations surfaced about forms of power. Students discussed city officials making decisions. They discussed large-scale developers coming to a neighborhood as visible and observable. They talked about CSX donating money to their school and Grace Chemicals providing funding for summer camps as forms of hidden power because it is invisible and often happens behind the backs of the public. One student said, "We come to see 'these donations' as acts of charity and think, 'Wow, they are doing good in our neighborhood.' To me that's invisible power." Another responded, "Yeah. Maybe they do this so we ignore the ways in which they pollute Curtis Bay." Throughout this book, I have chosen to refer to the illicit wheelings and dealings that connect the public to the private, that connect, for example, polluters to educators, and that confuse the categories of good investor/bad investor as "toxic entanglements." These are the toxic entanglements of industrial development. The Free Your Voice students used the power cube to create spaces for dialogue, first among themselves and later with political leaders. Within these dialogues, they were able to draw attention to many of the toxic entanglements in their community.

In addition to utilizing exercises in the classroom, students in Free Your Voice became ethnographers of their own communities. Murphy described how the five students in the first cohort of Free Your Voice explored the community and the facets or parts of the community where their neighbors preferred not to go alone. The peninsula did not (and still does not) lend itself to individual exploration due to its mix of industrial wasteland and high levels of crime and violence. So, Murphy and the students often went out and walked the community together. They walked and talked, or "journeyed," together, occupying (and thus reclaiming) spaces as a group that were intimidating to each individually. Equipped with notebooks and cell phones, they documented injustices and brought jottings, sketches, and photographs back to the group to share. Very quickly, students grew adept at identifying the structural injustices in and around them.

To document the "toxic brew" of industrial and residential dumping surrounding them, they sought and found data that was textual, but also olfactory, visual, and multisensorial in other ways. Destiny, who was in the original cohort and later returned as a leader of Free Your Voice, spoke about the ways in which she focused her senses early on to hear the sounds of the industrial peninsula. She described many of the sites along the route she took to get to school. "I remember walking through streets where truck noise was so loud, I could barely hear my siblings . . . but I didn't really think twice about it. It felt so normal." Crystal, like Destiny, was a student in the original Free Your Voice cohort and later returned as a leader of the program. She spoke of isolating smells the first year she was in Free Your Voice, of learning to home in on the scents coming from the industrial hub. These and other "thick descriptions" (Geertz 1973), or "five-sense notes" as we called them in Free Your Voice, produced by students provoked conversations about why heavy industry was located on and what it meant for the peninsula.

Even with rapport building and confidence boosting, followed by "liberating" exercises and ethnography, teaching students that the toxic entanglements they were learning to document were connected to their own lives and their own histories of trauma was a challenge. After years of learning that the toxicity of their community was "so normal" (Destiny's words), students needed to learn—more accurately, they needed to teach themselves, with their leaders as co-teachers and co-learners, according to Freire's pedagogy—that their experiences, individual as well as shared, were affected by the broader political economy of inequitable toxic "dumping."

"ROOT SHOCK" ON THE PENINSULA

The Free Your Voice program succeeded not in spite of but because of its location at Benjamin Franklin High and in a community devastated by deindustrialization and plagued by environmental injustice.[5] In 2010, Brooklyn–Curtis Bay was engulfed by heavy industry, yet lacked a single supermarket. The neighborhood had a crime rate of 81.7 per 1,000 residents (versus Baltimore City's rate of 61.4). While 54.9 percent of the residents had at least some high school education, the majority had not graduated, and 75.77 percent of Brooklyn–Curtis Bay residents were blue collar workers.[6] This same year, BFHS was ranked in the bottom 5 percent of Maryland public schools and was struggling to survive. The demographics at BFHS were comparable to the overall demographics of Curtis Bay: African American (43 percent), Latinx (32.9 percent), White (21.6 percent).[7]

In this setting, the halls of Benjamin Franklin became an obvious space for students like Destiny Watford to begin organizing other students. Destiny often shuffled as she walked through the hallways in her black dress flats. Her magnetic energy captivated her peers. Between classes, she would hand out informational fliers about environmental justice and housing inequalities. She started conversations with her peers about what she and the other students already in Free Your Voice were doing in the after-school program. Her efforts to recruit her peers into Free Your Voice brought some of the least likely students to the program, and as a result, Free Your Voice included both straight-A students who participated in many activities and students who were bored by school and by extracurriculars, and whose grades and attendance rates reflected this boredom.

These latter students, just like the A-earners, found many things in Free Your Voice that kept them coming back, including guidance for effecting change in and around their neighborhoods, and space and community for sharing, connecting, and healing. For some of the youth, trauma (historical and contemporary, physical and psychological) defined their everyday experiences.[8] Many youth living and studying on the South Baltimore Peninsula lived complicated familial lives. Some endured physical and emotional abuse in their households, while others grew up aware of drug use and prostitution inside the vacant homes on their blocks. Lawrence Brown (2021) labeled these experiences as "root shock," a phrase he used to describe the traumatic stress reaction to the loss of some or all of one's emotional ecosystem. While root shock can follow a natural disaster (think of Hurricane Katrina), on the South Baltimore Peninsula it was (and is) a human-made phenomenon. The disaster played itself out through racist, classist systems, practices, and policies that produced and reproduced inequities, contaminating not only the air the students at Benjamin Franklin High breathed, but also the housing they could and could not access, as well as their health care, education, and food systems.

Root shocks can paralyze an individual's physical body, and numb emotional and mental well-being. In the earliest days of Free Your Voice, Murphy recalls students of Benjamin Franklin High who put up walls, sleeping instead of engaging; focusing on iPhones during intimate sharing sessions; getting up and walking out of group dialogues. This prevented them from coming together as a cohesive community and presented Murphy with his first challenge: how to help students care about these inequalities and find unity in "collective struggle."

TERREL JONES'S STORY: MULTIPLE DISPLACEMENTS LED TO ROOT SHOCK

Terrel Jones was one of the first students to join Free Your Voice. He was also one of the first to share "his story" with his peers after Murphy and the group came up with guidelines for group discussions. Terrel remembered it being hard to open up to the group. A young Black man, he was so painfully shy that his body seemed to cringe, with shoulders slouched and rolled forward during the school day. When he occasionally spoke up, he often stumbled over his words. And he only rarely made eye contact with his interlocutors. Murphy described Terrel's mannerisms as being steeped in a sense of financial precarity and constant movement.

In Terrel's own telling, he grew up moving from one place to another and had spent periods of time living without shelter or, as he called it, "living on edge." He explained that he saw things no teenager should ever see while "on the streets," listing prostitution, gangs, drugs, and even murder. When he told his personal stories of displacement, Terrel fidgeted with nervousness. Terrel's experiences of homelessness (the result of a death in his family) and his movements from one household to another (including within the US foster care system) were not atypical among students at Benjamin Franklin High School. Many switched households frequently, and some also had experiences with homelessness.

Terrel spent the first three years of his life, from 1995 to 1998, in Murphy Homes, a public housing complex on the West side of Baltimore made up of fourteen-story high-rises. The year after Terrel and his family moved out, the complex was demolished—by city ordinance, and by 375 pounds of dynamite (Pelton and Oakes 1999). Terrel described Murphy Homes as the "Murder Homes," a place of crime, addiction, and violence. From the Murphy Homes, Terrel's family relocated to the mixed-income housing project known as Amberwood Homes in the Moravia area of North Baltimore. They were able to do this using a Section 8 voucher. Terrel described becoming much more self aware as a child while living in a first-floor apartment in Amberwood Homes. There, from 2008 to 2010 and as a young teenager, Terrel cared for his dying mother: "There were days I would stay home from school to be able to care for my mother. We hoped her health would improve, but it got worse. She went to several nursing homes, and I ended up living with my aunt in Anne Arundel County. My mom fell into a coma, and I remember the doctor saying it was induced by stress. It was here that my life started to spin out of control."

After Terrel's mother passed away, his family moved to Robstown, Texas in search of affordable housing. "My family relations became stressed, and I eventually ended up in foster care," Terrel explained. "The foster court case was resolved, and I moved to South Baltimore to live with my aunt and start at Benjamin Franklin High School. From 2012 to 2013, I lived in Curtis Bay on Elm Street with my aunt. She got sick and passed away, and that's when things got really bad. I started taking long walks to get away and find escapes from my life. I was so numb and hollowed out that I turned to marijuana." Forced to leave his aunt's abandoned home, Terrel became homeless. Some nights he would stay on Curtis Avenue with friends from Benjamin Franklin High School who likewise had nowhere else to go. At other times, Terrel's housed high school friends allowed him to stay with their families for short periods.

It was during this period of homelessness that Terrel heard about Free Your Voice and started attending the meetings and sharing parts of his lived experience with his peers. In the evenings after school, when he had nowhere else to go, he often wound up at Murphy's house where he could spend the night on the couch. (Murphy opened up his

doors to several of the youth when they needed a safe place to stay).[9]
Later, Murphy invited Terrel into his home for an extended period
of time. Terrel lived in Murphy's basement while working at a fast-
food restaurant and saving money to be able to rent an apartment of
his own.

CRYSTAL GREEN'S STORY:
SEARCHING FOR MEANINGFUL COMMUNITY

Crystal Green, who graduated from Benjamin Franklin High in 2012,
was another member of the original Free Your Voice cohort. After
graduating, she went away to college, but she quickly learned that being
away made her feel alienated from her community. She felt out of place
while at college. As a result, she returned to the peninsula. "I shouldn't
have to run from my community," she explained.

In 2015, after her return, Crystal took a job at an Amazon fulfillment
center located in South Baltimore. There she worked as a tech assistant
fixing broken computer monitors, but she felt like "a cog in a machine"
In contrast to this, Crystal remembered her time as a high school student in the Free Your Voice program as creative, innovative, and intellectually challenging. She described her experience at Amazon, with
its long hours, long days, and the growing alienation/mechanization
of those working on the plant floor, as undermining the sense of self-
confidence and self-determination that she had cultivated while a part
of Free Your Voice.[10] Therefore, it was with great intentionality that
Crystal returned to the after-school program in 2018: "I was like, oh, of
course I'm gonna do this. I liked what I was doing [at the high school].
It felt real and it felt right to me, so I did the whole interview thing.
I think even if I didn't get the job, I would still work—volunteer and
talk to [students in the program]—when I wasn't working twelve-hour
shifts at Amazon." Crystal Green was a gregarious teenager during
the early years of Free Your Voice. She remembered seeing Murphy in
school, walking up to him, and asking, "What do you do?"

"To myself I was thinking what is this white man doing in this community? Why is he even here?" Crystal recalled. She was fearless in her relationship building, posing provocative questions from the start, and unlike Terrel, she always stood upright, looking her interlocutors in the eyes when she addressed them. She remembered Murphy inviting her to come and learn with a group of youth after school. And she recalled bringing a group of friends along with her to the meetings when they first began. "I don't remember what exactly our conversation was about. But I remember we would usually hang out and talk. We started talking about what we saw in the community. I didn't feel at the time like it was a class on community poverty, but in a sense it was. We talked about where we lived and what we thought of the places where we lived. People talked about nothing good in the community, talking about drugs and people selling drugs in the community."

Crystal imagined the world of her mother, who grew up and came of age in 1950s Baltimore. Despite the fact that Baltimore was hyper-segregated, Crystal's mother spoke of a deep sense of community and how all the neighbors knew one another and took care of each other. Sometimes cooking meals, sometimes watching each other's children—these were part of the deep fictive kin relationships that residents built to survive and to thrive, according to Crystal's mother. While attending Free Your Voice sessions and listening to personal narratives recounted by her peers, Crystal reflected upon her own life and how seismic ruptures left her feeling lost and anxious. She wanted to recreate the kind of community that her mother described to her. She wanted a sense of home grounded in place and with fictive kin relationships. "I wanted to bring back what my mother had. I just knew drugs and violence plagued our communities, but it wasn't because people were bad. It wasn't just because people were born bad. It was things in their lives shaping them to make them feel like they had to do this to survive. I wanted to see what my mother had in terms of relationships and community."

Crystal's story of life as a teenager, like that of Terrel, was of frequent displacement. She told her story to her peers (and more than once to journalists) in bits and pieces. She described going into communities, living for a period of time, and then something would happen. Something like a gang-related outbreak of violence, for example, and "my mom would just run." Crystal wanted to establish relationships in high school, and to deepen and enrich those relationships. Crystal described how nervous she was when she first joined Free Your Voice, and then how thankful she was:

> My mom and I were not talking, and I was trying to deal with so much at the time. I didn't have anyone in my corner. It was only me, and I was trying to figure out all these things. But I still cared about what was happening. So many of us were struggling with basic needs like housing, where we were going to get meals from, how to support our families economically. It was really powerful when we could share some of these struggles. We were vulnerable. Talking with others about it made us realize that we were not alone. We felt for the first time that we weren't alone. It's not just me personally being affected by high rents. We are all dealing with it. Then when you begin to see there are bigger structures in place, that it's constructed, and it's not by accident—wow! That's powerful.

JIMMY BROWN'S EXPERIENCE:
FROM THE BACK TO THE FRONT OF FREE YOUR VOICE

Jimmy Brown joined Free Your Voice as a student in the Fall cohort of 2018, three years after the Free Your Voice program shifted to focus explicitly on Participatory Action Research (see chapter 4). Jimmy was a quiet but deeply thoughtful young man who sported different colored hairdos (sometimes purple, sometimes orange, etc.) with short dreadlocks. Jimmy lived in the Cherry Hill community, founded in the 1940s and '50s by the Housing Authority of Baltimore as a neighborhood for Black families migrating from the South in search of industrial jobs. It is located across the Hanover Street Bridge, south of the city of Baltimore less than two miles north of Curtis Bay. Jimmy's home was one of the many army-barrack-styled public housing units in Cherry Hill, properties that were turned into low-income housing following World War II. As Jimmy explained: "My mother worked for the government, and we were living in public housing because she could not afford rent. She was a single mom trying to raise three kids. There were so many problems with public housing. Our basement was flooded during a hurricane and the maintenance men never got there to fix the damage. . . . The refrigerator always leaked. There was mold in the shower. The shower was never hot. I learned to live with this."

I often picked Jimmy up for youth events and would park my car in front of his house to wait. From there, I sometimes picked up the smells of deep-fried foods and marijuana wafting down the street. Garbage was piled up on corners, local parks were covered in layers of graffiti tags, and on the block just before Jimmy's, discarded needles and ongoing drug deals were equally visible to passersby.

"I've been moving house to house my whole life," Jimmy explained.

> I thought it was normal, my mind could never connect the dots. I didn't understand that we were constantly being evicted because my mother who had no help and three kids couldn't afford to pay her rent. As I've aged, I started to see why we were being displaced. We were paying high rent for houses that had too many problems that housing [authorities] didn't want to fix. We eventually had to move into a two-bedroom house. This house was affordable only because the conditions were terrible: mold, and leaking problems. I, too, have faced eviction. It is very scary not knowing if you will have a roof over your head.

Often Jimmy came to class tired, worn out from working the night shift at Chick-fil-A in order to help his mom pay rent.

> I was working in Chick-fil-A in the tenth grade. I would work at 12 a.m., the night shift. So I would have to get up super-early to take a shuttle [from home to the light rail station] and then get all the way to [the airport] on the light rail. Even in my twelfth-grade year, I had to go to classes the next day, and I'd say to my group, "Please don't blame me, but I did not get enough sleep."

Jimmy described the working conditions in the back of the fast-food industry as "dehumanizing":

> The managers used all kinds of tactics of fear to keep us working fast and without breaks. Sometimes they tell us that we would be fired if we didn't work fast enough. Sometimes we couldn't even take bathroom breaks, so I would hold it during my whole shift.

Despite the hardships Jimmy described, and his narratives of growing up poor and, later, overworked and underpaid in and around Cherry Hill, passion radiated from him as he spoke. His eyes often told a story of their own, dancing with emotion, glimmering as he talked.

Jimmy described Free Your Voice, when he first joined, as not quite for him. "I just wasn't really interested." At the beginning, he admitted, he was just taking the class because it seemed like an easy credit for graduation. But when Destiny Watford (who was no longer a student at Benjamin Franklin High School but leading the program she once piloted along with Murphy) described the health effects of incineration, using a pamphlet from Global Alliance for Incinerator Alternatives (GAIA), something changed for Jimmy. He later described Destiny as "a bright light." "She had this awareness of the issues and such a sweet and kind way about her. I was drawn in." Jimmy explained that when Destiny talked to him about incineration in a way that allowed him to connect it to his own personal life, he arrived at epiphanies. "Wow, this is why our football team doesn't win, because of all the respiratory issues we have [on the peninsula]," Jimmy realized. "To me, it became very personal. I remember feeling very angry and scared, actually terrified, when I heard that incineration could cause birth defects." Destiny helped to channel Jimmy's anger into inquiry by posing the right kinds of questions and giving Jimmy work outside the space of the classroom to then bring back to the group. This independent work was, in Jimmy's words, "like a fire or something; it lit a spark inside of me, and I wanted to learn more." Among other things, Jimmy developed interests in the international alliance of grassroots organizations fighting to end incineration (chapter 3) and support zero-waste initiatives (chapter 4).

CONCIENTIZACIÓN AND CONNECTING
THE PERSONAL TO THE COMMUNAL

Sharing stories, as Terrel, Crystal, and Jimmy did, was emotionally cleansing for many of the students, but it also tethered the youth to one another. As Terrel Jones described:

> I realized by hearing other people's pain that I was not alone. I could express myself freely and not be afraid or ashamed of my conditions. I used to think that my problems were about individual deficiency, or these problems were my fault. But I realized it was a bigger beast. These conversations really helped build unity, and we started to trust one another. I could express some of these challenges, and I knew I had a team behind me that would support and back me up in any way they could.

Along with unity, the students built confidence from the personal discussions of pain and trauma. According to Murphy, Terrel progressed from "not being able to sustain a conversation . . . to really beginning to identify the problem in his personal life and to pose the right kinds of questions."

Paulo Freire called the process by which learners become aware of how poverty has numbed them into acceptance of a status quo and their oppression as *concientización*, or "to awaken a critical consciousness" ([1970] 2018). When trauma is relocated, no longer understood as something that lives inside individuals but instead becomes understood as something that is communitywide, or structural and systemic, this approximates what Freire meant by *concientización*. Murphy helped Free Your Voice students see poverty and inequality as trauma, and as a violation of their human rights. He worked to reveal to them the structures and interlocking systems of oppression at work in their lives. Sometimes students had to take these systems apart and study land or zoning practices separately and then put their findings together with macro-level understandings of industrial development to see how a policy, became entangled, for example, with an industrial polluter's business and a family member's asthma.

The students participating in Free Your Voice used their own stories to understand systems of oppression and then chose, together, to become more involved in a process of liberation for themselves and others in their community. As Murphy described, "leadership learning did not occur on the level of one person telling their story but rather people experiencing and critically reflecting on their own actions and relations and how this might relate to others in the group." The cross-conversations within the group made youth feel worthy. Seasoned leaders also challenged youth to disagree with one another, respectfully, about poverty and inequality, racism and injustices. From disagreement grew knowledge, and in Free Your Voice, it was the students who were positioned as knowledge makers.

CHAPTER THREE

Fighting the Nation's Largest Trash-to-Energy Incinerator

It was bitterly cold on December 18, 2013, when Free Your Voice students Terrel, Destiny, and Crystal led a group that included their peers, teachers, the principal of Benjamin Franklin High School, and other allies, down East Patapsco Avenue to the would-be site of a trash-to-energy incinerator. The incinerator was being proposed by the Maryland Department of the Environment and a New York–based company, Energy Answers International, with a scheduled completion date in the summer of 2014. Upon completion it would be the largest waste-to-energy system in the nation, importing garbage from all over the United States and permitted, by Maryland state officials, to emit up to 240 pounds of mercury and 1,000 pounds of lead per year (see https://stoptheincinerator.com). The students and their allies held massive banners reading, "We demand Fair Development." At the front of the group, Terrel, Destiny, and Crystal shouted into megaphones.

"What do we want?" the students cried.

"Clean air!" the marchers responded.

"When do we want it?" students asked in unison.

"Now!" the marchers responded.

The crowd chanted, "Clean air is only fair."

When the group arrived at the site where the incinerator was to be built, less than one mile from the high school, they stopped. There the students initiated a ceremony. They gathered community residents and allies together to honor those members of their community who had high rates of cancer, asthma, and other respiratory illnesses as a result of the toxic pollution in the neighborhood.

Next, Terrel took a megaphone, closed his eyes, and, trembling with nervousness, leaned forward and began to speak:

> Fair development is when the community has a voice in every decision that affects us. Charlie Chaplin in his movie, *The Great Dictator*, said it best. "We think too much and feel too little." More than machinery, we need humanity. More than cleverness, we need kindness and gentleness. Without these qualities, life would be violent, and all would be lost. The airplane and radio brought us closer together. The very nature of these inventions cries out for the goodness of men, cries out for universal brotherhood, for the unity of us all. . . .We are going to take a moment of silence to contemplate the incinerator, and envision development that brings out the goodness of men, universal brotherhood, and the unity of us all. We are going to envision fair development.

Ricardo Chavez, a Latinx organizer from The Worker Justice Center, ended the protest that day by asking the crowd to leave a yellow flower on the fence of the Food Machinery and Chemical Company (FMC) site,

> We want you to take a moment and think about all the people that have been the victims of failed development, all the people who have died and all the kids who have asthma in this area. Think about all the injustice. Because we have had enough. We have had enough!

In this chapter, I chart a student-led campaign to stop an incinerator from being built on the South Baltimore Peninsula, recognizing that this three-phase fight functioned as a school for low-income youth of color. The Stop the Incinerator campaign, in its first phase, emphasized education and outreach. Beginning in 2011, Daniel Murphy (representing The Worker Justice Center) spent more than fifty hours per week organizing at BFHS and bolstering the student-led Free Your Voice program from behind the scenes. It was during this phase of the campaign that students involved in Free Your Voice learned about incineration and became experts and teachers within the community.

In the campaign's second phase, students sought to expand their organizing work (and impacts) by connecting with their broader community. From 2011 to 2015, the project grew into a collaboration between students and organizers from The Worker Justice Center, eventually becoming an even more expansive coalition that participants referred to as "The Dream Team." During this second phase, students and their allies learned to use communal testimonials to see and then show structural racism through time. They learned to use the arts (including performance) to tell the stories of the impacts of toxic industries on their neighborhoods, including incineration. The narratives the students brought to life focused on local histories of environmental racism and the ways in which residents in frontline communities bear the health burdens of polluting industries.

The third phase of the campaign to stop the incinerator was marked by acts of civil disobedience performed by Free Your Voice youth, The Worker Justice Center organizers, and some allies. In this latter stage, the campaign evolved yet again. This time organizers identified and attacked the people financially invested in and/or politicking for the incinerator project. Organizers, including the Benjamin Franklin High students along with The Worker Justice Center staff and allies, placed significant pressure on the Maryland Department of the Environment (MDE) to rescind building permits for the incineration facility (which they had awarded to Energy Answers International in 2010).

Through each stage of the campaign, students who were enrolled in the Free Your Voice program played key roles in learning, teaching, building external alliances, and placing pressure on officials of the state of Maryland.

PHASE I: EDUCATION AND OUTREACH

In 2011, Free Your Voice cofounder Daniel Murphy organized a field trip to see a performance of Arthur Miller's adaption of Henrik Ibsen's nineteenth-century play *An Enemy of the People* at Baltimore Center Stage. From the beginning of the Stop the Incinerator campaign, art, theater, and literature were important vehicles for the students to connect both cognitively and emotionally, not only to one another but also to larger structural issues in their community. Art also became a way for them to communicate effectively and, in so doing, pull allies into the struggle. On the field trip that day, students drew important connections between the play and their experiences of living in a polluted community. "It just completely blew my mind," said Destiny Watford. "It was about this neighborhood and these two brothers—one is a politician and one is a scientist. The neighborhood is horribly polluted by their hot spring, but the hot spring is what brings so much wealth into the neighborhood. They were forced to ask this question: Are we willing to be poor and not have the hot spring and live longer? Or do we sacrifice the health of our neighborhood? I remember coming home from that play and talking to all my friends."

After the play, Murphy shared with students on the trip an article from the *Baltimore Brew* about the proposed Energy Answers incinerator.[1] The article laid out a plan to build the nation's largest trash-to-energy incinerator—in the students' backyard. "I took it home and I read it, and I was just blown away," recalled Destiny. "I remember coming to the [after-school] meeting where folks were speaking up and talking about the issue, and that became Free Your Voice." According to Destiny, the play "broke the numbness" that came with growing up amid so many polluting industries—and the article gave the students a sense of direction. They decided they wanted to do something about those industries.

Destiny remembered a group of about six or sometimes seven students, most of whom were awkward and shy and all of whom were in tenth and eleventh grades. The group was "really informal," according to Destiny. Often the students "just talked about crime and/or violence in the community, or personal problems." But they also asked bigger questions, like: What do we want out of this group? What do we believe in? What do we value in the world? "The incinerator issue was not the first or only issue that we talked about," explained Destiny. "We talked about a lot of other things going on in our community."

The group quickly came to the conclusion—prompted by Murphy's sharing of the UN Declaration of Human Rights—that incineration violated residents' basic rights—the right to clean air, the right to breathe, the right to prosper.[2] Destiny shared:

> This made it easier for us to understand and be motivated to learn the education and do the research. I remember, specifically, one student, Chris—who worked with us for a little while before going off to college—questioned us just as we were asking ourselves "Do we really want to do this? Can we actually do anything about it? We're just kids." He said, "If we don't do something, then what is the point of our group?" That really lit a fire under everyone, and we started doing that research and talking to people.

Two years after the field trip to the theatre, Destiny brought the *Baltimore Brew* article Murphy had shared to a Free Your Voice meeting where she presented it to peers who had not been on the field trip. At the time, the youth in Free Your Voice knew little about incineration. They decided they needed to learn more. Leanna Jackson, who was a member of the original Free Your Voice cohort and a sophomore in 2011, said: "I knew it burned stuff, but I didn't know what it burned exactly. I knew there were different types . . . so when we [were] doing research, we found out what an incinerator was. We learned about some of the stuff that it puts in the air like lead, mercury. . . . At the time, I remember us quickly relating it to illnesses." Destiny recalled, "As we all read the article, we saw these very clear connections, realizing like, 'Oh, this is happening right *here* in our neighborhood. We are being forced to make this decision. It's not a fictional story. It's reality.'"

Free Your Voice students learned through the *Baltimore Brew* article (Shen 2010) that Governor Martin O'Malley had signed an energy credit bill into law that gave the incinerator Tier 1 renewable status.[3] This status made the incinerator eligible to receive government subsidies and benefits, meaning it could receive the same kinds of subsidies as wind and solar panels. This was controversial because it placed waste-to-energy incineration in the category of renewable or "clean" energy. Industry representatives argued that incineration helped divert waste from landfills that produce methane, a much more potent greenhouse gas and invested heavily in lobbying politicians. Yet O'Malley had failed to consider the pollution that would be generated by increased use of diesel trucks moving through the community and the ash created by incineration that would inevitably line landfills on the peninsula.

Through further readings, students learned that the same year the proposed incinerator was given renewable status, Mayor Stephanie Rawlings-Blake received four thousand dollars from Energy Answers Baltimore, LLC—the company driving the incineration project—and four thousand dollars from the company's CEO, Patrick F. Mahoney.[4] O'Malley's campaign received one thousand dollars from Mahoney in January of 2010 (Shen 2012a, 2012b). Also, during the first six months after O'Malley became chairman of the Democratic Governors Association, Energy Answers International funneled a total of one hundred thousand dollars into the association (Shen 2012a, 2012b). Curtis Bay Community Association, too, seems to have been swayed by corporate dollars: members of the association pledged to support the incineration project after Energy Answers promised the association their own one hundred thousand dollars in funding (Shen 2012a, 2012b).

When Free Your Voice students learned that their community association pledged to support the incinerator, they learned, too, of a fundamental tension that ignites environmental debates: the pitting of job opportunities against residents' health.[5] From 2010 to 2011, the unemployment rate in Brooklyn–Curtis Bay was 11.8 percent, more than one and a half times that of the rest of Baltimore (Baltimore Neighborhood Indicator Alliance–Jacob France Institute2019). As a steelworkers' union leader Henry Lowry explained to me: "The steelworker union was incredibly supportive of the project. The lowest-paid job at Energy Answers would have been around thirty-eight thousand to thirty-nine thousand dollars. This is an entry-level position. We think that when you get into higher-skilled-level jobs, it would be about the seventy-thousand-dollar range." Lowry explained that Pat Mahoney, the founder, president, and CEO of Energy Answers became a close friend of his. "We communicated three, four, five times per week about the Energy Answers project. He agreed that he would not do anything anti-union. Again, these were good union jobs for a very depressed area of Baltimore."

When I asked Lowry explicitly about trade-offs between detrimental environmental impacts and job creation, he said,

> When the steel plants were built years ago, I'm sure they dumped a lot of stuff into those creeks. But you know what? We have environmental engineers and controls to reduce emissions. We have come a long way to support the environment. The problem here is the environmental community doesn't like anything that burns. It's either wind or solar.

Lowry's points were indicative of the industrial union perspective on environmental hazards and health concerns. In the short term, unionized jobs represented financial security (i.e., a way to keep food on the table) for laborers and were better than the alternatives: precarious jobs in the service economy or a shortage of jobs. The health and environmental consequences of such jobs were not short-term concerns but, rather, to be dealt with in the long run—by outsider experts such as "environmental engineers." Lowry told me that industrial workers were frustrated with environmentalists who refused to see the gray areas in development options and who were unwilling to compromise on their commitments to nature.

While the Curtis Bay Neighborhood Association agreed to support the incinerator project as early as 2009, they did introduce conditions to that agreement. Energy Answers International would need to route truck traffic around rather than through Curtis Bay. Additionally, the association expected the company to make donations to a local college scholarship fund for area high school students and to build a picnic area and a boat ramp in the local park. (In 2010, a resident of northeast Baltimore, Kelley Ray, cried out at a community meeting, "Shame on a community organization, selling out for a couple of picnic tables" [Shen 2012a].) To pay for these "amenities," the agreement specified that Energy Answers would pay fifty thousand dollars in the first year, and then an amount that increased by ten thousand dollars each additional year until reaching one hundred thousand dollars (which was to remain the annual investment made by Energy Answers into the community). The payments were to be managed by the Brooklyn and Curtis Bay Coalition (a local nonprofit community development corporation) as well as by the Curtis Bay Neighborhood Association and Concerned Citizens for a Better Brooklyn, Inc. (Shen 2012a).[6]

It is relatively common practice for large corporations in deindustrialized and impoverished neighborhoods to pay residents off with promises to build football stadiums, parks, community gardens, and summer camps (deMause 2015; Gonzalez 2016; Sanchez 2019; Shen 2020a). Yet the Free Your Voice students recognized how the payments to neighborhood associations were demobilizing activism by pitting community members against one another, and they refused to be appeased. They decided that to organize effectively against Energy Answers, they were going to have to tell human stories of pollution, and they were going to have to awaken residents, paid off or not, with these stories. As spokespersons for their community, they raised concerns about the human health costs associated with the Energy Answers proposal. Most pointedly, they raised questions about the destructive effects of capitalism, and of capitalist-backed, for-profit incineration, on their bodies, on their lungs, and on their breathing.

From December 2012 through April 2013, students expanded their research into the health impacts of incineration. "We learned that the incinerator would burn 4,000 tons of trash and release 240 pounds of mercury per year and 1,000 pounds of lead," Destiny told me. In April 2013, guided by Murphy, the students decided to request a health-impact assessment (a tool used to determine how decisions regarding the construction of the facility or plant might impact the health of a community) from the Baltimore City Health Department. Health Department officials responded to this request with a firm "no," claiming that the incinerator was scheduled to start construction and that health-impact assessments could not be carried out this late in the process.

Undeterred, Free Your Voice youth reached out over email to public health experts and environmental lawyers at the Environmental Integrity Project. While doing research online, they discovered an organization called Physicians for Social Responsibility. Physician Elizabeth Doran, president of the Chesapeake chapter of the organization, had been doing anti-incinerator work for years. When Doran heard from the Free Your Voice students, she expressed interest in collaborating. As she told me in the spring of 2020:

> When Free Your Voice youth contacted me, I was so excited to join their movement. It was extraordinary to see these kids take on such an important issue. The students had so much power. They didn't realize it. It was extraordinary. My sense was they were transformed by their work and that's what's just so amazing by the work you guys do. The idea of creating leadership—creating leadership! These students were connected to the community, the assault was going on around them. I don't know what their opinions were of growing up in Curtis Bay, Brooklyn, and other communities around there. But I suspect they may have had feelings in sort of blaming themselves and then the transformation of seeing not only were they victims of injustice, but they could become activists and fight to change what others were doing to them, y'know, like the government or

companies or whatever. To see that process is just extraordinary. Students have so much power.

PHASE II: USING EXPERTS, ALONG WITH HISTORY AND THE ARTS, IN PROTEST (2013–2014)

Free Your Voice students quickly realized that they needed public health experts to help them fill in some of the gaps in their knowledge about the human health consequences of incineration, as well as environmental lawyers who understood EPA laws and regulations. They began to assemble a coalition in 2013, soon referred to as the Dream Team, by reaching out to well-known public health professionals, professors, environmental lawyers, Sierra Club representatives, members of the nonprofit group Clean Water Action, and activists from the Institute for Local Self-Reliance. This is when I was approached formally by Destiny Watford and Daniel Murphy, who came to Towson University to ask me to join their growing team of experts, environmental activists, and allies. The team met on a biweekly basis in the Brooklyn Clubhouse (of the Boys and Girls Club) or Curtis Bay Recreation Center to strategize about the campaign. I participated in the biweekly meetings, built teams of Towson students interested in researching incineration with the Free Your Voice students, and helped shape a curriculum. While members of the Dream Team collaborated with the students, providing expertise and guidance when called upon to provide reports, materials, and/or testimonials, we also participated in marches, demonstrations, forums, and sometimes even civil disobedience. In addition to the outsider experts they assembled, the students continued to read and to listen to community members around them, especially their elders who were educated and informed by decades of living on the peninsula, as key parts of their knowledge-making process.

Free Your Voice students were empowered by the academic works written by faculty and students at the University of Maryland Law Clinic who had done previous environmental work in the area. Brenda

Blom's dissertation on the Wagner's Point buyout paved the way for Free Your Voice student research.[7] "History was critical to our campaign," claimed Destiny. "With an understanding of the role of economics and development, we learned that the incinerator and the facts of its location fit into a historical pattern of meeting the demands of the economy regardless of the costs." One particularly important source, according to the students, was the 1998 Diamond Report, an unpublished manuscript based on a research project by faculty and students at the University of Maryland Law School, which recounted the history of industrial waste on the Fairfield Peninsula from the 1800s to the 1980s. Many of the youth, previously unaware of the hazards of the industries surrounding their homes, were "awakened" by these histories. Later, the students wove information they pulled from the texts into their thinking and learned to explain how structural racism shaped industrial development decisions.

Making Connections: Fairfield Houses
and Environmental Displacement

As the students developed independent investigations, they discovered what had happened in the campaigns against toxins that preceded their own struggle against the incinerator. They learned that the Fairfield neighborhood, before being relocated to its current site, had been situated near to where Energy Answers was planning to build their trash-to-energy incinerator. At the time of the students' investigations, this area was an abandoned industrial site surrounded by heavy diesel truck traffic, polluting chemical and fertilizer industries, and abandoned brownfield sites.

Students read that the City had built basic infrastructure in Wagner's Point, the all-white (though poor and white ethnic, to be clear) community on the peninsula in the 1950s, nearly thirty years before doing so in Fairfield, which was located alongside Wagner's Point but all (or almost all) Black. As Destiny reiterated to me in the Fall of 2019:

Wagner's Point was predominantly white and Fairfield predominantly Black, but both communities were company towns, living in poverty, working in dangerous hazardous conditions, and forced to live in a toxic environment. . . . On the surface, this history can be read as a story of two communities, different in culture and race, facing the issue together. But this ignores the issue of racism that divided the two communities. For instance, Fairfield did not get access to plumbing . . . until well into the 1970s. This is an example of structural racism. It is also a story not told by our history books.[8]

The students talked in small groups about systemic and structural racism and unfair housing policies. They investigated the evacuation of Fairfield Housing.[9] They learned that former residents were forcibly relocated to public housing and were offered $22,500 for renters and up too $5,250 per household. They also received moving costs of up to $1,500 per household (Blom 213). When 14 households remained in Fairfield a decade later, then-Mayor Kurt Schmoke stated that he would prefer to move all residents out of Fairfield, but the city did not have any money for relocation (Matthews 1999c). This history provoked Free Your Voice youth to think beyond their community to how structural racism shaped citywide decisions and policies.

Despite attempts to integrate school systems in the 1950s and the passage of civil rights legislation in the 1960s intended, specifically, to mitigate racism in housing policies, the provision of public education and the regulation of housing practices remained uneven in the 1970s (and into the present). Students learned that in 1979 a CSX railroad car carrying nine thousand gallons of highly concentrated sulfuric acid overturned and the Fairfield Homes public housing complex was temporarily evacuated. That same year, they read, an explosion at the British Petroleum oil tank, located on Fairfield Peninsula, set off a seven-alarm fire. All of this led the students to deeper inquiry.

Figuring out the ways in which structural racism shaped contemporary ideas about people, bodies, and space is something that Destiny often referred to when speaking publicly. Destiny explained that studying "history allowed us to see our community in a way that gave us the ability to build power or collective strength. So, how do you confront this history, this marketplace?" Building power within the school was about "re-education," she said, but it was also about rebuilding social relationships across the community and helping residents to understand the structural conditions and histories sustaining inequities that others (especially white others) tried to explain away using racist stereotypes and tropes (e.g., Black youth as "thugs"; "they're poor because they're lazy"). These tropes subtly and not so subtly suggested racial and cultural inferiority.

As a group, the students worked to establish a presence in the community and to create spontaneous spaces for dialogue and discussion. They attended a Fairfield reunion in Curtis Bay Park during the summer of 2013, where approximately 150 former Fairfield Homes residents gathered to celebrate their history, reminisce, and have a cook-out together. Gathered on the grass next to the Curtis Bay Recreation Center, former residents reminisced about what life was like in the projects. At one point, an elder participant shared with Destiny, "Fairfield was the Cadillac of housing projects. . . . We were all a family, we took care of one another." The Free Your Voice students engaged with living history as they listened and learned.

For many of the students, the combined processes of reading texts and listening to elder residents' stories moved them from numbness to awareness. Being able to discuss what they learned in sophisticated conversations with their peers and the experts they sought out helped to build their confidence as activists and adult interlocutors.[10]

Arts and Performance in Movement Building: The Crankie

While analysis and study were key to building change campaigns, the students also recognized that building a sociopolitical movement of economically disadvantaged people required more than mobilizing bodies. To be effective, they were going to have to move hearts and minds.[11]

In 2014, Free Your Voice students decided to strengthen the emotional and relationship building aspects of their campaign by adopting art forms, including performance and storytelling, into their communication efforts. Destiny began a speech she delivered at The Worker Justice Center human rights dinner in 2015 by quoting W.E.B. Dubois: "'Art is not simply works of art; it is the spirit that knows beauty, that has music in its being and the color of sunsets in its handkerchiefs, that can dance on a flaming world and make the world dance, too'" (Watford 2015). Art—in the form of a vintage performance genre known as "the crankie" (see below) and rap songs—became a tool the students utilized to tell their stories to much broader publics and to boost emotional connections with their allies. Performances particularly allowed youth to be creative and inventive. Their productions were often malleable. Sometimes, Free Your Voice youth would rewrite a script based on audience feedback. As a result, their performances were often improvisational, and they invited residents to be a part of the storytelling. This allowed the student-performers to develop strong narrative structures and especially realistic characters.

Not only did students do art, but they also invited artists, including performers, to join the Dream Team to broaden both the appeal and impact of the Stop the Incinerator campaign. One artist at the Maryland Institute College of Art, Janette Simpson, spoke to me at length about the genesis of her commitment to Free Your Voice's organizing, and how that commitment deepened and extended her work with other campaigns originating with The Worker Justice Center. Free Your Voice students approached Simpson, with their teacher Daniel Murphy acting as their mediator, about incorporating her work in theater into their campaign.[12] They sent her a recent report on the environmental history of the peninsula and asked that she read it. That report became the hook that convinced Simpson to collaborate:

> I had been thinking about how art and artists can serve social movements, and how artists also have agency in the making of their artwork. Or maybe thinking about autonomy. Free Your Voice youth suggested I read the

Diamond report, which was written by a team of researchers from the University of Maryland Law School. I remember being like, Wow! What a story! All these visuals came to my mind . . . like the guano factories, the ships, these agricultural communities, this Black community versus the white community . . . the relationship to the water and the relationship to the city. So I decided I would try to illustrate a version of that report in a way. Like, what did people look like in 1800s, and what were they wearing? . . . Then I realized that this is not my history, who am I to tell someone else's story? I need to think more symbolically, and then it came to me to write this illustrative history as a fable or an allegory.

Which is what she did, alongside Terrel Jones (whose childhood lived experiences I detailed in chapter 2).

Terrel and Simpson created a crankie, an old storytelling art form popular in the nineteenth century that includes a long, illustrated scroll wound onto two spools. The spools are loaded into a box that has a viewing screen and the scroll is then hand-cranked, hence the name "crankie." While the story is told, a tune is played or a song is sung. Terrel and Simpson created a show for the anti-incinerator campaign that was performed throughout the city for audiences of all ages and walks of life. *The Holey Land*, as their show was titled, was an allegory about the powerful connection between people and the place they call home. In this tale, the Peninsula People and the magic in their land are threatened when a stranger with a tall hat and a shovel shows up with big ideas for "improving" their community. As storybook images scroll past the viewing screen, the vibrant and colorful pictures of a peninsula rich in natural resources, including orange and pink fish, slowly get usurped by those of the man with the shovel building his factories, and the Peninsula People are left to ponder the fate of their land. The story ends with a surprising twist, and a hopeful message about a community's ability to determine their own future.

While Simpson provided artistic expertise and creativity, Terrel (along with Destiny) composed the narrative. "I remember how introverted Terrel was," Simpson recalled, but somehow the performance brought him out of his shell. He performed it so many times. I don't know, we did it like thirty-five times in the span of several months. So that story was *in him*. He *really knew it*. I could see his growth in how he was delivering it. There was something about the familiarity of the crankie that worked for Terrel.

Art gave the students a way to express themselves, it democratized knowledge, but also gave them a genre (a mode or means) via which they were able to articulate their struggles against pollution and the cumulative impacts of environmental racism. "Art and the creation of it became what moved us, fueled us, and sparked our imaginations," Destiny believed: "The play *An Enemy of the People* was an eye-opener; it reminded us that through art we could show people a way of seeing our community. So, we internalized the issue of our struggle, our frustration, our fear, and worked together to tell *our* version of the story through many creations. We wrote speeches, made poems, created paintings and drawings, videos and songs. We even created massive flowers that symbolize our hope for fair development and carried messages from people across the city." Art also became a vehicle for transforming others, often outsiders, into audience members, thereby enabling them to better "see and to feel" the struggles on and around the peninsula, as they were brought to life by the students.

Arts and Performance in Movement Building: Free Your Voice at the Board of Education

In 2015, the Free Your Voice students learned that many public entities, including the Baltimore City Public Schools, were buying "energy futures" from Energy Answers.[13] The city schools were part of The Baltimore Regional Cooperative Purchasing Committee (BRCPC), which signed a contract for the purchase of twenty-five megawatts of power, or about 15 percent of the Fairfield plant's expected 160-megawatt generation capacity.[14] As Destiny told me, "We found out through research that the Baltimore City Public Schools and twenty-one other entities were buying energy in advance from the incinerator. We reached out to tell them that this was not okay and that a school system should not be buying 'dirty energy' that would be polluting our lungs." Much of Energy Answers' viability was dependent on this contract. Therefore, any wavering of commitment or suspension of the contract posed a significant blow to Energy Answers' revenue stream.

Free Your Voice youth and several environmental legal advisors on the Dream Team recognized that in order to make the project unprofitable, they needed to get all the public entities that had bought into the "energy answers" agreement by purchasing energy in advance to pull out of their contract. Free Your Voice mounted a massive public pressure campaign across the region, including a petition drive during which they collected the signatures, planned marches and demonstrations, and edited videos, all of which attracted media attention. Over time, a video report (Demczuk 2015) and op-ed (Williams 2015) in the *New York Times* amplified the voices of the anti-incinerator activists.

A part of the campaign was directed at convincing public institutions from the Baltimore City Public Schools to the public libraries to divest from the contracts they had signed with Energy Answers to procure energy from the future incinerator. While experts provided "health data," "technical support," or "artistic guidance" for the Free Your Voice team, the students took center stage, presenting their case at community meetings and public institutions. Bringing knowledge, art, and fiery testimonials into new spaces helped lift the voices of the Free Your Voice students and thereby empowered them. The stage became larger and more frightening as the Stop the Incinerator campaign advanced, but the students were now occupying closed meetings, like those of the Baltimore Board of Education, and transforming those bureaucratic sites into places of struggle. Many students described the deep anxiety they felt about speaking publicly before parents, allies, and bureaucrats.

Baltimore's Board of Education meetings were one early and critical space where students could "claim a space" and make their case articulating why the Board of Education and Baltimore City Public Schools should not buy energy from the planned incinerator. At the meeting on May 27, 2014, the Board of Education panel, consisting of a committee of board members, was confronted by activists holding four-foot sunflowers.[15] Each activist chanted one of three human rights principles: accountability, equity, participation. This was another art project that added color and design to the meeting.

Destiny Watford took the lead as speaker that day. Her words to the panel are worth quoting at length:

> We are here tonight to talk about choices. Two years ago, a group of students and I made the choice to join a group called Free Your Voice. This choice allowed us [to] learn more about the world we live in. We meet every week to study, reflect, and act together. We learned about another choice to build the nation's largest trash-burning incinerator less than a mile away from our school. At first, we were shocked because we didn't have any knowledge of this. Should we get involved in an issue this big, complex, and intimidating? We chose YES. . . .
>
> While studying the issue we came to learn about another choice. This particular choice makes what we are talking about today so important. In 2011, the Baltimore City Public Schools chose to buy energy from the incinerator. The same one that would be less than one mile from our school, the same incinerator that would be twice the size of the incinerator Baltimore already has, pumping 240 pounds of mercury and lead into the air every year. The fact that schools are supporting this forces us to reflect upon the meaning of schools. To be honest, I really hated going to school. I didn't see its purpose. I never grasped the meaning behind it. You see, I was educated through the public school system. And, although it has its flaws, the beauty of the system is that, at its core, it aspires to be a public place of education. I want to emphasize the word *public* because this means it includes *everyone, no matter what economic situation you were born into*. At its root, it is a system that springs forth from the principle of equity. It represents a choice that we made as a society to reach towards fairness. It provides opportunities to enlighten ourselves and allows us to look out at the world and question what we see. Which is exactly why we are here tonight.
>
> We are here tonight to make it clear that this incinerator threatens the very idea of equity that we students, teachers, parents, and board members share. We ask everyone here: Is it fair to build the nation's largest incinerator

in the community with the highest level of toxic air emissions in the state? Is it fair to build the incinerator in the community with some of the highest rates of death from heart disease, lung cancer, and lower respiratory disease in the city? Is it fair to build the incinerator in the city that has the highest rate of air pollution-related deaths in the nation? Is it fair to have your life cut short because of where you are born? We say that it is not fair, and more—that it is not right. The incinerator is failed development. (Destiny Watford, Speech delivered at the Board of Education, May 27. 2014)

Destiny explained that the bright yellow sunflowers that the students were holding in the room represented hope. Each of these flowers was held by a single person who expressed their opposition to the incinerator project.

The sunflowers had yet another function: they created a visual stage for Leanna Jones and her sister Rosalyn Drey to perform a rap they wrote for the occasion:

18-year-old girl living in the world,
where no one cares about the safety of the girl.
Money, money, money.
That seems to be the anthem destroying the world
And always taking it for granted.
No more greed.
All I can see is landfills.
I'm disgusted.
I can't believe we trusted the world.
But it's not too late to be adjusted.
We have our rights
According to the amendments.
But why do we feel
like we have been so resented?
Shoved to the side
where opinions don't matter,
where opinions only die.
It's time to stand up
And let our voices be heard.
Incinerator move because

You are not preferred.
This life starts
With the air that we breathe.
With everyone competitive
And trying to succeed
Just worried 'bout the money
Not the air that we need
When you think opportunity,
The eye is deceived . . .
If the incinerator takes
Away a breath
How many do we need?
Until there is nothing that's left
Until the smoke clogs up
And we can't feel our chest
And the ones who don't catch the symptoms
Are considered blessed.

Rosalyn confessed to me later that she had been anxious about her performance:

> I was really worried about disrupting the energy of the room, I guess. It was interesting. But after we performed, we got a standing ovation and after that it put them over the top in terms of not accepting and pulling out of the Energy Answers contract. These are Baltimore City school kids saying, '[We] do not want this.' Adults can always advocate for us, but it is different when kids articulate and advocate for themselves.

After the rap, Terrel performed a soliloquy he composed entitled, "To Burn or Not to Burn":

> To burn, or not to burn, that is the question
> Whether 'tis better for Baltimore to breathe the foul and toxic air
>   surrounding us
> or to stand up against incinerators, and by opposing stop them?
> To trash, to burn—waste no more, and by burning, to say we end the
>   mercury and the thousand pounds of lead that trash has within?
> No—an incinerator gravely to be opposed.[16]

The students' speeches and performances located abstract ideas about "equity" and "choice" in the physical bodies of young people living in a community. As the board members listened, their expressions shifted from cold and distant to warm and engaged. "Something happened," Destiny told me in an interview in 2019; the sincerity of the students "opened [board members'] eyes, their hearts, and their minds."

The Free Your Voice students successfully claimed a political space in the board meeting that day, disrupting the ritualized formality of the event with their performances while also introducing the pain and hurt of their community to the elite decision-makers. Art and performance were powerful vehicles for communicating the consequences of board decision-making and forcing some of the board members to more fully "see." This seizure of space gave visibility to the students' struggle, extending their cause from the Dream Team of allies to a group of city officials, inviting those officials to think critically about the ways in which their decisions made them complicit in toxic industrial practices, complicit in complicating the breathing and overall health of individuals, most often of color and including youth, living in already overburdened communities.

After the meeting, several board members agreed to tour the neighborhood on a bus the following week. That "toxic tour" (see Figure 5) illustrated not only how but where the incinerator would adversely impact residents' health. As Destiny remembers:

> The whole point was to get [the board members] to the neighborhood, and to show them that we are there, and we are watching them, but also [to] build that relationship. Yeah, I remember standing with them in front of the incinerator, the location where it would be built, and we were talking about the significance of . . . them siding with us. I remember Cheryl Casciani [from the Baltimore City Board of School Commissioners] specifically saying, "How soon can we get out of this thing?" And I remember thinking, "Wow, that was huge!"

For board member Cheryl Casciani, witnessing a growing sea of industry ever closer to homes produced an "a-ha" moment. Immediately

Figure 5. Toxic tour with Dante Swinton, Energy Justice. *Credit: The Baltimore Sun* Media.

following the tour, Casciani said: "I'm also on the sustainability commission, and we've had a chance to hear from a subset of the students as well, and we're definitely in support of what you're trying to do. . . . I think they are part of a number of other sustainability issues. We need to consider the source of our energy. We'll talk to people in the operations department so we can understand a little bit more about [the purchase contract]. So I'll look forward to hearing more about that."[17]

Although the proposed incinerator's future emissions would have met public health guidelines, producing cleaner energy than coal-fired power plants elsewhere in the state, Casciani determined that the project had not been evaluated in the context of the South Baltimore Peninsula, with its existing industrial base and history of contamination. In February of 2015, the Baltimore City Board (after much discussion with Free Your Voice activists and several trips to the community)

terminated their agreement with the Baltimore Regional Cooperative Purchasing Committee (BRCPC)—the entity in charge of selling Energy Answers' energy contracts to public entities including city
schools. Shortly thereafter, like a stack of dominoes, the leaders of other
public institutions chose to withdraw their support for the incinerator.

But teaching others to see and generating empathy as a result has
its limits. The Free Your Voice student activists knew early on that
they would not be able to defeat Energy Answers by relying on the arts
alone, no matter how impactful their performances. They were going
to have to threaten the financial interests of those advancing the incinerator project.

PHASE III: CIVIL DISOBEDIENCE
AS A LAW ENFORCEMENT TACTIC

Soon after the Baltimore City Board of Education withdrew its support
for the incinerator project, Free Your Voice students along with members of the Dream Team discovered that the permit that allowed Energy
Answers to build a plant at the proposed site had expired months prior.
When the permit was initially granted by the Maryland Department of
the Environment in October of 2013, it stipulated that construction must
begin within eighteen months. By mid-2015, however, construction still
had not begun. As public support for the Stop the Incinerator campaign
grew, the students and their supporters decided that their next target
would be the Maryland Department of the Environment. Their goal
was to convince employees of the agency to enforce the law and rescind
the building permit. This action required additional tactical planning.
The Worker Justice Center and their allies decided to give the Maryland Department of the Environment thirty days to rescind the permit. Shortly thereafter, in November 2015, the Environmental Integrity
Project (EIP) alerted state and federal environmental regulators that
they intended to file a citizen lawsuit demanding enforcement of the
permit's terms.

Organizers knew that state agencies were unlikely to meet the deadline. From July of 2015 through November 2015, movement stories big and small were lived, told, and transmitted through videos. These stories pitted fair development against ongoing attempts at a form of development that compromised the health of residents. Free Your Voice students created, filmed, and edited the videos. These then circulated on Facebook, Instagram, and Snapchat. The videos presented the Maryland Department of Energy with a choice: either continue to support "the unpopular" and dangerous polluter or enforce the law and side with fair development. Smaller demonstrations over time flowed into a big action on December 15, 2015, one that used the tactic of civil disobedience, and for which participants were to risk getting arrested. The organizers in collaboration with the Free Your Voice students planned the civil disobedience event ahead of time. A group of veteran organizers (including Daniel Murphy and Stuart Rosen from the Worker Justice Center) shared possible scenarios with the youth as they walked through "what-ifs?"

Failure to meet the deadline, the group decided, justified the ramping up of protests at the MDE offices. For the protesters, this brought transition to a new phase of mobilization: one of civil disobedience, placing activist-protesters at risk of arrest. The decision to employ acts of civil disobedience was not something the organizers took lightly. Rosen explained: "We don't do one-off stunts simply to get ourselves in the newspaper or on television. We are accountable to many communities who have entrusted members and leaders across a spectrum of organizations and networks to develop an effective strategy to resolve this crisis and move forward with fair development alternatives. To commit acts of civil disobedience and open up the possibility of a team of leaders getting arrested was treated with utmost seriousness." The tactical transition to civil disobedience, which took place in late fall into early winter 2015 required planning coupled with community buy-in. Free Your Voice students heightened public pressure to end the incinerator project, organizing demonstrations at the Maryland Department of the Environment offices that were intended to hold

Figure 6. Protestors gathered outside MDE headquarters. *Credit:* Free Your Voice.

state and city officials' feet to the fire. Rapidly, Maryland Department of the Environment's weak enforcement practices were translated into an organizing strength by linking it to health and safety threats to the South Baltimore Peninsula.

The day of action, December 15, 2015, was freezing cold. Free Your Voice youth, Dream Team members, and about one hundred other concerned citizens, gathered outside of the massive Maryland Department of Environment offices in Baltimore (Figure 6). They held colorful signs reading "No Incinerators" and "Fair Development for All." Numerous cars and trucks passed the protest and honked in support. The group chanted in unison "Arrest the Polluters!" and "Pull the permits!" The plan had been to enter the Maryland Department of the Environment office single-file dropping off petitions, but Maryland Department of the Environment security guards prevented protestors from entering the building. Two members of the group were allowed inside to speak with the secretary of the environment, Benjamin H. Grumbles. In that meeting, Grumbles made his position clear: no intervention or action was planned. A group of seven individuals eventually snuck past the guards to occupy his office, an act of civil disobedience that ultimately led to their arrests.[18]

The rest of us continued to protest outside. When we were told that the seven had been arrested, we searched for and found the police vehicle transporting the protestors to central booking. About a half dozen vans and a dozen police cruisers appeared on the scene, an exaggerated use of force to arrest seven nonviolent protesters. Among those arrested were Free Your Voice youth activists Terrel Jones and Luis Mendoza. Stuart Rosen, also arrested, described the aftermath a year and a half later:

> The seven of us who had decided to be arrested were taken into custody, handcuffed and placed in a paddy wagon around 6 p.m. to cheers and chants from our supporters. . . . The plastic handcuffs hurt and cut into my hands. We were finger-printed, photographed, and then placed in a cell. Terrel Jones, Luis Mendoza, both from Benjamin Franklin High School, were with me in a cell. The cell was all concrete, sound bouncing horribly off the walls, bright lights and unrelenting air conditioning. I should have worn more layers of T-shirts, but I mistakenly thought I could keep my sweatshirt. For what felt like an hour, I stood by the cell door. Then I leaned my head back into the corner of the cell and closed my eyes. After about eighteen hours in custody, we were released, and our Worker Justice Center comrades were waiting for us in the lobby.[19]

For many Free Your Voice students—and their parents—it was scary to put their bodies on the line for an environmental justice issue. Risking arrest and the possibility of a minor offense on their records was just one part of that fear. The sit-in occurred eight months after the Baltimore uprisings of April 2015, when appalled citizens took to the streets in response to the murder of Freddie Gray by the Baltimore Police.

Destiny, who had planned to be part of the civil disobedience action and get arrested, recalled getting a call on the day of the sit-in from her mother who was fearful for her life and for her future:

> When my mom was watching some of the coverage of the MDE protest on TV, she called my cell phone right away and said, "Please, Destiny, don't get arrested." In her mind she was still living with the fears and trauma of what happened to Freddie Gray. I get her deep-seated fears for my safety. She even sent my brother and nephew to go get me from the protest to make sure I was not arrested.

Destiny, empathizing with her mother's fears, chose not to get arrested in the end.

This particular act of civil disobedience proved successful. It was an exclamation mark of sorts for the campaign, something that "heated things up" according to Destiny, after several marches, demonstrations, petitions against the incinerator, and media coverage. In March of 2016, the Maryland Department of the Environment finally enforced the expiration date on Energy Answers' waste-to-energy plant project and pulled the permit. "After all the pressure we've been building, MDE is finally taking a step in the right direction," Terrel said; "I see this as an opportunity for the City and the State to work towards fair development alternatives to the incinerator."

Four months after the "Maryland Department of the Enviornment victory" (as the event became known), Destiny Watford won the Goldman Environmental Prize.[20] It is an award given annually by the Goldman Association to six grassroots environmental activists, one from each of six geographic regions: Africa, Asia, Europe, Islands and Island Nations, North America, and South and Central America. Destiny received the prize in April of 2016 for her organizing work in the Stop the Incinerator Campaign and gained national and international attention. I remember walking into Benjamin Franklin High with her at the start of the following school year and one of her former teachers ran up to her and said, "Now you and your mama can move out of Curtis Bay!" Destiny thanked him and without pause told him, "I'll never leave Curtis Bay!"[21] She told me later:

> In high school, I had this holier-than-thou attitude. I was too good for this space. I just wanted to get out of here. . . . It changed the way that I saw people. . . . But all the organizing work made me feel more human. I feel I can connect with people in a real way that I haven't been able to before. . . . It's just a different kind of experience and learning that you are not used to. And once you enter into this work, you are never gonna be able to stop thinking about it.

After winning the award, Destiny reiterated publicly and privately that the campaign had been a group effort. Being put on a pedestal as an "example" or "model activist," she said, failed to recognize the importance of the broader and more collaborative movement for environmental justice. To counter these impulses, Destiny said, "What I try to do is just talk about the work in a collective way as much as I can." While the Energy Answers project came to a conclusion, the campaign provoked other questions around the global struggle against incineration, especially how to dissolve a system in which polluting industries freely occupy community and residential lands and spaces and replace it with something better.

THE FUTURE OF THE FMC SITE

Despite the campaign victory, the Food and Machinery Chemical Corporation (FMC) brownfield and planned Energy Answers site remains abandoned in 2022 as I type this. Some people (especially developers and, sometimes, politicians) describe the rubble that remains on the site as a failure to produce economic development for the South Baltimore Peninsula (Shen 2016a). Henry Lowry from the steelworkers' union was similarly pessimistic: "This was a huge failure for economic development. Baltimore City is dying for jobs, and this could have been the biggest opportunity the city has seen in decades. Show me any other opportunity or project that would have supplied 150 to 200 jobs, would have been union jobs and entry-level positions at thirty-nine thousand dollars." Alternatively, environmental activists describe it as "a victory" for fair development. Destiny argued, "Instead of one more polluting industry, we now have shown the city that *we* can decide about the kind of development we want on this land." Free Your Voice youth learned through years of researching, working, and fighting that creating viable options for fair development is not an easy task. One member of the Dream Team, Neil Seldman from the Institute for Local Self-Reliance, wanted to use the site to build a recycled paper factory.[22] Some allies and peninsula residents supported this idea. However, the company imagined as leading this development effort "filed for bankruptcy because they were having trouble making recycled paper," Henry Lowry told me. "My biggest gripe," Lowry said, "was that they were promoting companies as alternatives that didn't really exist as a viable option." Beyond these concerns, many of the projects The Worker Justice Center and the Institute for Local Self-Reliance promoted required city- and statewide support, consistent funding streams, and developers willing to invest in construction. These hurdles and the complexity of implementation stalled efforts to create alternative forms of economic development on the peninsula.

Another member of the Dream Team, Angela Warren, who had worked for a solar firm and whose son was also a Benjamin Franklin High School student, proposed converting the site to a community-owned and community-controlled "solar farm." This idea gained traction with Free Your Voice students and much of the rest of the Dream Team in 2015. Warren drew several maps and a plan for what a solar farm might look like.

Evergreen Cooperative Representatives, a group that had community-controlled solar projects in Cleveland held meetings in Baltimore during the summer of 2015. Their mission was to create jobs, sustainable businesses, and wealth in low-income areas. The campaign membership considered working with Cooperative Solar, a partner member of Evergreen Cooperatives. Evergreen Cooperative employed residents through local institutions to become greener using solar power and weatherizing techniques to improve energy efficiency. Entirely worker owned and worker controlled, past projects had installed photovoltaic solar panels on Cleveland-area institutional, governmental, and commercial buildings. Evergreen catalyzed local, cooperative, sustainable companies providing employee-owners opportunities for personal, financial, and career trajectories. This kind of strategic, community wealth building was at least in part what Curtis Bay needed; the creation of meaningful jobs, keeping financial resources within the community and planting development seeds to rebuild the local economy. Sustainable companies and meaningful jobs offered a path to stabilize, revitalize and transform communities and individuals. The promise of the project was very appealing to our Baltimore-based team.[23]

While the blueprints for both the paper recycling plant and community-owned solar plant presented possibilities for residents of the peninsula, the team realized that FMC, which still owned the land, was refusing to turn the land permit over to the community. The phrase "holding the land hostage" has since become a rallying call within The Worker Justice Center, as organizers searched for ways to transfer control of the land and development decision-making power in Curtis Bay from absentee corporate owners to community residents. Environmental justice is not just about stopping one polluting industry, Free Your Voice students and their allies learned. It necessitates community control over development decisions, community investment in mapping agroecological green spaces, and supporting land trusts and zero-waste or green businesses and co-operative engines so that health and wealth can be built and shared equitably—as well as locally. In the next chapter, I explore Free Your Voice student investment in the "reclamation of land" and their fight for and then experimentation with land trusts as a viable option for fair development, including the establishment of long-term affordable housing.

Though it is an unfinished project, one that quickly gave rise to thinking about land ownership and land trusts, the trajectory of the Stop the Incinerator campaign produced important stages of success and collaboration. The Free Your Voice youth learned how to use history and arts to tell meaningful stories about the health impacts of incineration, while research gave them the tools to put pressure on the economic interests behind the project. Some labor unionists, including Henry Lowry, argued that it was not Free Your Voice but rather the low market price of gas that made the Energy Answers project unprofitable and thus stopped the incinerator. The majority of Baltimore City officials and public health experts, however, have recognized the key role of the high school youth in halting the project. Their work was honored by Baltimore *City Paper* as the "best activism in Baltimore" in 2014.[24]

CHAPTER FOUR

"Whose Land? Our Land!"

Land Trusts as Fair Development

After several years of organizing against and ultimately stopping the construction of the Energy Answers incinerator in their neighborhood, Free Your Voice students at Benjamin Franklin High School were adept in their thinking about land use, and critical of development decisions on the South Baltimore Peninsula. As Destiny explained, "We were thinking, 'Yeah, we stopped the incinerator but what happens now? How do we stop something else from happening?'"

The residents that the students interviewed when studying and later communicating the dangers associated with living next to a trash-to-energy incinerator (see chapter 3) had shared stories about the inhumane housing conditions on the peninsula. These individuals had talked about the proliferation of black mold and lead paint chipping off walls. They described housing in a free fall of decay, and landlords doing little, if anything, to resolve problems. Destiny recalled her mom sharing stories about struggles with landlords: "Suddenly, it became personal," Destiny remembered. Given the outpouring of narratives about housing injustices, the Free Your Voice students agreed that their next fight would be for the creation of community land trusts. In Destiny's words, "[We figured out that] owning the land in the neighborhood is the best way to improve the quality of the housing stock for the poor and assure long-term and affordable housing"

In this chapter, I describe the evolution of Free Your Voice student activism, from powerful youth-led organizing to end incineration to a grassroots collaboration with the nonprofit South Baltimore Community Land Trust (SBCLT) to build community land trusts. I begin this chapter by introducing the in-school program that led students to believe in land trusts, before defining land trusts and explaining how they work. I then juxtapose the history of failed development practices in Baltimore, practices that were racist and unjust and that students hoped to correct by adopting a community-led form of development. I describe redlining as well as city officials' overconfidence in trickle-down economics.[1] This latter resulted in the destruction of numerous public housing units (including the Gilmor Homes in West Baltimore and Perkins Homes in East Baltimore), while justifying glitzy, high-cost development projects for elite condo buyers looking to return to the city, including the $5.5 billion Port Covington venture, which is underway on Baltimore's "Gold Coast" as I type this.

After glossing the failure of private-sector development models, including Port Covington, I describe The Worker Justice Center–sponsored, quickly victorious 20/20 campaign of 2016, in response to which politicians promised (and sometimes provided) funding for land trusts in Baltimore.[2] I then focus on Free Your Voice student involvement in the fight to create Baltimore-area land trusts, starting in 2017. As Destiny explained, stopping one incinerator was significantly different from starting up an urban redevelopment organization: "I had been so focused, so much, on environmental justice that the housing stuff was a whole new area for me. . . . It's one thing to stop something, but it's a whole 'nother thing to create something new, something that has never existed before!"

ARCHITECTS GO BACK TO SCHOOL:
NEIGHBORHOOD DESIGN JOINS FREE YOUR VOICE

As do most things, the participatory action class known as Free Your Voice evolved two years after the success of the Stop the Incinerator campaign, the program had expanded to include new collaborators and a growing body of students. As a result of a partnership between Towson University just outside of Baltimore and Free Your Voice, beginning in 2017, students who participated in the yearlong, community-based research class obtained three college credits. Just as in the pre-credit, less formal past, the class was set up so that students defined research questions collectively, sketched the methodologies they would use, and then spent one entire year using qualitative and quantitative research methods to answer their questions. At the conclusion of the academic year, just as in the past, students disseminated their research findings to teachers, community residents, and their peers. Much of the data that students collected was incorporated into the Free Your Voice environmental justice movement work in the community. Student findings were used to bolster arguments that organizers presented at city council meetings, for example, and these findings frequently became the imagery and statistics drawn and written onto signage, held high at community protests.

In addition to becoming an in-school (as opposed to after-school) program and offering college credit, the Free Your Voice program evolved in other key ways. While outreach to the community in the program's early years was largely organic and informal, by 2015 Daniel Murphy and his students had developed lasting relationships with area experts. As a result, they began to use the classroom as a space for envisioning, designing, and then implementing solutions to more concrete and complex problems, including housing injustice and waste mismanagement. They called what they were doing "participatory design," a method of design that includes stakeholders in all phases of the design process (https://ndc-md.org/).

In the fall of 2018, architect Janette Love and intern (and artist and social justice activist) Maureen McDonald, both from the Baltimore nonprofit Neighborhood Design Center, began attending the Free Your Voice class twice per week in order to provide hands-on community design support to students tasked with envisioning uses for vacant lots in their community. Their presence in the classroom was part of the Place Matters and Community Design Works program, a venture that put Neighborhood Design Center employees into collaborations with community members interested in urban design. "There are fundamental values that lead the work," Love explained:

> Everyone has the right to good design, and participatory design and community-led design are critical to creating outcomes that are relevant and beneficial to the neighborhood. So, we try to pair the design professionals that have certain technical skills . . . with the neighborhood, to have [those professionals] expertise [for] what [community members] need and what they want and what will work.

Along with Love and McDonald, and sharing the Neighborhood Design Center commitment to community-led initiatives, were Daisy Thompson, a new hire for the Worker Justice Center, Towson undergraduates and anthropology majors Nicole Hughes and Stephanie Logan, and myself, a Towson professor and Free Your Voice activist.

As their major project for the 2018 school year, the students (with us as their interlocutors) chose to repurpose an abandoned and overgrown lot into a community land trust—the first on the South Baltimore Peninsula. Initially, many knew little if anything about land trusts, but as the students participated in The Worker Justice Center meetings and events, they learned how land trusts could provide stability for families. "The rent is so high in this area that often families cannot afford to stay for any period of time," Jimmy Brown explained to me in class one day. "The land trust makes it about home ownership, and it also makes it affordable for the working poor."

The lot the students chose to work on was an overgrown mess of shrubs and weeds. It was located directly behind Benjamin Franklin High School, in an area where local middle and high school students lacked a safe space for recreation, games, and gathering. Parents worried about their children roaming the streets at night, given the high rates of crime in the neighborhood, and often kept kids inside. Free Your Voice students saw, in the lot, possibilities for creating a safe, local, outdoor space for youth.

One year into the project, during the 2019–2020 academic year and after many Affordable Housing Trust Fund meetings, the Free Your Voice students continued to advance in their thinking as well as their collaborating.[3] They worked with Passive Design Housing experts at Maryland Institute College of Art (MICA) and, again, with the two employees from Neighborhood Design Center, Love and McDonald.[4] One major outcome of these collaborations was that the South Baltimore Community Land Trust (SBCLT), under the guidance of the youth and their instructors Daisy Thompson, Crystal Green, and Daniel Murphy was established.[5] The students spent many days inside and outside of the classroom learning about land trusts, their origins, and their more recent successes. The team of Worker Justice Center organizers pushed the land trust model and the nonprofit (501c3) organization that became SBCLT forward with the Free Your Voice youth advising throughout the process. Over time, the team of students and organizers translated their efforts into a broader vision for development without displacement (Brey 2021).

BUT WHAT IS A LAND TRUST?

Community land trusts became popular in the 1960s as a way for Black farmers, specifically, to work rural land for themselves and their families. The sharecropping system from a century earlier prevented Black farmers from owning land, so instead, many rented small plots of land, or shares, that they worked for white landowners in exchange for a portion of the crops at harvest time. As historian Mary Ellen Curtin explains in the documentary *Slavery by Another Name*, "High interest rates, unpredictable harvests, and unscrupulous landlords and merchants often kept tenant farm families severely indebted, requiring the debt to be carried over until the next year or the next. Laws favoring landowners made it difficult or even illegal for sharecroppers to sell their crops to others besides their landlord or prevented sharecroppers from moving if they were indebted to their landlord" (Pollard 2021). This was an exploitative system that perpetuated slavery and slave-like conditions for Black farm workers long after slavery was outlawed in the United States.

Community land trusts arose as a just alternative for families who could not afford or were prevented by outdated laws, including heirs' property laws, from owning land. They allowed multiple individuals of any race to own land collectively—making land ownership both legal for all individuals, regardless of race, and affordable. The first community land trust in the United States was established in rural Georgia in 1969 on land purchased by a small group of Black sharecroppers with some federal grant assistance (Axel-Lute 2019; Elliot 2019; Noor 2019). At the time, this became the largest single piece of land in the country owned by African Americans, and unlike in the sharecropping system, the landowners got to keep all proceeds from their labor. Although this particular trust, known as New Communities, Inc., was affected by drought and racism from the start and was forced to close in the late 1980s, it provided an example for the rest of the United States and, in so doing, inspired people to create similar organizations across the country (Cohen and Lipman 2016).

Today, the classic Community Land Trust (CLT) is an independent, nonprofit organization that allows a group of individuals to share ownership of a plot (or multiple plots) of land. Membership in a CLT is open to anyone residing within a specified geographic area that includes the plot(s) held in trust. While the CLT owns the land (typically, for ninety-nine years), members can agree to sell the home on a property to qualified buyers at a below market-rate price. When a buyer purchases a home from the land trust, they agree to sell the home, if and when they choose to do so, to a low-income purchaser at a reduced price, and to split the profits from the sale with the CLT. While there are direct beneficiaries of a land trust—those living and/or working on land trust land—a community land trust is accountable to its entire membership.

Classic CLTs have a tripartite board that is divided into three groups of representatives. One group is the leaseholders—people living on or using CLT land. Another is made up of other community members or residents. The last group consists of technical experts and funders or other stakeholders in the organization. Because at least two-thirds of the board is made up of local community members, the majority of votes are held by local residents at all times (preventing absentee ownership and control). The Worker Justice Center organizers argue that community land trusts are true community-led and community-controlled organizations.

The community land trust model allows for community ownership of the land and individual ownership of houses. Because a buyer isn't paying for the land (just the building), owning a home is much more affordable. Additionally, though not required, land trust organizations often provide down-payment assistance and low-interest mortgages to low-income families, making homeownership even more feasible. The model allows low-income residents to build equity through homeownership and ensures that they are not displaced when land speculation and processes of gentrification drive up urban housing costs. Community land trusts also greatly reduce rates of foreclosure (Medoff and Sklar 1994; Davis 2010; Green and Hanna 2018). Homeowners are less likely to experience evictions and displacements because they are not overwhelmed by the costs associated with conventional mortgages, upkeep, and utilities.

Further, affordable housing land trusts can provide a community with a range of amenities, including homeownership education programs, and commercial development projects. Many community land trust committees organize not only around affordable housing but also environmental sustainability, providing ecologically friendly design, including low-carbon housing solutions and community greening projects. The South Baltimore Community Land Trust (SBCLT), for example, is guided by dual commitments to housing and environmental justice, envisioning how to have green spaces alongside new housing constructions and to create homes that make breathing easier (Brey 2019; 2021).

The SBCLT's mission is to replace neoliberal, "trickle-down" development practices with community-led, people-centered, bottom-up development. The organization arose following the grassroots and youth-led Stop the Incinerator campaign, as a community response to the question: how do we begin to realize the forms of development we want as we continue to oppose the development that threatens our health and environment? The community land trust model seemed best suited to meet the needs of the residents of the South Baltimore Peninsula.

Since its founding, SBCLT members have worked to ensure access to the housing market for poor residents who earn less than 50 percent of the area median income (AMI) as well as community control of land. Like CLTs in general, SBCLT includes residents in the overall design and development of their future community. Through their decision-making, participants work not only to provide affordable housing but also to establish green spaces, parks and other recreational areas, and more. The SBCLT also organizes with other CLTs, including the Charm City Land Trust (CCLT) on the East side in McElderry Park neighborhood, which, partnering with the Amazing Grace Lutheran Church, has acquired and developed vacant lots on North Port Street as multi-use community gardens. CCLT, like SBCLT, is in the process of renovating vacant homes, transforming them to permanently affordable land trust homes.

The Free Your Voice students who first envisioned a land trust lot behind their school and who worked collectively with The Neighborhood Design Center architects in the classroom also worked with SBCLT. As a result of this collective project, they not only transformed one lot, but they also envisioned much broader change for the South Baltimore Peninsula. Starting with one small-scale project helped the students to imagine what might be possible with fourteen land trust homes to repurpose. Before I share with you their project, however, let me describe the troubled history of Baltimore City urban development initiatives, initiatives that were racist and classist (toxic to humanity and society) and environmentally devastating (toxic to the biosphere), and which the Free Your Voice students were trying to correct when they chose to participate in the land trust movement.

A HISTORY OF FAILED DEVELOPMENT

The most notorious, perhaps, of the unjust development strategies used throughout the twentieth century in the United States was redlining. Baltimore played a pioneering role in developing and implementing redlining practices, which first took form in 1937 as a result of the Home Owners' Loan Corporation (HOLC) "Residential Security" maps of major American cities. Mapmakers outlined "high risk" neighborhoods in the color red, using racial composition of the neighborhood as a key indicator of risk and equating Black people with especially high financial risk. Subsequently, residents in mostly Black neighborhoods were denied loans and capital investments. This wealth denial evolved into systemic disinvestment and decades-long neighborhood decline that is still evident in the present (Hillier 2003; Scott 2020; Plumer and Popovich 2020). Take for example, the case of Sandtown-Winchester, the Baltimore neighborhood that was home to Freddie Gray, the young Black man whose wrongful death while in police custody triggered a firestorm of protests throughout Baltimore in 2015.

As historian Emily Lieb wrote:

It was not so long ago, really, that Freddie Gray's [neighborhood of Sandtown-Winchester] was a livable neighborhood in a liveable city. At the turn of the 20th century, its streets were lined with pleasant rowhouses in which middle- and working-class families thrived. Every year, it seemed, the School Board built a new school or two to accommodate the neighborhood's growing population of children. . . . Brand new streetcars ferried workers and shoppers to and from downtown for just a nickel. Teams of city workers paved roads and sidewalks, dug sewer lines and picked up trash. (Lieb 2015)

Skip forward one generation and, by the end of World War I, Sandtown-Winchester was "well on its way to becoming a slum: dirty and decaying, with hazardous streets and crumbling schools" (Lieb 2015). Redlining denied neighborhoods including Sandtown-Winchester access to capital that would have allowed them to maintain their infrastructure, update housing stock and other buildings, and provide ongoing community services. Instead, these neighborhoods became sites for concentrated poverty and chronic social and environmental injustices.

Residents of redlined communities on the peninsula including Cherry Hill and Curtis Bay today are overly familiar with potentially deadly black mold and asbestos. Some have related health problems, especially asthma and other respiratory illnesses, but also cancers, heart disease, and skin infections, as a result of living for extended periods of time with these toxins (Mayo Clinic 2022a). Free Your Voice students talked at length about uninhabitable yet habited housing. They described hazards in their apartments that included collapsing roofs, leaky faucets, and chipped paint as the daily struggles of poverty. With regard to paint chips: Black neighborhoods in Baltimore, including those on the peninsula, experience some of the highest rates of childhood lead poisoning and lead paint violations in the city (Abell Foundation 2002; WYPR 2019b). According to the Mayo Clinic medical website, lead poisoning symptoms include developmental delays, learning difficulties, irritability, loss of appetite and weight loss, sluggishness and fatigue, abdominal pain, vomiting, hearing loss, seizures, and more (2022b). Youth from Free Your Voice spoke freely and frequently about the high levels of lead in their bloodstreams.

Juxtapose to this, the best (or grade A) neighborhoods on historic Home Owners' Loan Corporation (HOLC) maps, those that were colored green. In Baltimore, these neighborhoods included Roland Park, Homeland, Guilford, and Northwood, neighborhoods that still today represent centers of capital investment and intergenerational wealth accumulation. They are hotspots for desirable mortgages, beautiful parks, and outdoor green spaces (Pietila 2010: 67) with reliable infrastructure and an abundance of services provided by the municipality. Residents in these neighborhoods have homes with curbside appeal and well-manicured lawns and gardens. Their children, who have never seen a lead paint chip, receive top-notch public educations and have clean parks and other recreational areas nearby.

In his famous paper, "Two Baltimores," Lawrence Brown (2016b) outlined how accumulated advantage breeds investment, whereas accumulated disadvantage breeds disinvestment, decline, and eventual decay. Antero Pietila (2010) noted that for decades following the 1937 redlined maps, politicians found it easier to concentrate public housing in Black neighborhoods or atop environmental wastelands than to disperse them throughout the city. This exacerbated poverty in already impoverished neighborhoods, aggravating environmental inequality and other elements of unhealthy and uninhabitable housing. As a result, social and structural problems of racism and housing inequality map onto environmental and human health crises. The poorest and predominantly Black neighborhoods in East and West Baltimore, in addition to the Southern Peninsula, became (and many still are) epicenters for lead contamination, transit apartheid, food apartheid, school closures, loss of recreation centers, and expanding drug economies (Brown 2016b).

While the South Baltimore Peninsula experienced a heyday of industrial development during World Wars I and II that brought housing, new infrastructure, and even schools to the peninsula, these were short-lived. Quickly followed by deindustrialization and decline, blocks of boarded up vacants became a potent symbol of the disinvestment and decay in South Baltimore neighborhoods—a symbol that Free Your Voice students were quick to appropriate and then take advantage of.

The year that the architects entered the classroom, a subset of Free Your Voice students set out on a mission with Daniel Murphy to map the vacant houses in Curtis Bay. They went out with pens, paper, and maps, and marked on those maps (and in red) every home that was vacant. The youth photographed the vacants they observed and even walked the perimeter to record the sights, sounds, and smells of the abandoned properties. They also recorded the addresses of these vacants. In Curtis Bay alone, they found over five hundred homes that were vacant by identifying systematic and structural characteristics such as boarded doors and windows, structural damage, marked differences between neighboring properties, and abundance of trash outside and inside of the home. They cross-checked their findings with the City of Baltimore vacant property list and against code violations that the City of Baltimore Department of Housing and Community Development was supposed to enforce. The students located the names of current landlords and obtained their addresses and phone numbers. They used Google Maps to spatially locate the addresses on their map of vacants and drew red arrows outward to the states where the absentee landlords resided.

This map became a visual display of predatory forms of speculation. In 2000, Curtis Bay and Brooklyn had 16.1 and 16.3 percent vacancy rates, respectively, while the citywide vacancy rate was 14.1 percent. In 2017, while several neighborhoods in the city had decreased vacancy rates, including at or below 4 percent, the vacancy rates for Curtis Bay and Brooklyn were nearly double what they had been, at approximately 32 percent.[6] Making a bad situation much worse, the Free Your Voice students found, by going out and counting vacants and then comparing their findings to city data, that Baltimore City *underestimated* the number of vacants in Curtis Bay. This corroborated concerns published in a 2015 report by the Abell Foundation "that Baltimore Housing's metric undercounts the number of vacant properties and thus understates the city's vacancy problem" (Jacobson 2015).[7]

Following Paulo Freire's problem-posing education model, the vacancy research by the Free Your Voice youth prompted the students

Figure 7. A homeless resident from Hazel Street Homes, which burned down in 2018; many remain vacant and abandoned. *Credit:* South Baltimore Community Land Trust. Photo by Kyle Pompey.

to begin by asking, "How many vacant buildings are in our community?" and then to ask more questions: Why do landlords hold on to vacant properties? Why do landlords let their properties fall into disarray? Through qualitative interviews with residents the youth discovered that many of the absentee landlords engaged in land speculation and "flipping" (upgrading homes, often when market values begin to climb, in order to sell them at much higher prices than they were purchased for). Some landlords, the students found, held on to abandoned and vacant properties for decades, waiting for the land to increase in price. Again, many of these landlords lived elsewhere. Meanwhile, residents spoke to the students about how the pervasiveness of the vacants heightened their concerns over rising rates of crime and violence, illegal dumping, and loitering. Many reported having witnessed illegal activities like drug sales, sex work, and gambling in and around the vacants.

The maps that youth made of vacants became potent political symbols at 20/20 Fair Development events (described below), as well as other events, rallies and demonstrations. The maps of abandonment and decline drew attention to a model of development that was failing the majority of Baltimore's residents (see Figure 7). Many residents believed that land speculators were not just waiting passively but tried bringing a large-scale development project to the area to jump-start gentrification and increase the values of their properties. These beliefs proved to be well founded when developers proposed Port Covington Development, a multibillion-dollar urban "renewal" project that would include, most prominently, a "campus" where sports gear giant Under Armour would headquarter its company (Simmons 2022).

A TALE OF TWO SOUTH BALTIMORES

The Under Armour Port Covington Development is a classic example of large-scale development Baltimore style: designed for the affluent while promising fair and equitable mixed-income housing for the poor. Early on, this 235-acre mega-development project innovated by Kevin Plank, the former CEO of Under Armour, and the Sagamore Development company, promised a city within a city (a waterfront urban center south of downtown), with one thousand new residences, three hundred hotel rooms, 240,000 square feet of retail space, and multiple high rises, parks, and parking garages (Marton, Sherman and Pate 2018). Plank's Port Covington real estate project was (and is) one of the largest urban renewal proposals in the history of the United States, having amassed six billion dollars in local, state, and federal government support so far (King and Rich 2021).

According to Lawrence Brown,

> What we are seeing here is the Sagamore Development company [headed by Kevin Plank] is redeveloping the industrial waterfront Port Covington neighborhood with new Under Armour headquarters as its anchor. Yet they

are receiving $660 million from the City [in the form of Tax Increment Financing (TIFs)].[8] Corporate developers exploit local, state and federal economic development policies to enrich themselves under the guise of helping redlined Black neighborhoods (Brown 2021: 198).

This investment was nearly six times the amount slated to be spent on parks and recreation across the city in 2018 (Brown 2021). Recent legislation permits TIF breaks to be used to build affordable housing. But the Sagamore Development Company representatives fought housing advocates—including People Organized for Responsible TIFs, Tax Breaks, and Transformation (PORT)—in order to limit the number of on-site affordable housing units to be included in the project. Instead, the Sagamore TIF allocated $139.8 million to be spent on parks in Port Covington (the alliance of PORT and Build Up Baltimore argued this money would be much better spent on providing affordable and inclusionary housing). City officials celebrated the Port Covington victory and called the document outlining Sagamore investments a historic citywide benefits commitment and Memorandum of Understanding (MOU).[9]

As of 2022, on the Port Covington side of Hanover Street Bridge, the Sagamore Spirit Distillery and Rye Street Tavern, both of which opened in 2017, look outward over the water at Winans Cove. Nearby is an eight-thousand-square foot bus depot turned incubator and startup hub that opened in 2016 known as City Garage. In its expansive parking lot sits South Point, a seasonal, open-air market plus restaurant and event space with "epic sunsets" and FLOW yoga events (Jackson 2018). From the volleyball courts and the grassy hangout spaces of South Point, one can look across the water to the Cherry Hill and Westport neighborhoods on the other side of the Hanover Street Bridge, just across the Patapsco River, and see abandonment and disinvestment. Those who look closely see the vacant buildings that were counted by the students: homes boarded up with code violations dangling from unhinged doors. They might see uneven streets with potholes large enough to pop a tire. Unseen yet glaringly obvious, on the Port Covington side of the river, the median income is $109,000, while in Cherry Hill the median income is $24,000 and in Westport it is $37,000; in Brooklyn-Curtis Bay, just past Cherry Hill and Westport, the median income is $40,000 (King and Rich 2021; Brown et al. 2016).

Despite the fact that Plank and the Sagamore Development Company promised to build affordable housing, many activists believed Plank was building a massive retail empire that would only drive up rents and displace current residents. During the planning commission approval meetings, affordable- and fair-housing advocates such as Barbara Samuels of the Maryland ACLU, Anthony Williams of Housing Our Neighbors, and Adam Schneider of Healthcare for the Homeless testified to the need to include public housing residents and inclusionary housing in Port Covington planning as a step toward desegregating the racially and socioeconomically divided city. This proposal was rejected by the Baltimore City Council, led by council president Jack Young, and the Sagamore Development Company which resulted in the signing of an agreement with only 10 percent of total housing development allotted to affordable housing (Kravetz 2016; Brown 2021).[10]

Port Covington represents the world in a grain of sand. Large-scale economic development brings capital and investment to postindustrial and indebted cities and, perhaps, improves the overall or outward-facing image of a city. In the case of Baltimore, many US residents viewed these processes from their living room couches via *The Wire*, a TV series set in Baltimore that aired on HBO between 2002 and 2008. Yet residents on the South Baltimore Peninsula did not need an HBO series to understand that Port Covington was to bring development for some and displacement for others.[11] Most residents living in the six peninsula neighborhoods on the south side of the Hanover Street Bridge (known as the "South Baltimore Six") with whom Free Your Voice youth spoke expressed concerns about gentrification and displacement. Across the river from them (on the Port Covington side of the bridge) already, the corporate grocery Harris Teeter had replaced the local mom-and-pop grocery store. Neighbors talked about speculators and developers roaming their neighborhoods in search of blight. "It is like you build a community, especially in places like Lakeland where Latinx workers have put blood and sweat into community and local businesses, and then a big glitzy project like Port Covington comes along and bulldozes over everything you have created and you have to move elsewhere," explained Free Your Voice student activist, Dario Lopez.

In a letter addressed to the city council president, Jack Young, ACLU representatives Barbara A. Samuels and D'Sean Williams-Brown called Port Covington "a brand new racially and economically segregated city within a city, a virtual gated enclave inhabited by millennials and empty nesters who make an average of 100,000 dollars or more" (Samuels and Williams-Brown 2016). They concluded their letter by asserting: "The choice before the City Council is not one of growth or no growth. It is a choice between equitable growth and trickle down, between inclusive growth and continued segregation, between shared prosperity and growing inequality. In short, it is a choice between the unsustainable path of Two Baltimore's and starting down the road toward One Baltimore" (Samuels and Williams-Brown 2016).

Their curiosity piqued by the wording of the ACLU representatives, Free Your Voice students studied the "Two Baltimores" and found what they already knew: one Baltimore for the businessmen and other members of the elite class on the north side of the Hanover Street Bridge where young entrepreneurs kayaked on the water and played beach volleyball, and the other on the south side of the Hanover Street Bridge, where poor residents of color breathed toxic fumes from heavy industry dumped in their backyards and where asthma rates soared. The students recognized in this research the injustices of trickle-down development, and they began to envision land trusts as an alternative— as a strategy for maintaining the integrity of their community, bolstering it before processes of gentrification decimated the homes, businesses, and intricate informal social support networks that made their neighborhood theirs. The money that made their vision feasible,

and with which the SBCLT was founded, came as a result of the success of a citywide citizen initiative known as the 20/20 campaign.

THE 20/20 CAMPAIGN AND THE ORIGINS OF SBCLT

The demands at the center of the 20/20 campaign were for Baltimore
City officials to (1) invest twenty million dollars annually to deconstruct
vacant homes, replacing them with public green spaces, urban gardens, and environmental sustainability projects, and (2) dedicate another
twenty million dollars to create permanent, affordable housing (Figure 8). Hence the 20/20 in the name. Perhaps most importantly, the
20/20 campaign called for annual investment in neighborhood-driven
development and resident control of their communities so that prices of
homes (including rentals) would not increase above what residents could
afford. "This is an agreement that came from the power of the residents
on the ground," said Destiny; "This isn't an agreement that was made by
a wealthy developer coming in or [that] the City [made] behind closed
doors. This is our vision, and it's finally coming to fruition."

Ultimately victorious, the 20/20 campaign required long days of
campaigning and nights of strategizing by Free Your Voice students and
members of The Housing for All coalition. In less than six weeks, activists and volunteers gathered more than thirteen thousand signed petitions from registered voters to get the Affordable Housing Trust Fund
initiative on the ballot. And after 83 percent of voters approved the initiative, coalition members worked with the Baltimore City Council to
create a dedicated revenue source for the trust fund, to be managed by
the newly created Affordable Housing Trust Fund.[12]

"Equitable community development in our historically redlined
neighborhoods is at the top of my agenda," said Baltimore City Mayor
Brandon M. Scott when he came into office in 2021; "Community land
trusts are one tool to provide permanent affordable housing across our
neighborhoods, while helping close the racial wealth gap" (Baltimore
City Department of Housing and Community Development 2021).

Figure 8. Protest for housing justice in McElderry Park. *Credit:* South Baltimore Land Trust and Charm City Land Trust.

"These funds will support housing those who are at or below fifty percent of the area median income," explained Acting Housing Commissioner, Alice Kennedy; "Making quality homeownership a reality for lower-income residents of the city will not only stabilize these residents but will strengthen our neighborhoods" (Baltimore City Department of Housing and Community Development 2021). The citywide campaign with its growing political support—and more specifically, the money made available as a result of the campaign plus support— was the stimulus necessary to begin the South Baltimore Community Land Trust (SBCLT) development project.

SBCLT is, still today, a Baltimore-based nonprofit organization committed, first, to establishing community land trust homes in order to build permanently affordable housing for low-income residents in the community and, second, to zero-waste work. In the following chapter, I will detail Free Your Voice students' investments, along with those of SBCLT, in Baltimore's Zero Waste campaign. That Free Your Voice students got involved with SBCLT and land trust work, as they very quickly did, was in no small part influenced by the architects with whom they were in communication in the classroom as the Free Your Voice curriculum evolved. Equally important, at the time students turned their attention to land ownership issues, the Worker Justice Center, as a part of the Fair Development coalition, was organizing the 20/20 campaign I just detailed. Thus, the fact that the students of Free Your Voice—a Worker Justice Center program from the start—were excited about and active in land trust development had much to do with their program roots and the adults with whom they were in conversation, adults who had been organizing around housing justice for decades and who were excited by and/or active in the 20/20 campaign. I would be remiss not to include them in the picture. In addition to these influences, the students' own lived experiences and the data they gathered while participant observing in and around the South Baltimore Peninsula, all of which put into perspective for them the very long history of racist, classist, toxic housing decisions and practices in their city, bolstered student commitment to the cause.

AN EXPERIMENT IN BUILDING LAND TRUSTS

The very first "land trust" on the peninsula was a private house with a yard located behind Benjamin Franklin High that was legally owned by Daniel Murphy. Murphy bought the house in 2015, lived in it until 2016, and then began renting it at below-market rates to Free Your Voice students and their parents. While not officially a community land trust, Murphy utilized the property to run a land trust experiment of sorts. Initially, the home provided Destiny with low-cost housing directly behind the high school where she mentored youth in the Free Your Voice program. Once Destiny moved to Seattle in February of 2020, former Free Your Voice student Jimmy Brown and his mother and sister moved into the home. Jimmy described it as

> the best house I have lived in. The rent is very affordable. My mom is just handling those rent checks now. It's very stable and it's not something you have to think about or worry about.... With the land trust model, you don't have to worry about rent because it's very affordable and it's a stable home.

While the house benefited Destiny and then Jimmy and his family by providing subsidized rent and a healthy and environmentally sound home to live in, the empty lot behind Daniel Murphy's house functioned as an official community land trust lot, held in trust by the SBCLT, after it was gifted to the community by Murphy. On this lot, the architects from Neighborhood Design spent long days with the Free Your Voice youth, initially clearing the overgrown weeds and brush and taking measurements. In the classroom, they created model mock-ups of the activities that would take place in the safe space they were planning to create.

The students agreed that they wanted this lot to be a "fun space," or a "recreational space" where they could gather and work out together in an outside gym; they wanted a space where they could play together away from the violence in their neighborhood. As their brainstorming advanced, they began to build what they wanted in miniature form. Maureen McDonald recalled:

> We made little mock-ups for the lot. I still think that for many students, it was much harder to grasp the bigger vision. It's just a hard thing for students to do who are thinking about that kind of design for the first time. I remember one student spent the entire class period making this really lovely bench that was just like . . . really thoughtful and cared for and showed his skill. That showed how precise this person was: he really liked working on the building aspect of it. He made the benches out of little wooden pieces, he used toothpicks, hot glue, and pieced it together.

After nine months of planning from within the classroom, during the summer of 2019, twenty students (most from the participatory action class though not all) began building on the community lot. The students were hired by The Worker Justice Center–Free Your Voice using a Baltimore City Youth Fund grant awarded by the City of Baltimore to The Worker Justice Center in order to train youth from Benjamin Franklin High as community organizers. In effect, the students were paid as interns to build the space(s) they envisioned.

As Jimmy described, "This lot was overgrown land and debris; we had to clear it out first. People in the community often dump trash in these kinds of spaces. But kids knew that they wanted a nice place where they would not be harmed on the streets." Once they finished clearing the land, the students laid concrete for a basketball court and set up hoops. They built a miniature golf course and constructed a stage (using wood diverted from the incinerator and donated to the lot). The idea for the stage was to provide a platform from which students could perform spoken-word and rap songs, host community talent shows, and also do creative theater as community action. They wanted to perform oral histories of important South Baltimore figures.

Not only did providing the required manual labor help to solidify social relationships for Jimmy and his peers, but the work strengthened the youths' claims to space and place. Even for the students who lived outside of Curtis Bay, in Cherry Hill and Lakeland, for example, the collective work of "building together" fostered in them a sense of entitlement and of connectedness to the land and to geography. Their identifications with particular neighborhoods such as Lakeland or Cherry Hill were replaced by new senses of being from "South Baltimore" as they tore down brush and ripped up weeds, laid mulch, and constructed the stage along with a three-bin waste system on the property.

The students who worked on the project over the summer recruited members from the community who had the skill sets in construction they needed: some were contractors who helped with the manual labor of building the stage (Figure 9), others had skills to assist with the miniature golf course. Mia Sanchez, a young Latinx Free Your Voice organizer and a budding artist, painted a portrait of Harriet Tubman on

Figure 9. Community residents building the stage on the South Baltimore Community Land Trust lot. *Credit:* South Baltimore Community Land Trust.

the stage along with the word *Lead* in bold black lettering. In Jackson's words:

> Mia was just so talented. She really loves art. She has been working with me on building a full-scale mural in the community. I told her that I would recommend her for anything in the future.... People in the neighborhood [who]

work and contribute to the built environment and see the change physically [are] such a huge source of inspiration. That's why I'm attracted to The Worker Justice Center. The art, the political mobilization, and the education. Fuse those three things together to do community organizing. This is the essence of what makes life meaningful and what makes our life meaningful.

This classroom project fomented student aspirations for a much larger land trust project, and as a result, during the 2018–2019 school year, Free Your Voice students, working with Maryland Institute College of Art (MICA) and the Neighborhood Design Center, began to dream of expanding their work from the lot behind their school to Inner-Monroe Circle, an adjacent lot. At that site, the students imagined constructing eight to ten affordable housing units. With this in mind, they wrote a letter to the owner of the lot, pleading to buy the land with money they raised through fundraising and with the promise to take care of it and steward it for the community. The owner agreed to their price and now it, along with the lot donated by Murphy just next to it, are part of the SBCLT vision (Figure 10). Additionally, students from the 2018 cohort started to take a vested interest in the Affordable Housing Trust Fund meetings occurring during the year and began to advocate at those meetings for city funding to build properties as part of the growing community land trust.

COMMUNITY CONTROL OF LAND
AND FAIR DEVELOPMENT FOR THE FUTURE

Development practices that promise community benefits but instead lead to the displacement of poor people are a contributing factor to what many have named urban apartheid. Sociologists Douglas Massey and Nancy Denton, citing Thomas Pettigrew, wrote that "racial segregation is the 'structural linchpin' of American race relations" (1998: 147). In their book, *American Apartheid*, they argued that persistent structural injustices including hyper-segregation, increased social isolation, and the clustering of poor (and Black) people into geographic areas of highly

Figure 10. First passive house of South Baltimore Community Land Trust rendered by architects from The Neighborhood Design Center. *Credit:* Neighborhood Design Center and South Baltimore Community Land Trust.

concentrated poverty most accurately explain not only the persistence of an urban underclass but why Black and Brown people are disproportionately represented in that underclass (Massey and Denton 1993). Lawrence Brown has shown through his research that Baltimore's practices of segregation are a result of over one hundred years of governmental policies of racialized covenants, redlining, blockbusting, rent-to-own, and more physically and financially violent forms of displacement, in service to projects and processes such as urban renewal, gentrification, eminent domain and the demolition of public housing (2021).

Many residents on the South Baltimore Peninsula were weary of corporate promises to provide charity while constructing mega-million-dollar development projects.[13] "We know that this will not be inclusionary development," explained a middle-aged resident at the July 2018 protest against the Port Covington development who wished to remain anonymous.

> Many of us are concerned as we are seeing more and more of these community buy-offs. Strangers, developers come into our neighborhood and offer a very low price for the home. We know that they all see the Sagamore development on the horizon and this means we will all eventually be kicked out of this community. It has happened before, and it will happen again.

Sagamore (The Port Covington Project) broke ground in 2019, and while there have been a series of problems that have slowed development, most of the construction will be completed by 2023. South Baltimore, North of the Hanover Street Bridge, will see new shops, sparkling new offices, and residential dwellings in high-end condominiums and mixed-use apartment buildings. But if history is any guide, few if any working-class and poor families living on the south side of the bridge will benefit from the development.

Community land trusts, in stark contrast, provide a long-term, community-based, environmentally friendly development, the kind that can ameliorate "blight" and impede the displacement that accompanies processes of gentrification. Organizations like The Neighborhood Design Center are hard at work collaborating with community residents who imagine the kinds of neighborhoods in which they want to live, work, and raise their children. "What could development look like if poor people take ownership of land and resources?" This is a question that is also a point of departure for developers who are invested not in profits but in community members, especially those who have been failed by development again and again. And this is a question that community land trusts are able to answer.

Free Your Voice students are at the forefront of the South Baltimore land trust movement, calling for multiple units of affordable housing to be fit into land trust lots, designing green spaces on adjacent lots, and envisioning agroecology. Crystal Green said in July of 2020 to a group of housing and land activists from Philadelphia visiting the SBCLT community land trust site:

> Already here in this community where we stand, there's an incinerator, there's an open-air coal pile, there's a landfill, then a medical waste incinerator. And so, all of that is here in this one community.... We don't wanna be a dumping ground anymore. We don't want our lives to be disrespected. So we fought a massive incinerator and won and now we are fighting to do grassroots development. Our community matters. We looked at who owns the land in our community. We were like, "we wanna own this land!" We want to determine what happens in our community. So, where you are standing here now is land that we own!

After which, the crowd of Philadelphia activists cheered.

Increased community control of land is key to alleviating the problems that plague frontline communities. The fight for fair development must not only address land ownership, however; it must address the beliefs and practices that perpetuate the dumping of heavy industry and waste management facilities into communities like those on the South Baltimore Peninsula. For even when the community owns all the lands for sale, if a city builds its incinerators next door, and if those incinerators continue to burn an overwhelming majority of area waste, residents do not yet have justice. In the following chapter, I examine what was, perhaps, the inevitable next cause of the Free Your Voice students, that of zero waste. The Zero Waste campaign calls for reducing— and even eradicating—waste destined for incinerators. Among the zero-waste measures the students along with their activist allies on the South Baltimore Peninsula have imagined is the use of community land trust and vacant lots for farming, gardening, and composting, and thus, the land trust movement and zero-waste work very quickly become spokes of the same wheel, prongs of the same fork, skirmishes in the same, singular fight against a long history of uneven and unequal urban development.

CHAPTER FIVE

Compost! Learn So We Don't Have to Burn

Zero Waste Is Our Future

We have three incinerators here. One burns medical waste. One burns waste from out of town. And the third one is the notorious BRESCO, [which perpetuates] this myth that burning trash is green energy. But we know that is false, and it's causing fifty-five million dollars in health damages when we burn trash. They put incinerators in poor neighborhoods, but one thing about the wind is it does not segregate or discriminate. So what's the alternative to burning trash? Zero waste.

—Marvin Hayes[1]

During the 2018–2019 academic year, Jimmy Brown (introduced in chapter 2) and his classmate Kenneth Smith decided that, for their final project in Free Your Voice, they would initiate a campaign for zero waste by creating videos to educate their community members, including peers, neighbors, and city officials. *Zero waste* is a term that denotes, most simply, a radical reduction of the waste sent to landfills and incinerators, with the ultimate goal of eliminating it altogether.[2] Jimmy and Kenneth labeled their project the "Zero Waste Challenge," and made two-minute video clips encouraging their peers and neighbors to join them, not only by radically reducing the amount of food waste they generated and adopting reusable utensils in place of single-stream plastics, but also, by creating their own videos to encourage others to join the movement for zero waste. In his video, Kenneth used the following metaphor, followed by a call to action: "When I was young, right, my mother and father smoked inside the house. But, ah, my little brother Cameron was born with severe asthma. They stopped smoking in the house entirely. Think of Baltimore City as our parents, BRESCO as a cigarette and *us*, the people of Baltimore, as the children of the city. Baltimore, do the right thing, and stop smoking." At the end of his video, Kenneth encouraged viewers to join the Zero Waste Challenge and help to build a healthier and more sustainable future. In the months that followed, other students, teachers, nurses, home health care providers, public health experts, college professors, city officials, and state representatives took up the Zero Waste Challenge, declaring on camera their own reasons for joining the movement. "My mom has asthma," a student from Baltimore Polytechnic Institute told the camera; "I don't think that's a coincidence." A woman in a plaid button-down shirt asserted: "I see every day, as a pediatric nurse in the emergency room in downtown Baltimore, children who have to spend hours to days longer than that in the hospital as a result of living in the shadow of BRESCO" (Figure 11).[3]

One year after the founding of the South Baltimore Community Land Trust (SBCLT), Free Your Voice students and members of the SBCLT designed community land trusts not only as spaces for providing equitable housing but as spaces for environmental stewardship, education on zero waste, regenerative economics, and green cooperatives (i.e., eco-friendly businesses with members and/or laborers who share ownership as well as profits). The same racism and inequities that marginalized the poor in under-resourced communities where vacants abounded and infrastructure failed, the students and SBCLT members discerned, underpinned city and corporate practices of dumping waste (including toxic chemicals) into the backyards of the poor. Increasingly, they began asking: How can the community utilize lands in the South Baltimore

Figure 11. BRESCO burning trash. *Credit:* Photo by Kyle Pompey.

Peninsula for zero-waste infrastructure? How can we get from (1) burning natural resources to (2) a regenerative and zero-waste system built by poor and working-class Brown and Black Baltimoreans? Alas, Baltimore's long reliance on a burn-and-bury approach to waste management, along with the entrenchment of this system in city government, left the city ill equipped to oversee a just transition to something better.

In this chapter, I describe the Baltimore-based Zero Waste campaign that began inside Benjamin Franklin High School and the Free Your Voice classroom during the 2018–2019 academic year, and which evolved into a citywide plan to adopt zero-waste practices by the spring of 2020. I also chart mounting tensions—including a rift among leaders of the Filbert Street Community Garden and organizational conflicts within The Worker Justice Center—that left Baltimore's zero-waste movement vulnerable to closed-door dealings and political buyouts.

As a result—and despite incredible grassroots organizing work by Free Your Voice students and a coalition of allies that included public health officials, teachers and professors, eco-socialists, politicians, and other stakeholders—in the narrative I recount here, zero-waste campaigning ground to a halt, with organizers shifting strategies to instead minimize the amount of food waste entering the incinerator-bound waste stream. But let me start at the beginning.

Free Your Voice students, led by a cohort of peers interested in the problem of waste incineration, began the school year by studying health issues that arise as a result of incineration. Together, they worked with program leader (and former Free Your Voice student) Destiny Watford and public health experts to understand how toxins from incineration cause respiratory illnesses such as asthma and lung cancers. "Why do we continue to rely upon burning our waste if we know it is compromising human health?" they asked. Also: "How can we get food waste out of the waste stream?" Destiny suggested inviting Marvin Hayes, the Director of the Baltimore Compost Collective (BCC), into the classroom. BCC was an early hub for the zero-waste movement, and Hayes was someone to whom the youth could relate.

It is not accidental that Hayes ended up a compost fanatic in the middle of Baltimore. He grew up in Sandtown-Winchester, the West Baltimore neighborhood that was redlined in the 1930s, transformed from thriving community to racked by unemployment, crime, and over-policing, and where Freddie Gray was murdered by the police in 2015 (sparking the Baltimore uprisings of that same year). Hayes recalled struggling at Frederick Douglass High School, the oldest African American high school in Baltimore City, originally called the Colored High and Grammar School.[4] He acted up in his teenage years, and as a result, in 1988, he was enrolled in a drop-out prevention program called Futures. As a part of the program, students participated in Outward Bound, during which urban youth spent five days in the woods. Hayes recalled, "It had little ups and downs, but the last day we had to do this ropes course and I was scared to death. And I had this instructor,

I will never forget him. His name was Mike Beavis, and he was from London. He said, 'Marvin, just step out of your box.' I was scared to death! But I said to myself, I gotta get back to this Outward Bound Program and finish the rope course. And eventually I did." Once Hayes finished the Outward Bound program, it turned into other internships working for the Wilderness School in East Hartland Connecticut. This school provided at-risk teens an opportunity to take part in intensive hiking, backpacking, and canoeing in order to build confidence and self-sufficiency. Working with youth in this capacity exposed Hayes to veganism, composting, and even growing his own food. Hayes brought this and other lessons from Outward Bound and the Wilderness School back to Baltimore, eventually applying what he learned about environmental justice to his daily personal as well as professional practices.

When the Baltimore Compost Collective (BCC) was established in September 2017 by the Local Institute for Self-Reliance (ILSR) and Neighborhood Soil Rebuilders, Hayes worked in the Filbert Street Garden. He started as the driver and eventually moved into the position of program manager of BCC by the end of 2017. BCC was modeled after a youth-led, bike-powered, food scrap collecting enterprise in the Bushwick neighborhood of Brooklyn, New York, named BK ROT (for "bike rot"). Though BCC started small, Hayes's vivacious personality and contagious energy made him especially effective at communicating the urgency of composting food waste. Hayes worked hard to make the BCC into a laboratory from which he could demonstrate to city residents the benefits of composting food scraps on a small scale while inspiring them (especially youth) to join the movement for zero waste. In the initial three months, Hayes and two teenage employees, Juan Gonzalez and Damion Floyd, who made up the Baltimore Compost Collective staff, increased the program's outreach from eight residential customers to twenty-five residential customers and one commercial customer, Pure Raw Juice. Then, in the Spring of 2017, they moved the program into the Filbert Street Garden and launched an official website. The Worker Justice Center, through a Memorandum of Understanding (MOU), became the host for BCC.[5] This relationship, however, quickly became fraught with tension.[6]

On a cold winter's day in 2018, after receiving an invitation from Destiny Watford, Hayes entered the Free Your Voice classroom with Brenda Platt (from the Institute for Local Self-Reliance) to talk about composting. He explained to students what goes into compost buckets, how they separate food scraps and then turn them into "black gold" (or compost). He passed around a bag of this black gold, describing it as the final stage of the anaerobic digestion. The students were fascinated by the bags of compost at various stages. One student replied, "So basically, an onion peel and eggshell are food for our food?" Hayes turned to the student and answered, "Yes!" before adding, "All of this is food that can be reused, not burned in an incinerator." Hayes ended his talk that day by reciting one of his favorite phrases: "Compost!: We gotta learn so that we don't burn." He left the students asking themselves: What if composting was made more accessible in the city? What would it look like if we had curbside composting? Or effective recycling pickup?

After the visit, students decided that they wanted to see Hayes in action at the Filbert Street Garden, so Daniel Murphy and Destiny Watford coordinated a trip. A few weeks later, the Free Your Voice students walked from Benjamin Franklin High to the Baltimore Compost Collective, in one corner of the Filbert Street Garden. There they gathered around Hayes, who shouted out by way of a greeting, "Welcome to the Wakanda of South Baltimore." He was referencing the fictional, Afrofuturist land from which the Marvel character Black Panther hails. Hayes continued, "There's a quote from *Black Panther* that I love. He said, in times of crisis the wise build bridges, while the foolish build barriers. So, we are the bridge to lead Baltimore City to zero waste."

Hayes was a tall, strongly built, forty-something-year-old man whose black hands were stained from the soil he believed in and whose smile lit up crowds. His exuberant personality and passion for composting emanated from him like the scent of the raw vegetables and fruits he mixed daily to produce his potion of compost-rich soil enhancer he

Figure 12. Example of "black gold" made by the Baltimore Compost Collective. *Credit:* Photo by Kyle Pompey.

called "black gold" (Figure 12). With the Free Your Voice students as his audience, Hayes gave a lecture on carbons, nitrogen, water, and air. He showed the students the "three-bin system" and explained how compost sits for about a month while it is "cooking" before it's ready to be sifted. Two students that day volunteered to sift the compost Hayes indicated. "Look at this beautiful, beautiful Filbert Street black gold! This is the only soil enhancer you can put back into the soil!" Hayes exclaimed when the students had finished. "Starve the incinerator; feed the soil," was another of Hayes' favorite sayings.

While the tours Hayes led were a vital component of the Baltimore Compost Collective's education efforts, so too was the work of composting that Hayes performed along with his team of youth volunteers from South Baltimore.[7] Hayes and his team collected food scraps from residences in

Baltimore's Federal Hill, Riverside Park, and Locust Point neighborhoods—all gentrified areas on the northern end of the Hanover Street bridge (often referred to as the southern tip of the white L of Baltimore). Every week in 2018–2019, youth from the peninsula gathered approximately four hundred pounds of organic material from approximately seventy customers, who paid twenty five dollars for their monthly pick up service, the cheapest compost in the city. "We divert about eight tons of Baltimore City food scraps every year," said Hayes; "It was going to the Wheelabrator-BRESCO incinerator or the landfill."

Every week in 2018–2019, youth from the peninsula used a beat up van to gather four hundred pounds of compost.[8] Hayes often told tourgoers, "What's so special about our program is [it provides] an opportunity to work with youth, to transform them and give them a skill." He saw the garden as a space for training youth in green industries (economic activities that seek to minimize impact on the environment) and composting—and he hired many Free Your Voice students to work alongside him. When Hayes thought back to some of the very first Benjamin Franklin students he mentored, he recalled the ways in which BCC exposed them to places worlds away from the inner city and gave them additional opportunities for learning. Juan Gonzalez (a Dreamer, and a special education student at Benjamin Franklin), for example, was one of Hayes's first youth composters.[9] "At the age of seventeen, Juan had never left South Baltimore, let alone Maryland," Hayes explained, "but the Baltimore Compost Collective gave him an opportunity to go to Atlanta to speak about his environmental justice work. He never stepped on a plane, and he told me, 'Mr. Marvin—I have never left my mother,' and he started to cry. I replied, 'Juan, be brave for her.'" After describing this conversation, Hayes turned to me to say, "This is what we are able to do, give young people these opportunities to expand their horizons."

Listening to Hayes and experimenting in the hands-on workshops motivated a subgroup of Free Your Voice students already interested in zero waste to move from making video-based calls to giving live demonstrations and promoting their cause at local events. They began these efforts at the 2019 Youth in Action Leadership Day. Designed, planned, and implemented by Free Your Voice students, the event brought city actors, nonprofit stakeholders, teachers, youth, and scientists together to share youth-led visions for a just transition to zero waste. That day, students presented research findings related to a multiplicity of causes—not only zero waste. Importantly, however, it was at this event that Free Your Voice students pushed their zero-waste work beyond the classroom, launching a citywide Zero Waste campaign. Because it mattered to the movement, I recount the events of that day in detail here.

TRANSFORMING UNDER ARMOUR CITY GARAGE INTO A ZERO-WASTE FUTURE

The Youth in Action Leadership Day was held on March 16, 2019, at City Garage, a former South Baltimore bus garage repurposed as an "innovation space" (Gantz 2015). City Garage is part of a corporate headquarters complex designed for the Under Armour sports equipment company, located at the tip of the Hanover Street Bridge. Holding the Zero Waste Youth Day at the City Garage was a way for Free Your Voice students to transform this wealthy enclave into a populist site where they could be heard while illustrating the benefits of green infrastructure and zero-waste businesses. Also, by using this particular site, Free Your Voice youth hoped to bring attention to the fact that the corporate headquarters was not designed to benefit the community. The glitzy office spaces, brand new wood fixtures, and fresh carpets, stood in stark contrast to the students' messages about regenerative and sustainable economies.

The students spent weeks preparing for the event: refining their research, painting murals, finishing three-dimensional mock-ups and maps for display, and finding other creative ways to communicate their research findings. The day of the event, they arrived early, shuffling into a dark auditorium half filled with empty booths that they soon transformed. The students claimed their booths and decorated the space with colorful drop-banners and other signage that read "Fair Development" and "Zero Waste." They set up art projects and science experiments and activities they brought and/or planned in order to engage their audience members. At 1 p.m. Destiny took the stage to welcome approximately 250 guests:

Hi. My name is Destiny. I'm honored to be here with you today at our very first Youth in Action Leadership Day. I'm in the classroom at Ben Franklin High School every morning. Seeing their development and leadership grow has been a truly magical experience, and I am so proud of these youth and excited we could all be here because: We are the *first* generation that is experiencing the effects of climate change, and we are the *last* generation that can do something about it. We have to save our planet, and we are *running out of time.*

I grew up surrounded by polluting industries, from massive coal mountains that overlook our playground to chemical companies that were responsible for making dangerous explosives. Because of where I—and many youth that you will see today—live, work, and go to school, we're more likely to die of lung cancer, respiratory disease, to suffer from asthma. In fact, we can expect an entire decade to be shaved off of our lives, simply because of where we live. We must find solutions.

So, what's stopping us?

We live in a system and in a society that puts making profits ahead of meeting everyone's basic human rights. We see profit being made off of exploiting the earth and the poor and minority communities being forced to bear the brunt—whether that be Black neighborhoods flooded from Hurricane Katrina or a village in China where kids pick through our iPhones for valuable metals that were originally mined by children in the Democratic Republic of Congo, or Baltimore where the burden of pollution reduces our lifespans.

Seriously taking on climate change means taking on this system of exploitation and racism. What we are calling for is a *radical reimagining of what is possible—a radical change in our system* that puts our planet and our needs as human beings first.

So how do we make this radical reimagining of our land, policies, and resources a reality?

To seriously take on . . . climate change requires all of us: residents, youth, parents, faith leadership, neighborhood leaders, nonprofits, local businesses, city officials and legislators. No one can sit this one out. We all have a stake in getting this right. So, today, as you meet and talk and discuss all of the ideas in the room, I challenge all of us to find our places in this movement. How can we contribute? How can we take on this challenge and fight for fair development and end climate change?

When Destiny finished, the crowd roared with applause and whistles and then dispersed to visit the students' booths. The point that day was to connect what seemed like disparate themes—incineration and health, vacant housing and absentee ownership, failing infrastructure, polluting industries, food apartheid, and even community safety—to the need for a zero-waste master plan. At one booth, students displayed their photography of environmental justice, and injustice. Their imagery showed abandoned houses with roofs caving in and wood and lead paint visibly chipping onto porches, garbage piled up in front of the lots, and incinerators spewing smoke into the air. Others displayed the results of their year-long project measuring particulate matter, specifically $PM_{2.5}$, inhalable particles measuring one-thirtieth of a single strand of hair (Environmental Protection Agency 2021) emitted from vehicles and toxic stationary facilities near Benjamin Franklin High. Clay sculptures and three-dimensional mock-ups of vacant homes accompanied a map on which a team of students had documented absentee ownership of vacant houses on the peninsula. At the zero-waste booth, Hayes and his student collaborator, David Upton, illustrated the small-scale, compost collective work happening at the behest of the Baltimore Compost Collective. They placed "black gold" into the hands of guests, as they described the benefits of composting.

FREE YOUR VOICE BUILDS A ZERO-WASTE COALITION

The summer following the Youth in Action Leadership Day, Free Your Voice youth collaborated with Global Alliance for Incinerator

Alternatives (GAIA) and the Institute for Local Self-Reliance to build a community-led coalition for zero waste as part of the execution of Baltimore's Fair Development Plan (FDP).[10] Their goal was to create a new infrastructure for waste in Baltimore. Youth leaders saw the coalition and the added expertise of their collaborators as essential to convincing the City, first, to abandon the current practice of burning and burying waste, including single-use plastics, and second, to adopt instead an inclusive waste management system that would address the needs of *all* residents of Baltimore, while at the same time, bringing healthy, green, and unionized jobs to the South Baltimore Peninsula and other impoverished communities.

At the beginning of the summer of 2019, Free Your Voice instructors Daniel Murphy, Crystal Green, and Daisy Thompson interviewed and hired zero-waste expert Gary Liss as a private consultant to help formalize the zero-waste efforts in Baltimore.[11] Before coming to Baltimore, Liss helped over a dozen communities establish zero-waste plans and assist in the development of recycling, curbside composting, reuse facilities, and more. The Free Your Voice students who got to know him through a series of listening sessions described him as a quirky white man who wore dress pants with sneakers and a necktie made from recycled wood. In addition to the students, Liss met with The Worker Justice Center organizers, city officials, university faculty and administrators, faith leaders, heads of community development corporations, and private sector, for-profit developers during listening sessions held throughout the one week he was in town.

In their meetings with Liss, The Worker Justice Center spoke plainly about how the communities they represented were used as dumping grounds for illegal materials, while also being deluged by toxic emissions. The city and state legislatures did not have vision or initiative, the organizers told Liss. Officials were too beholden to private industry and private developers to back radical change. After a dozen listening sessions, Liss proposed a list of interventions (written into my field-notes as follows):

1. Equity: allocation of resources to communities that have been historically disinvested
2. Education for youth and all about zero waste
3. City buy-in and support
4. New infrastructure—large, medium-scaled to be viable alternatives to BRESCO
5. More centers for people to recycle stuff to decrease illegal dumping
6. Banning single-use plastic and Styrofoam

These then shaped the citywide "Baltimore's Fair Development Plan for Zero Waste," which was composed by members of the South Baltimore Community Land Trust (SBCLT) team along with other allies over the course of that same summer and functioned as a practical guide for Baltimore City officials and residents to achieve the goals of zero waste. Among those goals were: "create jobs with dignity, reduce greenhouse gas emissions, replenish the soil, and create healthy living environments."

ZERO-WASTE FORUM AT THE UNIVERSITY OF MARYLAND SCHOOL OF SOCIAL WORK

Baltimore's Zero Waste Plan was the first grassroots, fair development plan for zero waste in the United States. While the idea came out of earlier conversations between the Baltimore Housing Roundtable (now Fair Development Roundtable) and Free Your Voice students (tasked with creating and carrying out their own participatory-action research projects), the listening sessions organized for Liss led directly to Baltimore's Fair Development Plan for Zero Waste.

The Worker Justice Center and Free Your Voice youth released the report in March of 2020 at the University of Maryland School of Social Work in front of a crowd of 150 people (Dance 2020b), including Councilman Ed Reisinger, incoming mayor Brandon Scott, and other city officials. The speakers at the event were youth of color and women of color from the South Baltimore Peninsula. Like broader national conversations around the Green New Deal, the plan laid out how Baltimore City officials could create this just transition. More specifically, the report defined the priorities of a zero-waste system, including cleaning up the air, strengthening community power, reducing waste, and expanding job opportunities. The report called for 90 percent of all materials discarded in the city to be diverted from landfills and incinerators by 2040, and for the City to contract mission-based or worker-owned recycling and composting operators. It also called for elected officials, public housing administrators, school leaders, and the heads of community groups, businesses, and universities throughout Baltimore City and County to work in close partnership. Most boldly, perhaps, the new plan called for the City to cut its ties with the Baltimore Refuse Energy Systems Co. (BRESCO), the South Baltimore-based incinerator in which 80 percent of city and county waste was burned, when the city contract expired in 2021. Councilman Ed Reisinger told the crowd, "I wish we could close Wheelabrator-BRESCO tomorrow. . . . We support the plan and we're going to move it forward." Incoming mayor Brandon Scott and many of the other officials present at the launch also formally agreed to the zero-waste vision while there.

BRESCO GETS DIRTY AND FREE YOUR VOICE STUDENTS TAKE TO THE STREETS

In March of 2020, the Zero Waste Coalition (which included community residents aligned with environmental justice organizers, professors, and public health experts) got word that the federal courts had struck down the citywide Clean Air Act that had been unanimously passed by the city council one year earlier (in February of 2019). The act had required owners of incinerators to monitor twenty major pollutants in real time and to severely limit emissions of nitrogen oxide. The law, written by Mike Ewall, who was the executive director of the Energy Justice Network and an anti-incineration activist for thirty years, was designed to force BRESCO to install upgrades estimated to cost ninety-five million dollars, according to a City-commissioned report. The hope among activists and some city council members was that the upgrades would prove too costly for the facility to remain open.

Lawyers for BRESCO and Curtis Bay Energy (a medical waste incinerator, also located on the South Baltimore Peninsula) sued the City in April 2020, arguing that existing federal and state environmental laws do not allow municipalities to enact stricter emissions regulations than the state, and they took their case to the federal courts. Further, Wheelabrator lawyers said it would be impossible to operate BRESCO profitably under the law's emissions strictures (Shen 2020a). US District Judge George L. Russell III ruled in Wheelabrator-BRESCO's favor in April 2020 (Muñoz 2020), concluding that the law undermined the authority of state and federal governments to regulate air pollution and, thus, was unconstitutional.

The interim mayor, Jack Young, failed to appeal the federal decision despite repeated pressure from grassroots organizers pushing for an end to incineration and citywide commitment to zero waste. That pressure took several forms, including a light show, something organizers called an illuminator protest, during which they projected the words *toxic, public health crisis,* and *I can't breathe* onto the massive smokestacks of the BRESCO incinerator.[12] And a few weeks later, in April 2020, a massive "die-in" was staged by Free Your Voice youth and their allies (Figures 13 and 14). While wearing masks and social distancing (precautionary measures given the COVID-19 pandemic), the Free Your Voice students along with other members of the coalition used their bodies in acts of resistance, pretending to die while holding brightly colored signs that read "I Can't Breathe" and "Zero Waste Now." Others read, "Mayor Young: Protect the Clean Air Act" and "BRESCO Kills." "The bill was created to protect this community," Crystal, a Free Your Voice lead organizer at the time explained later: "We have been trying to protect ourselves against these polluting industries coming and polluting our neighborhoods. These communities are made up of people of color and low-income people. And so, when this bill was rejected by federal

Figures 13 & 14. Protestors at the April 2020 Earth Day die-in in front of BRESCO. *Credit:* Photos by Kyle Pompey.

courts, we knew we had to come together to protect this bill because this signified us taking back our communities and us taking back our right to clean air which we have not been provided for a long time" (Dance 2020a).

In both of these examples, the students and their allies were able to transform a toxic site into an active stage for protest and dialogue. Then, on July 30, 2020, activists blocked garbage trucks from entering BRESCO facilities in an act of civil disobedience that was their biggest and boldest move yet. It was another attempt at forcing city officials to terminate the contract with BRESCO. I and others present that day refer to the BRESCO event as part of Blockadia, a term coined by Naomi Klein in her 2014 book *This Changes Everything: Capitalism vs. the Climate* to denote the increasingly frequent and global examples of human beings putting their bodies on the line in protest of fossil fuels and related industries. The next section describes the event as it unfolded that day.

SCENES FROM BLOCKADIA

A massive smokestack billowing nitrogen oxide, $PM_{2.5}$, and lead into the air rises high above highway I-95, one of Baltimore's major arteries. Though it passes just meters away, making it easy to drive by BRESCO, it is hard to get to the facility. Intersecting roads twist and turn and do not connect with the highway, giving way, instead, to back streets and alleys. On the day I describe here in July 2020, activists from the Zero Waste Coalition did in fact get to the facility, having arrived early to stand their ground at the entrance to the incinerator. There they held hands, becoming a human chain that prevented easy entrance and exit from the building. Many clutched signs reading "Zero Waste Now" and "By the People" and "BRESCO Closed." Department of Public Works (DPW) employees in orange shirts cut through the crowd trying to communicate with drivers of giant green garbage trucks that were backed up, caught behind the protestors whose locked arms were intended to prevent the trucks from entering and exiting the facility. Crystal Green, dressed in black workout pants and an all-black top and wearing a blue disposable face mask, screamed into her megaphone: "What do we want?" "Zero Waste!" the crowd responded. "When do we want it?" cried Crystal again. "Now." From one chant, Crystal rolled immediately into the next.

"No justice, no peace," she continued, bouncing up and down with a contagious energy, her large hoop earrings dancing against the tops of her shoulders. Still later: "Shut it down," she demanded, in unison with the crowd at the top of her lungs.

The City's contract to supply waste to the BRESCO facility was set to expire at the end of 2021 and the disobedience was a last attempt to dissuade Mayor Young from signing another ten-year contract with incinerator owners. "We cannot let this contract be extended because it would be detrimental to the zero-waste future, and we've all been trying to create a new future, a zero-waste future in Baltimore," Crystal declared.

That late July day, as temperatures reached ninety-five degrees Fahrenheit, the Department of Public Works' sanitation workers grew angry at the protestors for interrupting their work flows, and truck drivers revved their engines with impatience while the sweaty bodies of the protestors prevented the vehicles from getting through. Activists chanted in the faces of DPW workers. "No deal!" and "We must appeal!" One protestor remarked, "Even though we are dying in this heat, I'm here because my nephew has asthma and one night he said, 'Auntie, I cannot breathe, I think I'm gonna die.'"

Complicating the event that day, BRESCO's executives paid a handful of men and women to stand outside and oppose the protestors with signs that read, "BRESCO = Energy," "Get the Facts," "We are Part of the Solution," and "Wheelabrator-BRESCO Powers the City." The all-White executives, sporting button-down shirts, hovered over the counterprotesters. They had hired Black men and women, almost exclusively, to illustrate their allegiance with Black, low-wage laborers.

Drivers and garbage collectors from the Department of Public Works (DPW) grew angrier as they waited in their vehicles. They were accustomed to waiting in a long line for their turn to dump the city's garbage, but the protestors standing between them and the incinerator drop-off site increased wait times exponentially. One driver whose patience was exhausted screamed, "Get the fuck out of my way, or I will run right over you!" Other garbage truck drivers asked the zero-waste activists, "What about our jobs?" Though several activists tried explaining: "This has nothing to do with workers and everything to do with the system; we want you to have clean and green jobs," and "You will be *part* of the just transition." These answers failed to win converts. One DPW dump truck had a decal on its fender that read "Patience is the key to my lord," an especially ironic message in the scene, as the drivers' tempers flared.

Marvin Hayes stood tall and strong that day, wearing a green Baltimore Compost Collective T-shirt. As the nearly paralyzing July sun beat on his head, sending beads of sweat rolling down his forehead he led the crowd in chants and cheers. Crystal yelled from a megaphone, "I'm not afraid! Nothing scares me. We are all here because our mayor is backstabbing us and trying to do a backdoor deal. Settlement that has been poisoning us for years. . . . This is a war against BRESCO, not a war against workers!" She continued, "We want large-scale compost facilities. We must have clean air for the residents of Baltimore City." Hayes joined in, "Starve the incinerator. Feed the soil. Feed the community."

As Hayes shouted to the truck drivers, Daisy Thompson set up dozens of paper tombstones, handmade and painted by Free Your Voice students, in the field adjacent to BRESCO. They read, "Zero Waste," "I cannot breathe," "BRESCO is racist," "RIP My Baby," "Asthma Kills Us," "We Can't Breathe," and "No Deal, Shut it Down, Fund Zero Waste" (Krauss 2020).

Months later, in October 2020, Sunrise Movement activists (a national climate-justice movement pressing politicians to divest from fossil fuels) in solidarity with the Free Your Voice students and the South Baltimore

Community Land Trust Movement gave then interim mayor Jack Young a 5 a.m. "wakeup call."[13] They banged pots and pans together and played instruments in front of Young's house, waking up neighbors who came to their porches to see the commotion. The activists screamed, "Wake up, Jack! It's 5 a.m." from behind a banner that read, "This is an emergency. Act like it." The wakeup call, like the blockade, was designed by protesters from the Zero Waste Coalition to pressure Young to end the contract with BRESCO. However, escalating protest tactics did not materialize into a grassroots victory like the Stop the Incinerator campaign five years before.

TOXIC ENTANGLEMENTS: INFUSIONS OF CAPITAL SET THE STAGE FOR BRESCO TO WIN

As part of a massive propaganda campaign, Wheelabrator-BRESCO executives sent fliers to homes across the city in 2019, claiming to be a healthy, renewable, and green company. Seeking ways to divide and conquer resistance, they infiltrated spaces of movement building, paying leaders and organizers and sometimes even disguising these payments as awards for services. Additionally, they attended community association meetings where they argued that incineration was the only viable waste management option (Shen 2020b). And BRESCO representatives negotiated deals with politicians on the side. Senator Brian Feldman received $4,500 from BRESCO, for example. And Senator Kathy Klausmeier received a total of $3,050 from Covanta Holding Corporation and Wheelabrator Group (Andrews 2020; Kurtz 2021). While these attracted media attention, there were no doubt other politicians and corporations were receiving financial benefits as well.

Backdoor deals proved effective months after the die-in and the subsequent wake-up call when, in a public Zoom meeting (made necessary by the COVID-19 pandemic), the Board of Estimates signed off on the $106 million contract with Wheelabrator Technologies following a 3–2 vote (which also took place on Zoom) by board members. Despite strong arguments from the opposition, Mayor Jack Young pushed the contract through, and as a result, the city's trash will now continue to be burned at Wheelabrator-BRESCO through 2031. Young called the contract "a fair balance between fiscal prudence and social responsibility."[14] Because the meeting was open to the public, grassroots organizers on the call took to shouting, "Zero waste, zero waste!" before they were muted. "My father died from lung cancer, so I understand all of this," Young said at the end of the meeting, purportedly to the activists who opposed the decision. "But we have to have somewhere to send our trash" (Knezevich and Condon 2020).

"It is mind-blowing that a decision of this magnitude was made without answering any of the questions about compliance, about monitoring, about impact," Daniel Murphy told me shortly after the decision. Mayor Young refused to hear the Zero Waste Coalition members, claiming: "Lame-duck status or not, I have to make sure the city continues to run and run well, and I think I've done that." In the aftermath of the renewed contract with BRESCO, the Zero Waste activists had to reconfigure the movement. Because ending the contract with Wheelabrator-BRESCO was no longer a viable goal, they set about finding a strategy that would allow them to "starve the beast"—that is, to get as many institutions in Baltimore as possible to support diverting waste, particularly food waste, to zero-waste infrastructure.

RE-STRATEGIZING ZERO-WASTE WORK

The Zero Waste Coalition including Free Your Voice students spent months re-strategizing after the November 2020 decision to renew the BRESCO contract. Instead of solely focusing on anti-incineration, they began considering food diversion. "What if we can divert enough of the food waste from our waste stream to make BRESCO unprofitable?" they asked, and as they considered the possibilities, they found new motivation and a new path to environmental justice. Essentially, their new focus was on how to drive BRESCO to extinction. Free Your

Voice leaders invited area university faculty, including me, to participate in a working group for rethinking waste management. Together
we discussed the feasibility of diverting 100 percent of food waste from
incinerators. "Is this possible?" we asked, and "If so, how?" We began
with the knowledge that most of the regional institutions compost at
very low levels and often mix food waste with trash that ends up being
burned at BRESCO or buried at the Quarantine landfill. Changing this,
it seemed to us, could begin with getting area universities, including
anchor institutions like Johns Hopkins and the University of Maryland
(UMD) to buy into the zero-waste initiative. With prominent thought
leaders striving for zero waste on their campuses and, ideally, pushing
for a zero-waste city (and world) at the behest of their own researchers
and research findings, Baltimore City officials will be far more likely to
invest in building a regional composting site on the South Baltimore
Peninsula. And this seemed, to us, a good place to begin. Bringing a
composting site to the peninsula—one that is scalable, and thus can
grow as demand expands—will not only provide the infrastructure necessary to divert food waste from other types of waste management sites,
but it will also produce jobs for area residents. If established as members of the working group imagined, the composting site will be the first
experiment with zero-waste business to be unionized, and employees
will be assured decent salaries, health care, and retirement benefits.

While the loss to BRESCO forced members of the Zero Waste Coalition to rethink their strategies for eradicating incineration, many
newer and often younger activists wanted to understand what went
wrong with the campaign. These activists pressured SBCLT members
for a deep and self-reflexive, "postmortem" discussion of the years they
spent organizing against incineration—more specifically in relation to
the defeat at the end—so that future organizers might avoid some of
the coalition's missteps. "We would like to go back and think about how
and why we lost," a member of the Zero Waste Coalition told me. "We
really do want to win! But we need to look at our work over the years

and evaluate the holes. How can we strengthen our team? What kinds of information do folks feel they need to understand the issues at hand? What might be solutions to disseminating information?" Those pushing for discussion suggested it would be a way to strengthen the team as well as improve strategies and even modes of governance. It is hard to understand why the postmortem discussion never occurred, though the COVID-19 pandemic was certainly one factor, but moving forward is, historically, the way of organizing work.

Nevertheless, as a result of our failure to slow down and concretely identify what went wrong, outsiders—and disappointed insiders— suggested that the SBCLT could have allowed community members and a new generation of activists into the history of the conflicts and tensions with The Worker Justice Center activism. Instead, members of the Zero Waste Coalition accused the mostly white leadership of The Worker Justice Center of reproducing the same race, class, and gender inequalities that fracture society as a whole, and allies worried that new activists, activists of color specifically, were brought into the struggle as pawns rather than as valued and trusted leaders of the coalition and the team.

One ally of the Zero Waste Coalition who wished to remain nameless articulated her thoughts:

> My thoughts are that the environmental movement ecosystem in Baltimore is fractured, and thus not as strong as it needs to be. This is not the fault of any one entity. But an organizational analysis of how solidarity has been built and where solidarity has broken down is key. We need structures of participation—I think group norms about decision-making and power sharing must be established. Other climate and environmental justice movements actually do a very good and deliberate job building leadership within their structure of organizing. While I don't think it's the role of allies to dominate the strategy of the SBCLT, I do think there is a lot of talent in that zoom room that isn't necessarily being used. It is the role of the leadership of the group to draw out people's talent and empower them to feel ownership over the work. (December 7)

The inability to work through conflict and tension poses an ongoing challenge for SBCLT, as it does for many community organizations. Movements are messy, complicated entities made up of human beings with distinct personalities, behaviors, values, and so on. Sometimes activists align, but more often than not, divergent personalities pull organizers in distinct directions. Sometimes "collective" strategies win, but oftentimes dominant personalities drive the organizing work.

What came out of this experience was the need for SBCLT to reflect more upon our losses and lean into the tensions to deal with some of our inner conflicts instead of allowing friction to fester and eventually explode. Explosions distracted us from the true enemy, the corporate enemy. Activists need to be able to critique themselves, and in turn critique the movements we are a part of, for if we cannot do this, then our organizing remains static. We fail to be malleable and flexible. We fail to think through how we might do things differently next time.

Conclusion

In the beginning, the Free Your Voice curriculum helped students to focus inward, providing time and space for self-reflection, for sharing experiences, and ultimately, for finding commonalities and thus community among peers. Daniel Murphy described the first days of the afterschool program as follows:

> It wasn't me coming in and saying this is what we are striving for. Although, I did come with The Worker Justice Center model or our human rights curriculum, which borrowed from the United Nations Human Rights framework. This is what we're striving for. For example, polluting industries should not exist in our communities. This is a violation of our human rights. . . . There needs to be a starting point. But from early on, we were simply trying to build relationships and see that there was a shared struggle. We needed to find our own footing first, and finding our footing meant establishing meaningful relationships.

In the program, students moved from individual experiences of pain and trauma to establish a collective or shared sense of selfhood, one that empowered them to identify a need for and then enact change. By sharing their lived experiences and related senses of vulnerability, and with the help of a few key adults, students were able to build rapport with one another. In so doing, they came to understand themselves as united, and as members of a single community.

With these understandings came a shared awareness of injustices, social as well as environmental, and these motivated the students to dig into the systemic issues plaguing their communities. Students began to ask questions, using their personal narratives as a kind of a roadmap for identifying what to ask. One question led to another question. Just as Paolo Freire said would happen when educators ditched the banking system of education and adopted instead a problem-posing model.

The Free Your Voice students used qualitative research methods and arrived at new ideas and deeper understandings as a result of their research. Their early research charged them with a sense of purpose. As Daniel Murphy stated, "Like we had this mission. Adults have failed. Society has failed in these various ways to allow this incinerator system to be developed. Our school system is really, really isolated; the variables of the problem the youth are dealing with is overwhelming; often youth are left detecting this as a symptom of a rotten and broken system." As a result, the students of Free Your Voice became knowledge makers. They borrowed from The Worker Justice Center's human rights curriculum, though they added their own photographic, artistic, and musical talents to their activism. Armed with data from their citizen science projects, they articulated connections, at first, between toxic emissions and respiratory illnesses and, later, among environmental injustices (in all their complexity and diversity) and the sociostructural inequalities they, their families, and their neighbors endured on a daily basis. As they made these connections, the students began to draft and demand alternatives—to incineration, to historically unjust housing and development practices, and to waste in all of its forms.

Perhaps the most important moments of the Free Your Voice student-led campaigns and activism were those when they occupied key spaces of decision-making, persuading, for example, representatives of the Board of Education that environmental justice issues are equity issues. Their voices, their art, and their creativity infused unlikely spaces with their stories, their knowledge, and not to be underestimated, their raw emotion and pain. It was through art and research that Free Your Voice students built alliances, and it was also through art and research that they communicated the pain and trauma born of environmental racism. Getting the Maryland Department of the Environment to eventually pull the permits for Energy Answers was a major victory for the movement; some even called it a David versus Goliath victory. But more often than not, the daily grind of movement building and community organizing is about small victories and a whole lot of losses. This is to say: the Stop the Incinerator victory achieved by the Free Your Voice students was remarkable. Often activists work tirelessly, day and night, only to learn that city politicians cut backroom deals with private industry.

WHERE ARE WE NOW?

Since the 2016 success of the Stop the Incinerator campaign, much of the rest of our organizing has felt like a slow crawl toward a difficult-to-see finish line. As many of the youth activists have noted, fighting against something (an incinerator) is reactive and responsive to what's already there (polluting industries). The fight for fair housing and zero waste proved to be far more complex, longitudinal, and messy.

Housing work continues to be in a stage of design and development; South Baltimore Community Land Trust broke ground in the Spring of 2022. As of the Spring of 2023, there will be 15 community land trust homes. The South Baltimore Community Land Trust will continue to work on land trust education for community members, including education on credit/mortgages, and will draft an application for residents who might want to buy into the land trust model. Youth continue to work on their Baltimore Broken Glass project, getting more and more Baltimoreans to commit to zero waste.[1]

Zero-waste work continues with Mayor Brandon Scott and the new DPW director, Jason Mitchell, hinting at building zero-waste infrastructure. In 2022, The Department of Public Works piloted curbside composting projects at various sites throughout the city. As Brandon Scott argued, "The pilot program is essential and necessary to propel Baltimore on a path of zero waste, and I commend Director Mitchell and the Department of Public Works for making this a reality . . . creating innovative and sustainable practices for Baltimoreans today will pave the way for a greener and healthier tomorrow" (Baltimore City Department of Public Works 2021). While the City is experimenting with curbside composting and Free Your Voice has been administering local curbside composting drop-off sites in South Baltimore, the larger goal for the zero-waste work is to create a regional compost facility. Free Your Voice students and allies see this as an opportunity to shape how the transition takes place and what values/principles the city upholds. Unless there is a significant push from grassroots activists, city officials are unlikely to prioritize community needs and labor.

The harder and more grueling labor demands that the City take action, turning a sixty-four-acre DPW site located in Curtis Bay over to the South Baltimore Community Land Trust to build compost infrastructure with good, unionized jobs. The Zero Waste Coalition in the Fall of 2021 organized a public action in front of City Hall where activists and allies delivered personal testimony about why incineration was harmful to environment, community, and human health. The grassy area in front of the building was filled with sunflower placards and colorful signs that called upon the City to invest in local compost infrastructure and end their addiction to incineration. As folks gathered in a large circle, Crystal Green took center stage, stating, "There is a simple solution . . . not a complex problem. What we need from Baltimore is a local compost facility right now. This will create jobs for residents here, many jobs, while diverting waste that is being burned and buried. We need government, we need labor, and we need anchor institutions and when we organize, we will win."

Speakers made clear that the City needs to divert money and resources toward this local compost infrastructure. As Dr. Lawrence Brown stated, "I am here to support the efforts of the community land trust and all the

South Baltimore communities being negatively impacted. . . . As a public health professional, I believe in the public health of the community. We need Mayor Scott and the DPW director to follow through, and the way they can is to divert some of the budget dollars all the way to the compost facility. If they aren't talking about twenty to thirty to forty million dollars towards the compost facility, push them to allocate the resources." Baltimore received $641 million in Fall 2021 as a one-time funding to respond to the COVID-19 public health emergency and its negative economic impacts. Many made clear that some of this money could be used to develop green industries like the local compost facility. The Mayor's Office immediately established the Recovery Programs to administer this funding on behalf of the City via an application process.[2]

The next phase of the zero-waste work calls upon anchor institutions in the University of Maryland System and Johns Hopkins University (all major food waste producers) to divert 100 percent of their food waste away from incineration, including by committing food scraps to local compost facilities (current as well as future). The questions that Baltimore zero-waste activists pose are: Will institutions pretend that they cannot coordinate among themselves [even though they often organize collective procurement when it benefits them]? Will they put money and resources up in advance to attract other investments to build a multimillion-dollar compost facility? No one is taking the lead on this, so it puts leadership in the hands of community and the coalition. As Daniel Murphy said, "It is very difficult and grueling work. The City's role is to be in the background and to say the right things, but they have not taken any action yet. We are building up public pressure and trying to create the framework." This is not an economic development project for private organics but rather a way for universities to pledge food waste and be leaders in this community-driven development agenda. Murphy declared,

> That is the work we are trying to navigate and direct community benefits from composting that would go directly into the housing work. We are trying to mitigate environmental harm while building up alternatives in a

proactive way. We have only had a successful reactive campaign against what we didn't want. But we would [always] end with the things we are reacting to. So here we are looking at multiple things to react to and we need to build the tools for the alternatives.

While Johns Hopkins University and Towson University students have been organizing to pressure their universities to pledge a minimum tonnage of organic waste to the community compost facility, as of yet, no university president or provost has officially made a pledge or monetary commitment to the facility.[3] A pair of students at Hopkins in a recent op-ed wrote:

> Complacency is neglect. Neglect is violence. The University has a long history of exploitation in Baltimore, including medical racism and unethical research as well as gentrification. Hopkins is at a crossroads. This is an opportunity for the institution to truly serve its community and take real action rather than make empty promises. A Baltimore-based compost facility would permit local institutions to divert compostable waste, save the money and the fuel it takes to truck waste over long distances and support environmental justice in the city.
>
> We, students and faculty at the University, have the power to insist that Hopkins commit to zero-waste infrastructure in Baltimore, alleviate pollution and tackle environmental racism and health disparities. We demand that Hopkins commit to sustainable waste infrastructure by pledging a minimum tonnage of waste to the local composting facility envisioned by the community-led, zero-waste movement in the city.[4]

There are rarely immediate successes in organizing. It can take years and sometimes decades to see the change we work for daily come to fruition. To see the changes we work for daily requires rethinking, reinventing, and redesigning our proposals; it requires patience and diligence to see the most mundane of our actions as part of a long-term and holistic solution, and to privilege the long-term over short-term and quick-fix solutions. Unfortunately, techno-fixes are all too common in today's world. Billionaires like Jeff Bezos and Elon Musk back "space tourism" as both a money-making endeavor and a quick fix to global climate crisis (Noor 2021). The youth on the South Baltimore Peninsula, in contrast, know there is no shortcut to resolving our climate, housing, and educational crises.

WHY THIS STORY OF YOUTH ORGANIZING MATTERS

What can we take away from the story of Free Your Voice organizing? When I teach undergraduates, I often say, "While this political and economic moment of climate crisis and global pandemic might feel depressing, I don't want to leave you depressed. I want to leave you with hope. I believe in grassroots movements, and I believe in structural change." While I might overwhelm my students with depressing statistics about an overheated planet, floods and dangerous droughts, and disruptions to our ecosystems, the toolkit they build is filled with lessons and resources from the grassroots, many of which inspire optimism. I want students to leave my classroom hopeful, not in a romantic way but in a practical and tireless way. I want them to see what can be possible when young people come together to study the problems of their neighborhood, learn qualitative and quantitative research methodologies, analyze their own data, and then utilize that data to build movements for systemic change, the kinds of change that will liberate poor Brown and Black folks from historically entrenched racism, classism, and environmental harm. As Free Your Voice student Dario Lopez wrote about the urgency of zero-waste infrastructure in an op-ed for the *Baltimore Brew*,

> Because of City Hall's ongoing choice to rely on burning and burying, my neighbors and I have a greater chance of developing asthma, lung disease and other medical issues. I see these health problems in real time afflicting many of my classmates already. These are kids who use inhalers and cannot participate fully in active sports. The neglected communities in South Baltimore are no longer willing to host these landmarks to environmental injustice. That is why we have been taking action.

Dario speaks for a community that is hopeful. And for a community that has had enough.

What would it look like if anthropologists handed over all our methodological tools to grassroots activists and social movement organizers? What if our methodological toolkit was *put to use* in political work, not defined and utilized by the anthropologist but defined and utilized by activists, including high school students, who are hell-bent on eradicating the injustices that surround them? While many activist anthropologists came to study movements through intellectual questions or academic pursuits, I came to this work inspired to be a part of structural change. I was guided by young people. They were my teachers, my mentors, and my interlocutors in a journey to understand how to redesign communities, how to build equitable land trusts and alternative housing structures and sustainable waste infrastructure. And at the end of our work together, I have thought more about "the extinction of anthropology." How can we, as anthropologists, get out of the way? I keep wondering.

Eric Jackson, director of Black Yield Institute, a grassroots organization fighting food apartheid in Cherry Hill, often says that "academics need to get out of the way of movement activists." At a public discussion on the "Right to the City," held at Red Emma's Bookstore in November 2021, he asked, "What would it look like for academics to utilize the financial, academic, intellectual, and other resources to support grassroots organizations?" In other words: How can we facilitate access to resources, tools, and machinery so that young people can generate the data they need to create systemic change? How can young people from frontline communities utilize anthropological methods in order to create their own toolkits of knowledge and political movements for more just futures? Interactive maps, interviews with residents, engaged documentary filmmaking, and photography can all help youth (and the rest of us) tell alternative stories, and in so doing, they can help dismantle the unjust systems and structures that have historically overburdened low-income neighborhoods and communities of color.

An undergraduate student who worked with me on the peninsula for several years once asked me, "Doesn't this project make anthropology irrelevant or extinct?" She was referring to the participatory action research course that is explicitly centered on liberation. And perhaps this is the utility of anthropology today: to make research for the academy extinct and to turn it over to the public.

As we are in political, climactic, economic, and even public health crises, young people from frontline communities are coming up with the solutions to our planetary problems. It's not about escaping or fleeing. Unlike Jeff Bezos, who builds rocket ships, searches for signs of life on Mars, and dreams of a new wave of colonization (Noor 2021; Kramer 2021), the young people with whom I have worked and alongside whom I have learned realize there are no quick-fix technological solutions to climactic crisis.[5] Rather, these youth are studying interlocking systems of oppression, and in so doing, building power, building collective strength, designing with architects, and creating just transitions to a better planet Earth, one on which air, land, and waterways are clean.

Legislators like Alexandria Ocasio-Cortez (D-NY) push forward a Green New Deal—a comprehensive plan for utilizing federal dollars to transition us away from the fossil fuel industry and build urban and rural landscapes of renewable energy, guaranteeing climate-friendly work, no-carbon housing, and free transit. Ocasio-Cortez has suggested we need a Green New Deal for public housing that includes retrofitting all ailing and environmentally unhealthy infrastructure to provide social housing for the poor. Moreover, Representative Jamal Bowman (D-NY) introduced legislation for a Green New Deal for K–12 which includes some of the same proposals for ailing schools. It is within this climate of progressive "squad" members proposing a Green New Deal that perhaps youth movements like Free Your Voice can serve as a kind of model for how to do this engaged learning tied to environment and climate policy work. Bowman unveiled in July 2021 his Green New Deal for Public Schools, which would put $1.4 trillion in federal funding—redirecting $446 billion in grant funds over ten years—toward decarbonizing and retrofitting the nation's K–12 schools, particularly in high-need and socially vulnerable areas. Bowman's three impact areas are health and environmental equity, educational equity, and economic equity. The jobs will be given to local residents from construction to retrofitting to educating. These retrofits will turn schools into neighborhood resiliency hubs, making them key nodes of overall green community infrastructure, and of zero-waste infrastructure (Rodriguez et al. 2021). This is precisely the work we have been pushing forward in Curtis Bay for nearly a decade.

POSTSCRIPT

A Letter of Confession to the Activist Scholar

In the summer of 2020 there was a growing conflict between South Baltimore Community Land Trust and The Worker Justice Center (as I hinted in chapter 5). Eventually this led to an organizational and fiscal split. Destiny and Crystal along with many other youth from the South Baltimore Peninsula came forward with video testimonials, letters, and accusations of ongoing verbal abuse and mistreatment by veteran organizers within The Worker Justice Center.[1] They spoke of harsh working conditions and the inability of White organizers to "care" for them, including giving them time off when they were sick. These young organizers from South Baltimore built a team of allies— "the accountability allies"—with a goal of holding The Worker Justice Center accountable for their "toxic work environment." In a series of letters (which were published on Facebook, Twitter, and Instagram), the young activists explained the inequities within the organization and called upon organizers to hold certain leaders accountable for their abuses. Daniel Murphy and Destiny Watford simultaneously posted South Baltimore Community Land Trust organizers' testimonials on The Worker Justice Center website and the Fair Development Roundtable Facebook page which were quickly taken down.

Destiny later wrote a letter to The Worker Justice Center Council about the paradox of the cover-up that followed:

> At the same time my story was being deleted from the Worker Justice Center Facebook page, the same webpage features my image and my story. The Worker Justice Center has received and continues to receive benefits for using my likeness—in forms of funding, speaking, and networking opportunities. . . . The list goes on and

on. My image and story have been used to push our movement forward, no matter how difficult the message I was trying to convey was. The video [I posted] was no different—but now, because what I had to say was too hard of a pill to swallow, you try to silence me.

So, I want to be clear: My image, my story, and my name are not anyone's property. I am not owned by the Worker Justice Center. My story is my own (personal letter written in July 2021).[2]

Destiny's letter serves as a powerful reminder that human stories of pain and trauma can get commodified and exchanged, even speculated upon, just like the abandoned buildings in low-income neighborhoods. Black blood and sweat have "exchange value" in a broader nonprofit industrial complex in which organizations compete for limited funding from private philanthropy and each aspires to appear inclusive of the communities in which they work. "My story is my own. I am not anyone's property" was an acknowledgment by Destiny of her liberation from The Worker Justice Center and from white power structures, even inside an organization supposedly against such power structures. It was also an assertion of her "control" over her narrative. Other Black women organizers, too, aware that they were rarely the decision-makers, questioned the extent to which and the reasons for which they were valued at The Worker Justice Center at this time.

Of course, the Worker Justice Center were not and are not the only ones using the lives and faces of those for whom they purportedly fight to promote their causes—and woo donors. And the other complaints Destiny had, too, were not unique to the Worker Justice Center. Far too many activists have experienced being overworked, undervalued, and sometimes even verbally abused by coworkers inside of social justice organizations. That racism is a problem inside nonprofit organizations, just as it is everywhere else, should not be a surprise. "Toxic masculinity" is another accusation that has been leveled at leaders of social and racial justice organizations more than once.[3] While the problems that plagued The Worker Justice Center were not unique, unfortunately, neither was the organization's response to these problems. Despite multiple serious attempts made to hold individual leaders of The Worker Justice Center accountable for their mismanagement and exclusivity, the organization ultimately chose not to deal with its internal issues through restorative justice. They hired an outside LLC to deal with some of the ongoing HR concerns and restructure the organization with a new executive director.

Many leftist scholars and activists might argue that in a moment of rising fascism with the paramilitary right taking up arms in cities and rural areas throughout the United States, this is not the time to hold leftist organizations accountable for internal dynamics or behaviors. And, in fact, collectively The Worker Justice Center continues to do important housing and renter justice work across the city of Baltimore. Yet the toxicity of a few organizers can infect the larger organization (even the wonderful organizers alongside whom I have been privileged to work for a decade). And this is why restorative justice is so important. Calls for leadership accountability do indeed threaten well-intentioned organizations, undermining important political work for racial, housing, and environmental justice. If we do not deal with our internal conflicts, and if we maintain the racialized, class-based, gendered, misogynistic, and even hierarchical values of the capitalist system within our organizations, we reproduce the same power structures we purportedly seek to replace and reimagine via our organizing and activism. If organizational leaders fail to create truly transparent and participatory mechanisms to hold themselves accountable in moments of crisis, then how can the general public trust these leaders to build solidarity and achieve economic equity and racial and gendered justice in their communities?

The egos of predominantly white, predominantly male leaders have defined leftist organizational spaces for far too long. Poor people and people of color have been used as pawns, often in multiracial coalitions that uphold white-centric, capitalist-centric organizational models despite fighting for racial and economic justice. That toxic work culture does not represent racial justice or multiracial coalition building. This has to do with the ultimate failure to dismantle models of hetero-patriarchal structures of white supremacy. To say that The Worker Justice Center is a movement led by frontline communities, led by poor Brown and Black Baltimoreans, means that white middle-class organizers would have to take a backseat in decision-making and grant writing, and ultimately would be guided by the political education and ideological development of those in the trenches, not white academics and white organizers. This means that poor Black and Brown organizers form and shape the ideological and political manifestos of the organization. It also means that we learn directly from the poor and from people of color. As a result, it might mean that we give up the millions of dollars in philanthropy and other sources of funding from donors who don't like to rock the boat. But in so doing, we heed to the direction of those who have directly been impacted by apartheid systems and structures (Brown 2021).

"Putting poor people up on a pedestal"; extracting "exchange value" by writing people of color into grants or utilizing their imagery; and commodifying stories of environmental racism, trauma, and/or abuse all undermine the broader intentions of a social justice organization. Anthropologists have also been in the business of extractivism for far too long, extracting stories of poverty and pain in their endeavors not only to "give voice" but also to build fame and accrue capital in a market economy of the academy (Simpson 2014; West 2016; Todd 2015; Loperena 2016, 2017).[4] Often academics circulate these stories inside the five-star hotels where professional conference meetings take place annually. As they do so, they ignore the Brown and Black underpaid hotel workers serving water or cleaning the rooms after the panel. Or they circulate these stories within the ivory towers of academia, utilizing "sexy" theory that is readily "consumed" by like-minded academics. These are spaces and places far removed from the poor communities we "study." Our inaccessible conference papers and the peer-reviewed articles will not create structural and systemic change. In fact, writing solely for the academy excludes a large number of people who are struggling economically to survive from being a part of these conversations. These peer-reviewed and insular articles will only exacerbate inequality, as those in the academy debate theoretical stances while those on the streets struggle to survive.

In a recent article, "The Case for Letting Anthropology Burn," Ryan Cecil Jobson (2019) argues: "The case for letting anthropology burn entails a call to abandon its liberal suppositions. Sociocultural anthropology in 2019 encountered a moment in which its investment in a titular ethnographic Other is no longer sustained by a 'stable foil' of liberal democracy and humanism (see Mazzarella 2019). . . . To let anthropology burn permits us to imagine a future for the discipline unmoored from its classical objects and referents."[5] This paper became a catalyst for a webinar-based conversation sponsored by UCLA and the Wenner-Gren Foundation, aptly called "The Case for Letting Anthropology Burn," where several leading anthropologists of color discussed several topics: the history of anthropology and this political and economic conjuncture of empire, disposability of Black bodies, police un(accountability) and what the response from anthropology should be. Some talked about the nature of the discipline to find temporary fixes like the state fix, these technological and quick fixes serve merely as band-aids over deep wounds. Others spoke of the ways in which "numbness is caked into the discipline and we tend not to notice and not to observe" the "brokenness of the world around us" (UCLA 2020).

While I agree with Ryan Jobson (2019) and the panel of anthropologists about how these multiple and intersecting crises (economic, political, racial) should lead us to a new path forward for anthropology, I have some ideas that extend beyond their discussion of race and that incorporate class, political economy, and the state into a frame of analysis.[6] At the intersections of race, class, and urban regimes of inequality, we can see the complex dynamics of abandonment and dispossession of Black and Brown people. But this comes in multiple forms, not just state violence, but rather from community residents being pitted against one another, as well as city officials, developers, educators, and state bureaucrats. It is not so easily identifiable and is always shape-shifting. Perhaps it's not about anthropology or our over-theorization of where the discipline should go, but rather about building critical solidarity and utilizing our skills to advance the goals of social movements fighting for Black and Brown liberation with concrete plans as to how to get there from land reclamation to agroecology to passive housing and community land trusts.

I ask the panelists at the UCLA webinar: Where is our accountability? I have seen many social scientists and journalists come and go, searching for stories in Curtis Bay. Just like those toxic industries spewing heavy metals into the air, these same public health academics, anthropologists, and so-called community-based scholars are part of the broader economy of capitalist extraction and toxic overburden. It is not just the industries but also the academics and journalists that lurk in the background of layers of toxicity, searching to make careers off the backs of Brown and Black people and environmental injustice.

What can critical solidarity look like? What do long-term, meaningful relationships look like as we build critical solidarity? How can we construct collective projects of meaning that defy the individualism of the academy? How can we hold our institutions accountable and write to and for the general public? How do we avoid the tendency to write or advance ideas for an insular group of scholars? What are the stories we tell? Who are our audiences? And why does that matter? Just as the tools of anthropology can be handed over to the grassroots, so too can the pen, so movement activists can write their own stories. If we want to create social, environmental, and economic change, we need to understand that writing and theorizing unfortunately will not change the dire circumstances of those who have been historically marginalized and dispossessed, but grassroots organizing and movement building can.

These are questions I ask over and over. As I return to this, I reflect upon a decade of being an activist anthropologist and resisting the norms of the academy and of my discipline. So, what does it mean to be an activist? Or what does it mean for our teaching and writing to be tied directly to social change agendas? Our classroom material should inspire young people to want to get involved in movements and want to create change. Not in a White savior complex or a voyeuristic way, but in a way that engages over a long period of time in critical solidarity.

Baltimore's streets, community gardens, toxic industries, and sites of tourist development have become my classroom. These are the basics of popular education from a Freirean perspective. But what does it mean to show students a political economy of inequality through sight, sound, touch, and taste? What does it mean to thrust them into neighborhoods where they feel uncomfortable and to force them to walk around in other people's shoes? We are moving them into spaces of discomfort not simply so they can study and report back in a classroom but also to model relationship building and world making. We must be present over long periods of time in these communities and put in the hours of physical labor alongside our students. For example, during the COVID-19 pandemic, I labored for a year in the soil (planting, harvesting, and bringing food to market for the Pop Market) alongside my Towson students on the Black Yield Cherry Hill Urban Community Garden (CHUCG). This laboring together was part of our commitment to Black Yield Institute, but it also allowed for a liberatory form of education that is not possible within the bounds of our institutions. If we want students to feel inequality, to experience it, and to realize that this is not a one-off community engagement assignment, if we want them to see how they can become lifelong learners in and of communities, listening to the sounds of the street and hearing the cries of neighborhoods at war, then we, too, must put in the time with them. We ultimately want them to become engaged citizens in a world that is highly unequal and needs empathetic young people to reboot and reimagine our political and economic system. These are things you cannot learn in a college classroom. Perhaps, these are the things you will never learn in graduate school. For in graduate school, we do not learn how to teach or how to inspire young people to create change. There are limitations to Blackboard lectures and documentary films. These platforms do not illustrate the complexities of everyday life, the daily battles for survival, and the ongoing challenges of working toward social change. I want to make some interventions at the end to collectively carve, alongside grassroots organizations, a new path forward. This comes from decades of conversations with organizers.

In the form of a letter to the scholar activist, addressing all those contemplating or at the early stages of an academic career and wondering if and how they can negotiate the demands of political engagement and academic performance, geographer Laura Pulido (2008) wrote honestly and wholeheartedly about her own lived experiences at the crossroads of academia and activism. I borrow three of her astute points to elevate a few of my own more than two decades after Pulido composed her letter.

I. IT'S NOT TEACHING FOR THE SAKE OF TEACHING OR WRITING FOR THE SAKE OF WRITING. EVERYTHING WE DO CAN ADVANCE A POLITICAL AND SOCIAL CHANGE AGENDA. Critical solidarity is about building meaningful relationships. Relationship building is especially hard when the tenure clock is ticking. Perhaps, I had more flexibility to be spending full days and weeks down in South Baltimore when I was not located at an R1 university with the demands of publishing for an insular world. I was able to be creative in building programs and I was supported by my colleagues for this creativity. But no matter what, even as R1s struggle to do community-based research, they fail to truly engage in a praxis of solidarity through building deep relationships of trust. This comes from long periods of "deep hanging out," listening, sharing stories, doing manual labor together and working toward collective change. Ruthie Gilmore defines oppositional work as "talk-plus-walk: it is the organization and promotion of ideas and bargaining in a political arena" (2008: 35). What is important here is how we walk alongside our interlocutors in their daily struggles. How do we show up beyond the class? How do we provide emotional, mental, and physical support to our comrades overburdened by organizing? How do we take some of the burden off by providing on-the-ground support as it is needed?

Laura Pulido argues in her 2008 letter that "accountability refers to the fact that scholar activists are not lone mavericks. Indeed, the idea of a scholar activist operating alone is something of an oxymoron. The whole point of being a scholar activist is that you are embedded in a web of relationships, some of which demand high levels of accountability to a community. [seeing yourself as part of a community of struggle, rather than as an academic who occasionally drops in]" to me seems essential (Pulido 2008).

For me, it wasn't about being a "lone maverick" but rather being present *in* the community and seeing myself as an active member of this community (Pulido 2008). For one, I showed up at all protests, events, marches, demonstrations, and political education schools. But it was more than this. It was about being present when my South Baltimore Community Land Trust friends saw the injustice within the broader organization and called for accountability. It meant stepping up as a member of this community in those hard situations and disrupting the status quo even if it meant taking risks and losing friends and, sometimes, institutional support. My children had grown up inside the spaces of The Worker Justice Center politicking, so this was not an easy ask to publicly hold organizers accountable. It also meant the risk could be greater than personal gain. Calls for "accountability" could mean that right-wing, private developers, and even city bureaucrats might benefit from such organizational "weaknesses." Left-wing organizations might not survive such a push toward accountability. But that is a risk we were all willing to take for justice to be served and for new structures of equity to be created. Great risk is not easy in teaching, in politics, or in organizing work. However, it is perhaps the backbone of all social change work. Thrusting yourself into situations that might endanger you or those you love may mean risk to your own physical body, risk to your sense of safety and positionality, and even risk to those you are accountable to. Beyond being *in* and of community, another intervention is thinking about our labor as "collective," not as individual. This is an ongoing challenge when our culture values hyper-individualism.

2. BUILDING LONG-TERM AND MEANINGFUL RELATIONSHIPS NOT BECAUSE THERE IS AN "EXCHANGE VALUE" FOR THE ACADEMIC BUT BECAUSE WE ARE ALIGNED WITH MOVEMENT VALUES, GOALS, AND OBJECTIVES. COLLECTIVE PROCESSES YIELD CO-CONSTRUCTED NARRATIVES. It also meant thinking about our work as collective labor and collective, public production and dissemination. It meant our teaching had to be together—Free Your Voice and Towson University—in building our participatory action project, in teaching at Towson University, in organizing and in writing. Our collaborative work had to matter: it wasn't a "one-off" classroom activity but part of a long-term "collective project" that should advance the goals of our team, not my individual goals as a scholar. Much of this everyday and collective labor does not count toward tenure, and much of it is not measured quantitatively as "outcome" in the academy. It is considered "lost" time to those who evaluate your performance, but perhaps it is the most valuable to those in the community. Building trust, sharing our histories, showing up, taking someone out to eat, and laboring together are the only ways to do this work honestly and ethically. Yet there is no measurable outcome to what the academy sees as "lost time." Time outside of "individual productivity" is not measured on the tenure clock and not valued inside the political economy of the university. The time that is measured has to do with "service" work to the university, advancing the goals of our neoliberal institutions, not

solidarity work outside of the university. Service work creates even more of an enclosure of the commons. However, "laboring together" and in community, while it is not valued in the extractive political economy of the university, tethers our individual lives to one another and to a broader social change agenda.[7] Now is the time for new forms of measurement and new "markers" of value or ways of seeing and thinking about time. Perhaps the work of the new generation of scholar activists is to transform how universities measure and evaluate public-facing scholars. Perhaps we might even envision measurements outside of the purview of our neoliberal institutions, including panels or committees of community partners who evaluate with qualitative measurements.

In 2019, Free Your Voice youth, Kyle Pompey, two graphic designers, and SBCLT members created a photographic book about the South Baltimore environmental and housing struggles.[8] This allowed youth to arrange their photos in the way they wanted and to tell their story in their own words. The photobook will be used for fundraising and for raising awareness about the issues of environmental justice in Curtis Bay. This is one of the many examples of collective outcomes that fail to be measured within the academy. Yet the impact will be great in the public sphere as youth utilize this story for building out the zero-waste and housing justice campaign work. We have also created interactive maps used for negotiations with city officials as well as reports that outline our goals for housing and zero waste. All may be considered a "waste" of time within the political economy of the university. However, this was the most valuable time spent for our movement work as it produced something "useful" and "exchangeable" for activists.

Revitalizing neighborhood history and stories of resilience can provide motivation for students—as it did for those of Free Your Voice, who did not realize the strength of community knowledge until they began systematically studying it. As Baltimore-based writer and abolitionist Bilphena Yahwon stated at a panel discussion at Red Emma's Bookstore and Coffeehouse in November 2021,

> Knowledge does not begin and end in our institutions. When I think about academia, there's the idea that all academics are sitting inside institutions. They are not. Political prisoners have been knowledge producers and academics. We think about the intellect that exists in Black communities that has no access to schools. . . . Intellectualism is formed and curated outside these buildings.

This community knowledge, these community stories, are part of preserving the integrity and culture of communities in the face of large-scale development and serial displacements. Communal testimonials should remain in the community where students excavate them.[9] This community-knowledge is helping to define the kinds of worlds young people want to build. We are working on a Curtis Bay public archive where all the photographs, newspaper articles, and testimonials will remain in the community. It will not be bulldozed, demolished, and displaced like the people of Fairfield or extracted by the academy or mass media to advance knowledge for some at the expense of others. Youth continue to build upon this public archive year after year. Eventually, we envision a kind of interactive museum filled with the rich history of Curtis Bay, exhibits of community-informed, and community-controlled development and even interactive participatory design all tied to the high school.

3. TURNING THE LENS TOWARD THE UNIVERSITY AND DISMANTLING OUR OWN HIERARCHIES OF OPPRESSION AND EXCLUSION. ORGANIZING TO RETHINK AND REDESIGN THE PUBLIC UNIVERSITY FOR THE PUBLIC. When my South Baltimore Community Land Trust team wanted me to organize at Towson University, it meant focusing and thinking about the university as a field site.[10] The field is not "out there," but rather right in our own institutions. I have always thought about how to redistribute the resources and wealth of the university to communities in which I organize (As Moten and Harney advise doing in their 2013 book). But this was different. This was turning the university into a site for organizing students and staff. How can students come to understand that our waste cycles have a direct impact upon poor Black and Brown people?[11] Our over-consumption in northern Baltimore and in the county is burned or buried in South Baltimore. I cannot teach about social and environmental justice without coming back to us, to our own consumptive lives and disposable cultures by getting students involved in these struggles. Not as voyeurs, not as outsiders, not as poverty tourists but rather as part of a broken and unequal system that reproduces itself from generation to generation and fails to provide all of us with healthy air, lands, soils, and waterways. In order to break the cycles and systems, students need to see themselves and their institutions as part of a broader political ecology of inequality and waste.

Pulido asks at the end of her letter,

> How do people transform the world? What are my own commitments to antiracism, workers' rights, environmental justice and anticapitalist policies? ... I have tried to address some of the most frequently asked questions, as well as those that seem pertinent for anyone considering becoming a scholar-activist. ... Becoming a

scholar-activist entails daily acts of courage—particularly the determination to live your truth—attentive to your emotions, thoughts, and consider how they affect your attitudes, values, and behavior. (Pulido 2008)

At the end of this book, I would like to amplify what one Baltimore freedom fighter and intellectual said at the panel at Red Emma's in November 2021, which my Towson University colleagues and I organized about social movement activists talking back to anthropology. Eddie Conway—former Black Panther Party member and prisoner—argued that his community of Sandtown-Winchester, where his grassroots organization Tubman House is located, is a war zone. He said,

> A year after we started organizing, Freddie Gray got killed right there on that corner. Six years later, yesterday, a young woman we had been working with for several years . . . thirteen-year-old Molina got shot six times and died yesterday. . . . So it is with anger and a heavy heart that I come before you all because we have been talking about this stuff for a decade. We have been looking at this stuff for decades. We have been sitting around tables for decades. . . . We have been talking about the evil institutions and what we need to do about them and how we can fix them. I would suggest organizers and academics bring "their asses" down to the community. Go down and start working with people down there. . . . Find out what the problems are and organize with people in the community. . . . We're in a critical stage of history right now. We're in a stage where we are looking at the face of fascism. The face of fascism is not just white supremacy. It's also Black neocolonialism . . . and neocolonialism of all colors. If we do not organize among the masses, if we keep talking about how to do it right, then we are doomed. The key is getting down there and bringing resources to fix houses, to create co-ops or create freedom schools.

I end with Eddie Conway here because while academics love to write and talk about social and systemic inequality, what is desperately needed are "getting our asses down there" and figuring out how to redistribute resources. Organizers know what their communities need; follow their lead. Perhaps part of our work as engaged academics is to redistribute money and resources to build alternative engines of employment, to fix houses, to create food cooperatives, to build political education and freedom schools.

I would add one more thing to Pulido's thoughtful letter about being a scholar activist: we are not separate and severed from the communities we work in. We cannot create artificial boundaries between North and South, suburban versus urban, good school districts versus failing school districts. We all breathe the same air, drink the same water, and throw away the same kinds of items, which in turn harm all of us. However, once we begin the collective labor of understanding this shared planetary reality, we realize that we are ecologically connected: our "good life" of consumption and leisure connects to the highest rates of asthma in the nation. Our teaching, our service, and our politics cannot be severed from the everyday and lived experience of the communities have been used as our dumping grounds. We—those occupying historical spaces and institutions of privilege—have made it difficult to breathe and contributed to high rates of Black and Brown death. It's our responsibility to be public scientists and to utilize our fields of anthropology, public health, architecture, design and everything else we study toward a 'common good,' finding and rebuilding community from the ground up. Not just dreaming of just transitions or teaching about it in our classrooms but putting in hours of labor or "sweat equity." As I say to my students, "Boots on the ground and hands in the dirt" is my philosophy. If we realize that we are in a planetary crisis and the solution requires all of us to prepare the lands for harvesting local foods, to carve and chisel the green infrastructure, to demolish and rebuild retrofitted housing, to construct participatory models of governance, it is our collective duty to hammer and sow a more just future. Let us learn from the great Eddie Conway who states, "We cannot keep on doing the same thing and sitting around the same table. It's really late in the day. You are gonna wake up in '24 or '25 and find Hitler and it's gonna be too late." Let us learn from the Baltimore Algebra Project where Jamal Jones (co-executive director) tells us that "It's about paying young Black men a living wage and creating jobs that facilitate empowerment." And finally at the center of this book, let us learn from the Free Your Voice students in Curtis Bay and other young people living in frontline communities who push us to see that development should not be imposed from above but driven by community residents, with their values driving the engines of job and housing creation. Let us follow their leads as we build this more just and equitable world.

NOTES

I. NIMBY (Not in My Backyard) is an acronym used to describe individuals who oppose undesirable or, sometimes, hazardous development projects in their own neighborhoods yet are seemingly unbothered by the same types of developments in other neighborhoods. These individuals are often, though not always, residents in White suburban areas.

INTRODUCTION

1. Note that Port Covington was added as another community during the negotiations over Under Armour but for the purposes of this book I will only refer to the six communities.

2. Curtis Bay, where the South Baltimore youth attend high school, 44.84 percent of the residents are white, 40.4 percent African American and 4.67 percent mixed race, 8 percent other races including Latinx and 1 percent Asian. While other neighboring communities like Cherry Hill are 89.9 percent African American. The Cherry Hill community was a direct product of systemic racism and white resistance to African Americans living in their neighborhoods after WWII: "The relocation of a proposed public housing project for African Americans after World War II to the city's southern tip was a move that civil rights groups protested because of environmental hazards" (Noor et al. 2021). Yet the Housing Authority of Baltimore City declared that "there was no other politically acceptable vacant land site for Negro housing" (Winbush et al. 2015). Today Cherry Hill is still predominantly

African American with shocking levels of poverty and inequality. The percentage of families living in poverty is 57.2 percent and the hardship index was 74 percent (Baltimore City Health Department 2011, 2017a, 2017b).

3. For more on environmental justice, see Bullard 1994, 2000, 2008; Checker 2005, 2020; Pulido 2016, 2018; Pulido and de Lara 2018; Sze 2007, 2018a, and 2018b; Taylor 2014

4. For more on state-based violence, see Julie Sze 2007, 2020.

5. Because of this, perhaps, the South Baltimore Peninsula has been erased from the historiography of Baltimore. Often, we read about East and West Baltimore and the racialized dynamics of the city but fail to incorporate the industrial South. In erasing this geography, we also erase how poor Whites (many of whom were migrants from Eastern Europe and their descendants) lived alongside Black and Brown people, fighting the intrusion of toxins into their lungs and homes.

6. A Harvard TH Chan Study found that long-term exposure to air pollution increases COVID-19 mortality rates (Wu et al. 2020). For more on how air pollution has exacerbated effects of COVID-19, see Parshley 2020.

7. For more on the right to the city, see Harvey, 1989, 2008, 2012; Lefebvre 1996; Purcell 2013; Spence 2015, 2018; Boggs and Boggs 1966.

8. Destiny Watford's name is not a pseudonym because, after receiving the Goldman Environmental Prize, she became a public figure. In all other cases, I use pseudonyms for the Free Your Voice activists, in order to protect their privacy and preserve their anonymity.

9. From the Goldman Environmental Prize website: "The Goldman Environmental Prize honors grassroots environmental heroes from roughly the world's six inhabited continental regions: Africa, Asia, Europe, Islands and Island Nations, North America, and South and Central America. The Prize recognizes individuals for sustained and significant efforts to protect and enhance the natural environment, often at great personal risk. The Goldman Prize views "grassroots" leaders as those involved in local efforts, where positive change is created through community or citizen participation. Through recognizing these individual leaders, the Prize seeks to inspire other ordinary people to take extraordinary actions to protect the natural world."

10. Fair Development is an idea that came out of earlier conversations within the Baltimore Housing Roundtable (now the Fair Development Roundtable), a group formed to create "development without displacement" and promote community development that "highlights [the] key benefits of community ownership strategies" (Fair Development Roundtable 2019).

11. Benjamin Franklin High School was considered a failing school and in 2010–2011 it was determined that the school would be designated a turnaround and a

community school, which is one that not only addresses the whole child but also recognizes the importance of family, neighborhood, and community. It imagines the school as the center of a web of services and relationships that address the many and diverse challenges enrolled children and their families face. In addition to a fully functioning day care system at BFHS, there is a trauma and mental health team, familial supports, food pantry/food access services, and college readiness programs and supports.

12. There is a rather large literature on activist anthropology (See Speed 2006; Hale 2001, 2002, 2008, Schuller 2010; Loperena 2016, 2017; Stuesse 2016; Berry et al. 2017). While this literature has inspired my work with Free Your Voice, much of the activist anthropology literature surfaced out of the anthropologists' intellectual and academic inquiries seeking collaborative relationships that produced written reports. Activist research is often conducted alongside and with disenfranchised communities such that a specified group can actively participate and learn the methodology, collect data, and take an active role in knowledge creation. My work with Free Your Voice was about political convictions, not academic inquiry. I never intended to write articles or even a book about this. In the postscript, I reflect back on my ten years of Baltimore-based activism to offer suggestions for transforming anthropology and our universities (see Jobson 2019).

13. These intersecting crises are a result of our neoliberal economic system, which idealizes markets, capital, and individual needs and desires over communitarian notions of belonging or justice (Sze 2020).

14. My methodology merged activist or "collaborative" anthropology with Critical Participatory Action Research (a model of research that uses quantitative and qualitative research methodologies to advance the goals of social justice movements). My inspiration came from researchers like Michelle Fine, Maria Elena Torre, Brett Stoudt, and Madeline Fox at the Public Science Center at the Graduate Center of the City University of New York (CUNY). I took several leaders from Free Your Voice in 2017 to a five-day intensive PAR training at CUNY which covered the history, theory, and ethics of PAR, along with in-depth discussions of participatory methods, conditions for meaningful community collaborations, and examples of effective research designs (Fine et al. 2003; Torre et al. 2012).

CHAPTER I. FAILED DEVELOPMENT
ON BALTIMORE'S TOXIC PERIPHERY

1. The Solvay company grew from a family operation begun in 1863 that innovated production of soda ash, used to make glass and detergents, and continued to

expand over time. The unit is called Novecare, which launched in 1950 as part of Rhodia, another chemical company. Solvay bought Rhodia in 2011 as a means of entering new markets after having sold its pharmaceutical operation to Abbott Laboratories in 2009. The Baltimore site of the Brussels-based conglomerate Solvay S.A. is part of a business unit that specializes in cosmetics and other personal care items, as well as plastics and other products. Today it is one of the world's largest chemical companies, with thirteen billion dollars in sales (Cohn 2017).

2. The City began to use the Marine Hospital as a pest hospital—that is, as an isolated place where people with often fatal contagious diseases could be housed. Poor people who were ill but not afflicted with contagious diseases were also sent to the Marine Hospital. The hospital was not inspected by any city officials and consequently was poorly managed (Diamond 1998).

3. I take this idea of historical trauma or root shock from Mindy Thompson Fullilove (2016). She borrows the concept of historical trauma from a Lakota scholar Maria Yellow Horse Brave Heart. Trauma occurs when an external force inflicts damage on an entity. According to Brave Heart, the social, economic, and emotional wounding resulting from damage inflicted by a powerful group onto the vulnerable can be passed on from generation to generation.

4. Yale Rabin's study of historical zoning decisions documented numerous instances where stable African American residential communities were "down-zoned" to industrial status by biased decision-makers, allowing inappropriate land uses near residents and ruining the social fabric of the neighborhoods. Rabin found that local zoning bodies in the early part of the century routinely zoned as "industrial" many residential Black communities, even as they zoned as "residential" similar White areas. These zoning practices permitted the intrusion of disruptive, incompatible uses and generally undermined the character, quality, and stability of the Black residential areas. Such "expulsive zoning," as Rabin called it, permanently alters the character of a neighborhood, often depressing property values and causing community blight.

5. Besides Old Fairfield and Wagner's Point, there were two other communities on the peninsula that deserve some mention. The first of them is Freetown. Whereas Fairfield was the site of the first pre–Civil War community of free African American landowners in the South, Freetown was the first free African American pre–Civil War settlement in the country. The historical record on Freetown is almost nonexistent: the major source is a report by the town's fifth graders in the early 1950s. At that time, Freetown was similar to Fairfield, though it claimed to have an extremely high rate of home ownership (Diamond 1998; McCraven 1997). Masonville, a tiny workers' community (even by peninsula standards), seems to have lasted only for about half a

century. The community was located between Brooklyn and Old Fairfield, directly next to the B&O Railroad switching yard and surrounded by sizable landholdings of Frank Furst, a local businessman and powerbroker. It also was an extremely tight-knit immigrant community.

6. Since the county was more lax about restrictions on weekend amusements, Wagner's Point was filled with adult entertainment. Beginning in the 1840s, recreational spaces such as Jack Flood's Park, Acton's Park, and the Walnut Spring Hotel grew up along the water in Baybrook. These geographic regions were filled with gambling houses and political hangouts, which sold alcohol as well as vaudeville performance spaces (King 2014).

7. Coal trains release heavy diesel fumes into the air, and these toxins find their way into soils where children play.

8. This data comes from Dr. Elizabeth Doran, who led a toxic tour in the Fall of 2020 with my Environmental Justice class at Towson University. Doran explained during the tour that coal dust, like other fine particulate matter, such as $PM_{2.5}$, gets lodged deep in our airways and over time can do great harm. She told the group, "We know that CSX, the owners of that pier have a permit from the Department of the Environment to allow emissions into the environment of the coal pier." As indicated in a *Baltimore Sun* article, this is approximately 1 ton a year of $PM_{2.5}$ (Wheeler 2013). The more $PM_{2.5}$ we breathe (EPA PM pollution), the more likely human beings are to get sick. The health effects as a result of long-term exposure can cause cardiac arrest and death (El Morabet 2019; Lockwood 2012; 2017). $PM_{2.5}$ increases emergency room visits and hospital admissions for respiratory infections and chronic lung disease, worsening lung function and increasing probabilities that one will develop asthma.

9. The Bethlehem Shipbuilding Company was created in 1905 when Bethlehem Steel of Bethlehem, Pennsylvania, acquired San Francisco Union Iron Works. In 1917 it was incorporated as Bethlehem Shipbuilding Corporation, Ltd. By 1940, it was the largest of the big three shipbuilders in the United States. In 1964, the corporate headquarters moved to Sparrows Point, Maryland.

10. The city of Baltimore eventually bought out the remaining residents' homes in Fairfield in 1988–1989, due to the environmental hazards, but there was a "bidding war" between Condea Vista and FMC, who were competing over buyouts for fear that they would be held liable for environmental contamination (Matthews 1999a).

11. This is an important reference because the language of "dump" or "dumping ground" is found in anti-integration discourses. Black bodies, represented by the language of "city trash", would contaminate your neighborhood. The idea of literally turning Fairfield and Wagner's Point into a dumping ground for the city here

is structural (in terms of location) but also cultural (in terms of how discourses and culture-of-poverty tropes circulated about White ethnic communities and predominantly Black communities).

12. By the 1960s Baltimore also had to manage the rubble from some of the urban renewal sites (see Cumming 2021).

13. An empowerment zone is an economically distressed community eligible to receive tax incentives and grants from the federal government under the Empowerment Zones and Enterprise Communities Act of 1993 initiated under Bill Clinton. Lester Spence argues that "the empowerment zone initiative, therefore, is a central part of a broadly coordinated strategy. With business people in mind, [these kinds of plans] seek to make places more attractive for new investments." (2015: 34)

14. The basketball coach of their local high school told me (years later, in 2019) that she didn't have enough healthy young people to make up a full squad for a basketball team because of such high cases of asthma.

CHAPTER 2. FREE YOUR VOICE

1. Children often describe the smoke coming from Wheelabrator-BRESCO and other factories as "cloud-making" machines. In December of 2021 there was a massive explosion at the CSX coal pier (see Fabricant 2022). There were two City Council hearings to hold CSX accountable for safety hazards during the summer of 2022.

2. From the hanging of laborer David Thomas in 1854 to the hanging and mutilation of field worker George Armwood in 1933, at least forty-four lynchings took place in Maryland, according to research conducted at the Maryland State Archives, the Equal Justice Initiative, and Bowie State University (See *Baltimore Sun* 2018).

3. I quote throughout the book from personal conversations with my cast of characters. Most of the quotes come from face-to-face conversations in which I participated.

4. Free Your Voice came out of The Worker Justice Center, where they developed a South Baltimore human rights hub. The Worker Justice Center was (and is) a human rights organization founded to organize homeless people evolved into a labor movement fighting for day laborers in Camden Yards. The organization focused on political education, which was a school of thought for poor people, political campaigns centering on labor, housing and environmental justice, and city-level policy. For the history of the Worker Justice Center, see Rosenthal 2013.

5. Benjamin Franklin was slated to close in 2008 due to overall poor performance. But the school never closed; instead, the community petitioned to have it stay open and helped it transition from a middle school to a high school. The name of the school was changed to Masonville Cove Community Academy to draw attention

to the environmental focus of the school and its partnership with Masonville Cove Education Center. It was also meant to draw attention away from the poor performance over the years. The community was upset about the name change, and the district settled on naming it Benjamin Franklin High School at Masonville Cove.

6. Data on the neighborhood profile come from the Baltimore Neighborhood Indicator Alliance (BNI) website: https://bniajfi.org/.

7. Data from Benjamin Franklin High School come from the Baltimore City Public Schools website: https://www.baltimorecityschools.org/schools/239.

8. Lawrence Brown (2021) discusses historical trauma as a conceptual frame first developed by Lakota scholar Maria Yellow Horse Brave Heart, who described trauma as an external force that inflicts tremendous damage on the affected entity, thereby threatening health and viability. Trauma can be passed on from generation to generation.

9. Many of the youth described Murphy as their mentor, and Murphy served as a stable family figure for several of them. Murphy recounted sleeping alongside a student in a hospital room, after that student attempted to commit suicide. He visited youth in mental health institutions, bailed youth out of the criminal justice system, and even opened his basement in Curtis Bay to those who needed a place of refuge. Murphy accumulated a tremendous amount of respect and admiration from the youth and their families during more than a decade of organizing, assisting, and living in the community. However, relationships are often complicated. Youth struggled to figure out who they were in relationship to Murphy. Some felt that they were simply an extension of Murphy's interests. Finding their own voices alongside this strong mentor was an ongoing challenge.

10. Shane (2019) argues that Amazon is a "many-armed titan reaching into Americans' daily lives." It is the number one supplier of electronics, clothes, groceries, information, music, and even security. Greater Baltimore accounts for 1 percent of sales nationwide.

CHAPTER 3. FIGHTING THE NATION'S LARGEST TRASH-TO-ENERGY INCINERATOR

1. It is important to note that The Worker Justice Center organizers like Daniel Murphy played a big role in directing the youth toward certain groups across the city and introducing them to new research venues, outlets, and even databases. The Worker Justice Center also played a key role in helping youth strategize about next steps in the campaign. However, youth always had autonomy in decision-making.

2. Daniel Murphy introduced youth to the human rights framework and curriculum of the Worker Justice Center by pushing them to ask lots of questions about basic rights to breathe clean air and basic rights to decent housing.

3. The renewable portfolio is divided into two tiers based on the electricity generation resource. Tier 1 renewables include solar, wind, biomass, anaerobic decomposition, geothermal, ocean, fuel cells powered through renewables, small hydro, poultry-litter incineration facilities, and waste-to-energy facilities.

4. Keeanga Yamahtta Taylor (2019) elaborates upon the dynamics of Black political leadership "Ascendance of Black electoral politics also dramatizes how class differences can lead to different political strategies in the fight for Black liberation. There have always been class differences among African Americans, but this is the first time those class differences have been expressed in the form of a minority of Blacks wielding significant political power and authority over the majority of Black lives. This raises critical questions about the role of Black elites in the continuing freedom struggle—and what side are they on" (Taylor 2016, 2019).

5. Bill Barry, a Baltimore labor historian, spoke to an audience at a Baltimore Museum of Industry event, "Mapping Dialogue." about the red dust coming out of the steel mills at Sparrows Point, which he described as the "color of money." Steel workers sacrificed environmental and human health for a good job" (WYPR 2019a).

6. Concerned Citizens of Better Brooklyn is a nonprofit doing the work of protecting community interests of residents and neighborhood improvement in the community. Curtis Bay Neighborhood Association and Concerned Citizens for a Better Brooklyn are spaces where residents come together to make decisions about the community. Often, they have leaned more in the direction of working alongside private and polluting industries in order to reap the economic benefits of donations and trinkets.

7. Brenda Blom and environmental scientist Rena Steinzor were incredibly helpful in locating historic documents about the Fairfield and Wagner's Point areas and even allowing students to interview them in 2021.

8. For the full Human Rights Dinner Speech, see Watford 2015.

9. These events, exacerbated by deindustrialization and plans to turn the entire peninsula into an industrial zone, contributed to Fairfield Homes experiencing a steep decline in both its quality of life and more specifically, levels of pollution. In the 1990s, the City finally relocated all residents due to the levels of pollution. After a voluntary City buyout of Old Fairfield in 1988–1989, few people remained in the vicinity. As mentioned in chapter 2, in 1997, the long uninhabited Fairfield Homes public housing complex was demolished. In its place vacant lots of approximately

twenty acres per site remained a constant reminder of wasted urban space requiring development.

10. The Worker Justice Center built their educational model on a Freirean pedagogical approach, based on Paolo Freire's *Pedagogy of the Oppressed* ([1970] 2018) which criticizes the "banking" model of education, mentioned in chapter 2, in which facts are deposited into the minds of passive students, much like the capitalist system, whereby students produce a paper or an assignment and they receive a numerical grade as part of the exchange process. Here, however, the labor of learning was considered collective, and could be about socially beneficial work. Training typically took place in small groups with lively interaction and embraced not only the written word but art, music, and other forms of expression. The Worker Justice Center drew upon Freire as a pedagogical inspiration but also utilized Antonio Gramsci's (1971) idea of developing organic, grassroots intellectuals.

11. There is a wealth of literature on the importance of the emotions for social movements (see Goodwin, Jasper, and Polletta 2001; Jasper 2011; Goodwin and Jasper 2006).

12. Some part of youth interest came from Augusto Boal's *Theater of the Oppressed* (1979); just as the group was influenced by Paolo Freire's *Pedagogy of the Oppressed*. Boal developed the concept of Theatre of the Oppressed (TO) as a series of games and exercises devised to give people a new "language" or medium to discuss, analyze, and resolve oppressions. With the premise that theatre is political, Boal disrupted dramatic techniques to subvert the oppressive nature of traditional theatre. Theater then becomes a common tool or language people can use to work together in a synergistic way to solve problems, share joys, learn about themselves, and take charge of their communities.

13. Baltimore Neighborhood Indicators Alliance (BNIA) aggregates census data from both Curtis Bay and Brooklyn as if they are one neighborhood.

14. BRCPC was a regional purchasing committee composed of regional public schools, community colleges, county agencies, cities and towns, and other organizations. Since 2005, they have been working to reduce energy costs by "collectively" purchasing power and buying electricity directly from the wholesale market, rather than via traditional retail markets. By working together, they are able to combine purchasing power and procure more advantageous contracts for electricity. Energy Answers presented them with one of those contracts for cheaper electricity.

15. Youth chose sunflowers as the symbol because they were beautiful and represented hope. These sunflowers represented the world they wanted to live in and encapsulated one goal of beautifying their communities.

16. Quoted in Brickell 2014.

17. Quoted in Brickell 2014.

18. For more, see Shen 2015 and Fritts 2020.

19. Personal Correspondence with Stuart Rosen

20. See Watford 2016, 2017; Shen 2016a and 2016b.

21. When Destiny Watford won the Goldman Environmental Prize, Global Alliance for Incinerator Alternatives (GAIA)—a worldwide alliance of more than eight hundred grassroots groups, nongovernmental organizations, and individuals in over ninety countries whose ultimate vision is a just, toxic-free world without incineration—became more involved in the work in Curtis Bay. The Global Anti-Incineration Alliance influenced Free Your Voice youth to begin to envision alternatives to incineration in the form of zero waste.

22. The Institute for Local Self-Reliance is a Washington, D.C.–based think tank that produces reports and assists local community grassroots groups in launching locally owned businesses and locally owned and controlled banks. For more on The Institute for Local Self-Reliance, see https://ilsr.org/about-the-institute-for-local-self-reliance/.

23. For more on the mission of Evergreen Cooperatives, see http://www.evgoh.com/mission-vision/.

24. See Cassie 2014 and Smith 2014.

CHAPTER 4. "WHOSE LAND? OUR LAND!": LAND TRUSTS AS FAIR DEVELOPMENT

1. Trickle-down economics, or "Reaganomics," is the idea that the free market (with the reduction of government spending, reduction of federal income tax on the wealthy, and a scaling back on all government regulation) will provide a rising tide that lifts all boats out of poverty. Those who support this model of economic theory argue that a deregulated market and a large money supply incentivizes venture capitalists and employers to invest money in projects that create jobs. In this way the private sector accumulates more wealth and eventually their wealth (in the form of job creation) "trickles down" to the rest of the American public (Casiano 2017).

2. For more on the 20/20 campaign, See Fair Development Roundtable (2020).

3. Free Your Voice youth attended nearly every Affordable Housing Trust Fund meeting. There was always a space at the end of the meeting for public commentary and this is the time where youth occupied the space and made their concerns known to the commissioners.

4. In order to maintain consistent and comfortable indoor temperatures through-out the year, passive buildings use high-performance windows and extra insulation, and they consider window orientation in their design. Passive buildings also use ventilation systems with heat and moisture recovery for increased air quality and efficiency. Passive homes use up to 85 percent less energy for heating and cooling than the average home. Beyond reducing the ecological footprint, these energy-efficient homes provide optimal comfort, especially for sufferers of asthma and other respiratory illnesses, by eliminating damp and mold (which has been plaguing public housing for generations). See South Baltimore Community Land Trust at www.sbclt.org.

5. I became an "official" part of the South Baltimore Land Trust as well. I served as secretary in 2018–2019 and have continued as a member since then.

6. Baltimore Neighborhood Indicators Alliance (BNIA) research has shown that nearly all communities in the city that grew between 2000 and 2010 had vacancy rates at or below 4 percent. Although 4 percent signals a tight market, that goal can help inform efforts: approximately 140 vacant buildings would need to be occupied or demolished to achieve it in Brooklyn and Curtis Bay. Residents only want to see demolition where absolutely necessary for safety or for redevelopment. Addition-ally, keeping vacancies low requires helping people remain in their homes (Balti-more City Department of Planning 2019).

7. According to the City, a building is considered vacant or unoccupied if it is unsafe or unfit for people to live or work inside the building, has two code violations that have not been addressed, or has six code violations in the past year (Baltimore Heritage 2017).

8. A TIF is a method of financing large-scale infrastructure projects through the use of special obligation bonds that are repaid using the estimated future value of the development. A TIF is an increasingly popular local redevelopment policy that allows municipalities to designate a "blighted" area for redevelopment and use the expected increase in property (and occasionally sales) taxes there to pay for initial and ongoing redevelopment expenditures, such as land acquisition, demolition, con-struction, and project financing (Casiano 2017).

9. The developers also entered into a Memorandum of Understanding with the City of Baltimore—which is unprecedented in scale and impact—that includes more than $100 million in commitments to fund priorities such as workforce development, education, economic development, and affordable housing. It is the largest citywide benefits package negotiated in Baltimore's history. The community-benefits agree-ment signed with the South Baltimore 6 (SB6) Coalition—a nonprofit organization

that represents the surrounding communities of Brooklyn, Cherry Hill, Curtis Bay, Lakeland, Mt. Winans, and Westport—outlines how these communities will benefit from the project. The developers of Port Covington suggest that 20 percent of the residences in this phase of Port Covington will be affordable housing and that of $36.5 million awarded for infrastructure work, contracts totaling $27 million have gone to minority-owned firms and contracts totaling $3 million have gone to women-owned firms (Gantz 2015).

10. After much negotiation, 20 percent of housing at Port Covington was allotted to "affordable," doubling Sagamore's original offer of 10 percent. But ACLU representatives of Maryland also noted loopholes in the final agreement suggesting that the language of "affordable" included as high as 80 percent of the area median income for the entire Baltimore region, or $83,2000 (Lanahan 2020).

11. Baltimoreans in this next phase of Port Covington development will see shops, offices, apartments, and a communal market, and all are due to open starting in late 2022. The hope is for Port Covington to transform some of these individualized shops and apartments into a full-fledged community (Gantz 2015).

12. The Affordable Housing Trust Fund supports both rental and for-sale affordable housing for very-low- and low-income households. The Trust Fund requires that all revenue be used to help those with incomes at or below 50 percent of the area median income (AMI) as established by the US Department of Housing and Urban Development (HUD) (approximately forty-six thousand dollars for a household of four in 2018) and that at least half of the funds be used to help those with incomes at or below 30 percent of the AMI (approximately twenty-seven thousand dollars) for a household of four in 2018. The trust fund comprises money (partially) from transfer tax on property sales above one million dollars, but the tax thus far has not generated as much as the City hoped; in part the pandemic has affected commercial real estate (Fair Development Report).

13. Marc Weller (Sagamore Ventures developer) stepped away from the Port Covington project in May of 2022. In a carefully scripted press release, Plank stated that the Weller team would be replaced by a team of "leading women-owned and Black-owned development firms." (Ruetter 2022) "MAG Partners, a New York-based woman-owned firm, and MacFarlane Partners, a San Francisco-based Black-owned development and institutional investment firm, will leverage decades each of national experience in taking the reins from Weller Development Co. for leasing, marketing and "placemaking" campaigns for the current $500 million, 1.1 million-square-foot phase" of development of Port Covington, Sagamore said (Mirabella 2022).

CHAPTER 5. COMPOST! LEARN SO
WE DON'T HAVE TO BURN

1. Personal correspondence, 2017. Marvin Hayes is the program manager of the Baltimore Compost Collective. There was no pseudonym used for Hayes.

2. Zero waste entails the conservation of all resources by means of responsible production, consumption, reuse, and recovery of products, packaging, and materials without burning, and with no discharges to land, water, or air that threaten the environment or human health (See the GAIA website for more on zero waste: https://zerowasteworld.org).

3. The Baltimore Refuse Energy Systems Co. (commonly referred to as Wheelabrator-BRESCO) is an incinerator located in Mount Winans, South Baltimore, that burns waste from the entire city of Baltimore. Mount Winans is five miles north of Curtis Bay.

4. For more, see https://www.thepealecenter.org/the-colored-school-at-the-peale/ and Frederick Douglass High School; https://www.baltimorecityschools.org/schools/450.

5. An MOU is a type of agreement between two or more parties that converges their interests; it is often not a legally binding document. In this case the MOU was between The Worker Justice Center and Hayes outlining the terms of agreement for the fiscal sponsorship.

6. There are ongoing conflicts between the Baltimore Compost Collective and The Worker Justice Center. The Worker Justice Center, according to Hayes, has failed to provide resources, administrative assistance, and other supports, who was currently looking for a new fiscal sponsor—or to turn the compost collective into an autonomous co-operative, As of October 2021, Hayes now partners with Ridge to Reefs, a Maryland-based environmental NGO that works on protecting and restoring ecosystems.

7. For more, see BioCycle 2020; Flin et al. 2021; Ramos 2021.

8. Michael Dorsey, one of the Directors of Chesapeake Center for Youth Development (CCYD) allowed Marvin to use the vehicle on the weekends with the understanding that it belonged to the CCYC after-school youth program. Many residents in South Baltimore communities thought Marvin and his youth were stealing buckets from homes but then quickly began to refer to his team as the "compost guys."

9. A Dreamer is a young person who has lived in the United States without official authorization. People of this description who met certain conditions would be

eligible for a special immigration status under federal legislation first proposed in 2001.

10. For more on Baltimore's Fair Development Plan, see Fabricant and Hax 2020.

11. Gary Liss (no pseudo name was used for Liss) had over thirty-nine years of experience in the solid waste and recycling field. He is the founder and president of the National Recycling Coalition (NRC) and was solid waste manager for the state of California. He developed their recycling programs into national models, which are currently diverting 62 percent of their overall waste stream. He is one of the leading advocates of zero waste in the nation.

12. This kind of illumination has been a strategy of movements seeking to raise awareness about social justice issues. In the South Bronx, through a participatory action project called the Morris Justice Project, researchers used a massive illuminator—a van first used in the Occupy Wall Street protests—that helped to project data onto local apartment buildings in the form of an open letter to the NYPD revealing the numbers of young men who had been stopped and frisked by police. This data disrupted everyday flows and forced people to read and take notice of the disparities in policing. Neighbors gathered on street corners to discuss what it means to live, work, raise kids, and pray in a community that experienced over four thousand police stops in 2011 (see Daniels 2013).

13. The Baltimore Sunrise Movement has been active in stopping climate change and creating good-paying and green jobs. They have been involved in state legislation for climate justice and alternative energy, and since 2019, individual Sunrise Movement leaders have been involved in the Zero Waste Coalition (Shen 2020a).

14. For more, see *Baltimore Sun* Editorial Board 2020.

CONCLUSION

1. Baltimore Broken Glass project is a youth-run enterprise that utilizes recycled glass to create art. Free Your Voice youth sell their art to Baltimore residents where 100 percent of the profit goes to support the South Baltimore Community Land Trust and zero-waste work. For more on their artwork, see https://www.etsy.com/shop/BaltimoreBrokenGlass

2. This was provided to the City of Baltimore as part of the American Rescue Plan Act (ARPA). For more on the mayor's recovery program, See https://arp.baltimorecity.gov/about-3.

3. By the end of the Spring semester of 2022 Johns Hopkins University, University of Maryland–Baltimore County, and Towson University had all committed to sending their food waste to the soon-to-be-built compost facility possibly in Curtis

Bay or elsewhere. The challenge is also getting anchor institutions to formally support a labor-benefits agreement, which would ensure decent and healthy jobs.

4. See Santoro and Abiral 2021.

5. Thea Riofrancos and Mark Paul (2021) argue that there is no final frontier. Capitalism inherently and constantly produces new extractive frontiers and environments to exploit and sacrifice, and it does so at every possible scale. The fantasy of escaping this condition through spatial fixes is the environmentalism of fools.

POSTSCRIPT

1. For the full video testimonial, see https://vimeo.com/126284175.

2. This personal letter was written to The Worker Justice Center and leadership council, September 4 2020.

3. For example, many #metoo Baltimore Facebook posts (2018) accused a prominent leader of the Black-led think tank Leaders of a Beautiful Struggle of raping a Black woman in 2015. This woman only came forward when several young women claimed that they too experienced sexual abuse by said leader of the movement (#MeToo Baltimore 2018). Leaders of a Beautiful Struggle leadership team officially responded two years later with a letter acknowledging the allegations (Leaders of a Beautiful Struggle 2020). Sunrise Movement Baltimore also underwent a public reckoning (See Sunrise Movement 2021) addressing white supremacy as well as DSA-Baltimore in January 2022.

4. PhD candidate in women and gender studies and organizer with Village of Love and Resistance Lenora Knowles stated at our forum at Red Emma's, "There needs to be deep recognition for the fact that people are building careers and political and social capital off the stories and bodies of low-income poor Black folks and that needs to stop. I also think intellectual questions need to come directly out of the communities most impacted" (See Red Emma's 2021)

5. Jobson starts with the American Anthropology Conference that took place in 2019 in the midst of some of the worst fires in California. Anthropologists could not breathe and had to wear N95 masks. Instead of canceling the conference, the American Anthropology Association decided to continue as "normal." Some anthropologists turned toward social media to critique the conference. Indigenous anthropologist Zoe Todd tweeted, "If breathing in the smoke of burning trees, homes, cities doesn't convince us that we need radically different ways to engage beyond conference center model . . . I don't know what will" (Todd 2019). Todd uses this conference as a point of departure for asking several provocative questions about

anthropology's colonialist history, anthropology's fixes "including obsessions with liberalism," and the new ontological turn.

6. In 2019, many anthropologists followed the trend toward a decolonial anthropology. As Daniel Goldstein and colleagues argue, anthropology has "yet to engage fully with the decolonial challenge" (Goldstein et al. 2019), as it continues to "endorse a model of scholarship in which the lives of cultural others constitute the legitimate objects of scholarly inquiry and to practice forms of research that distribute power upward, from those being studied to those doing the studying." In 2020, many now follow the wave toward "abolition." I also worry that abolition has become a new go-to theory in anthropology, with comfortable White liberals hiding behind the cloak of abolition instead of decolonization. Theories come and go and shift in academia. The language of abolition becomes a powerful way of performing solidarity but not doing the actual work of building alternative political and economic systems (Jobson 2019).

7. Perhaps, we need new value systems and new forms of measurements within institutions, especially public institutions, toward tenure requirements. Measurements could be created alongside community residents who determine the value and categories necessary to reach their goals for policy changes. In a moment of ecological and environmental crisis, it seems that social scientific research should advance the needs of frontline communities first. Universities should be accountable to the communities that they are in such close proximity to. R1 public institutions should be accountable to the broader public instead of using them as playgrounds for gentrification and leisure. These ideas have come from conversations with my two dear friends, comrades, and interlocutors Lawrence Brown and Eric Jackson.

8. Kyle Pompey, who runs NiceShot Media, has been a part of our collaboration since 2018, teaching youth photographic skills and turning cameras over to them to document the injustices in their community (Pompey 2017).

9. Many of these ideas have come out of conversations with Nicole King and the UMBC public humanities program.

10. Many anthropologists have become involved in movements on their campuses such as "Cops Off Campus" or supporting graduate students in their struggles for adequate wages and benefits. This is all noble work. But many sit in spaces of great privilege and we need to systematically understand the political economy of our institutions to push this activism work to align with community-based needs.

11. Free Your Voice saw the university/educational institutional sector in Baltimore City and County as positioned to play a critical role in supporting the development of needed infrastructure as both major food waste generators with procurement power and as entities that play a role in shaping the local political

landscape. As Free Your Voice articulated, "We are talking about 400,000-plus students collectively and 100,000-plus tons of food waste generated. We don't have a total dollar amount, but it's safe to say millions in procurement dollars are going for waste/recycling contracts and a tiny sliver going to organics diversion. We want universities to come together voluntarily to solve this problem and center zero-waste infrastructure that meets both community and labor's needs" (conversation Spring 2021).

REFERENCES

Abel, Joseph

 2019 "Building a Bridge of Ships: Fairfield Shipyards." *Baltimore Museum of Industry*, September 17, https://www.thebmi.org/building-a-bridge -of-ships-fairfield-shipyard/.

The Abell Foundation

 2002 "Childhood Lead Poisoning in Baltimore." *The Abell Report* 15(5). https://abell.org/sites/default/files/publications/arn1002.pdf.

Agency for Toxic Substances and Disease Registry

 2014 "Mercury." *ATSDR Toxzine*, May 23. US Department of Health and Human Services. https://www.atsdr.cdc.gov/sites/toxzine/mercury _toxzine.html.

Ahmann, Chloe

 2018a "Cumulative Effects: Reckoning Risk on Baltimore's Toxic Periphery." PhD diss., George Washington University.

 2018b "It's Exhausting to Create an Event out of Nothing: Slow Violence and the Manipulation of Time." *Cultural Anthropology* 33(1):142–71. https://doi.org/10.14506/ca33.1.06.

 2019 "Waste-to-Energy: Garbage Prospects and Subjunctive Politics in Late Industrial Baltimore." *American Ethnologist* 46(3):328–42. https://doi.org/10.1111/amet.12792.

Andrews, Owen Silverman

 2020 "Dumpster Fire in MD Senate Fueled by Corporate Cash." *Medium Opinion*, February 7. https://osilvermana.medium.com/dumpster -fire-in-md-senate-fueled-by-corporate-cash-3e607b762667.

Archibald, Katherine

1947   *Wartime Shipyard: A Study in Social Disunity.* Berkeley: University of California Press.

Axel-Lute, Miriam

2019   "New Communities, Inc. at 50: Thoughts on Identity and a Different Way Forward." *Shelter Force*, October 11. https://shelterforce .org/2019/10/11/new-communities-inc-at-50-thoughts-on-identity -and-a-different-way-forward/.

Baker, Mike, et al.

2020   "Three Words, 70 Cases: The Tragic History of 'I can't breathe.'" *New York Times*, June 28. https://www.nytimes.com/interactive /2020/06/28/us/i-cant-breathe-police-arrest.html.

Baltimore City Department of Housing and Community Development

2021   "City Announces Community Land Trust Award." March 24. https:// dhcd.baltimorecity.gov/news/news/2021-03-24-city-announces -community-land-trust-awards.

Baltimore City Department of Planning

2019   "INSPIRE Plan: Baybrook Elementary and Middle School" INSPIRE: Investing in Neighborhoods and Schools to Promote Improvement, Revitalization and Excellence." https://planning .baltimorecity.gov/sites/default/files/Bay%20Brook%20INSPIRE %20Plan_FINAL%20lo-res_2.pdf.

Baltimore City Department of Public Works

2021   "Baltimore Launches Pilot to Reduce Food Waste." Press release, July 9. https://publicworks.baltimorecity.gov/news/press-releases /2021-07-09-dpw-launches-pilot-reduce-food-waste-baltimore -residential-drop.

Baltimore City Health Department

2011   "Neighborhood Health Profile: Cherry Hill." Last modified June 8. https://health.baltimorecity.gov/sites/default/files/7%20Cherry %20Hill.pdf.

2017a   "Allendale/Irvington/South Hilton." Baltimore City Neighborhood Health Profile. Last modified June 9. https://health .baltimorecity.gov/sites/default/files/NHP%202017%20-%2001 %20Allendale-Irvington-South%20Hilton%20(rev%206-9-17).pdf.

2017b   "Brooklyn/Curtis Bay/Hawkins Point." Baltimore City Neighborhood Health Profile. Last modified June 9. https://health

.baltimorecity.gov/sites/default/files/NHP%202017%20-%2004
%20Brooklyn-Curtis%20Bay-Hawkins%20Point%20(rev%206
-9-17).pdf.

Baltimore Heritage

2017   "Vacant Buildings 101." Series of workshops. Last modified May 9.
        https://baltimoreheritage.github.io/vacant-buildings-101/.

Baltimore Neighborhood Indicator Alliance–Jacob France Institute

2019   "Vital Signs for Brooklyn, Curtis Bay and Hawkins Point." https://
        bniajfi.org/community/Brooklyn_Curtis%20Bay_Hawkins
        %20Point/.

Baltimore Sun

2018   "Lynchings in Maryland." https://news.baltimoresun.com/maryland
        -lynchings/.

Baltimore Sun Editorial Board

2020   "Incinerator Compromise Was Baltimore's Only Realistic Option."
        Baltimore Sun, November 5. https://www.baltimoresun.com/opinion
        /editorial/bs-ed-1106-waste-energy-bresco-20201105-galydqe6
        kfaannam7rjb6cqaym-story.html.

Berry, Maya et al.

2017   "Toward a Fugitive Anthropology: Gender, Race, and Violence
        in the Field." *Cultural Anthropology* 32(4): 537–65. https://doi.org/10
        .14506/ca32.4.05.

BioCyle

2020   "Community Composting Key in Baltimore's Waste Strategy."
        Community Composting and Food Waste Archives, August 12.
        https://www.biocycle.net/community-composting-key-in
        -baltimores-food-waste-strategy/.

Bloom, Brenda

2002   "How Close to Justice? A Case Study of the Relocation of Resi-
        dents from Fairfield and Wagner's Point." PhD diss., University of
        Maryland.

Boal, Augusto

1979   *Theater of the Oppressed*. New York: Urzien Books.

Boggs, James, and Grace Lee Boggs

1966   "The City Is the Black Man's Land." *Monthly Review* 17(11), April.
        https://monthlyreviewarchives.org/index.php/mr/article/view
        /MR-017-11-1966-04_4.

Braben, B et al.

1994   "Respiratory Morbidity in Merseyside Schoolchildren Exposed
            to Coal Dust and Air Pollution." *Archives of Disease in Childhood.*
            70(4): 305–12. http://dx.doi.org/10.1136/adc.70.4.305.

Bradley, Stephen, and Nicole King

2012   "Mapping Baybrook: A Digital Humanities Project." Univer-
            sity of Maryland Baltimore County, Department of American
            Studies. https://mappingbaybrook.org/about/.

Brey, Jared

2019   "Baltimore Advocates Keep Up the Housing Demands." *Next City,*
            August 1. https://nextcity.org/daily/entry/baltimore-advocates
            -keep-up-the-housing-demands.

2021   "Baltimore Land Trusts Plug Away at Vision for Development
            without Displacement." Next City, April 6. https://nextcity.org
            /daily/entry/baltimore-land-trusts-plug-away-vision-development
            -without-displacement.

Brickell, Allison

2014   "Making Music from a Plea about Airborne Mercury and Mate-
            rialism." *Baltimore Brew,* May 29. https://www.baltimorebrew
            .com/2014/05/29/making-music-from-a-plea-about-airborne
            -mercury-and-materialism.

Brown, Lawrence

2016a   "Protect Whose House? How Baltimore Leaders Failed to Fur-
            ther Affordable and Fair Housing in Port Covington." *University of
            Baltimore Journal of Land Development* 6(2): 161–69.

2016b   "Two Baltimores: The White L vs. the Black Butterfly." *Baltimore
            Sun,* June 28. https://www.baltimoresun.com/citypaper/bcpnews
            -two-baltimores-the-white-l-vs-the-black-butterfly-20160628
            -htmlstory.html.

2021   *The Black Butterfly: Harmful Politics of Race and Space in America.* Bal-
            timore: Johns Hopkins University Press.

Brown, Lawrence et al.

2016   "The Rise of Anchor Institutions and Threat to Community
            Health: Protecting Community Wealth, Building Community
            Power." *Kalfou: A Journal of Comparative and Relational Ethnic Studies*
            3(1): 80–100. https://doi.org/10.15367/kf.v3i1.88.

Bullard, Robert D.

1994   *Unequal Protection: Environmental Justice and Communities of Color.* San Francisco: Sierra Book Clubs.

2000   *Dumping in Dixie: Race, Class, and Environmental Quality*, 3rd edition. Boulder, CO: Westview Press.

Bullard, Robert D. et al.

2008   "Toxic Wastes and Race at Twenty: Why Race Still Matters after All These Years." *Environmental Law* 38(2): 371–411.

Burnett, Ava-Joye

2017   "Curtis Bay Area Residents Shelter in Place for Two Hours after Acid Spill." CBS Baltimore, September 18. https://baltimore .cbslocal.com/2017/09/18/curtis-bay-hazmat/.

Campanale, Claudia et al.

2020   "A Detailed Review Study on Potential Effects of Microplastics and Additives of Concern on Human Health." *International Journal of Environmental Research and Public Health* 17(4): 1212. doi: 10.3390/ ijerph17041212.

Campbell, Colin, and Scott Dance

2017   "Acid Cloud Leaks from Chemical Plant in South Baltimore, Prompting a Shelter-in-Place Alert," *Baltimore Sun*, September 18. https://www.baltimoresun.com/maryland/baltimore-city/bs-md -ci-hazmat-leak-20170918-story.html.

Carbone, Michele et al.

2012   "Malignant Mesothelioma: Facts, Myths and Hypotheses." *J Cell Physiology.* January 227(1): 44–58. doi: 10.1002/jcp.22724.

Casiano, Michael

2017   "The Financialized City: Public Debt and Local Organizing. United Workers Leadership School Materials." Unpublished Paper.

Cassie, Ron

2014   "The Best of Baltimore." *Baltimore Magazine*, August. https:// www.baltimoremagazine.com/section/bestof/best-of-baltimore -news/.

Checker, Melissa

2005   *Polluted Promises: Environmental Racism and the Search for Justice in a Southern Town.* New York: New York University Press.

2020   *The Sustainability Myth: Environmental Gentrification and the Politics of Justice*. New York: New York University Press.

Cobb, Jelani

2015   "City Life: What Racism Has Done to Baltimore." *New Yorker*, May 11. https://www.newyorker.com/magazine/2015/05/11/city-life-what-racism-has-done-to-baltimore.

Cohen, Helen, and Mark Lipman

2016   *Arc of Justice: The Rise, Fall, and Rebirth of a Beloved Community*. New Day Film. DVD. https://www.arcofjusticefilm.com

Cohn, Meredith

2017   "Baltimore Plant Involved in HAZMAT Incident Is Part of a Global Chemical Giant." *Baltimore Sun*, September 18. https://www.baltimoresun.com/business/bs-bz-solvay-chemical-company-20170918-story.html.

Cole, Teju

2012   "The White-Savior Industrial Complex." *The Atlantic*, March 21.

Crenson, Matthew

2017   *Baltimore: A Political History*. Baltimore: Johns Hopkins University Press.

Cumming, Daniel

2021   "Health Is Wealth: The Rise of a Medical Metropolis and the Remaking of Racial Inequality in 20th-Century Baltimore." PhD diss. New York University.

Dance, Scott

2019   "Where Will the Trash Go? Baltimore and Surrounding Counties Consider Alternatives if incineration closes." *Baltimore Sun*, February 14. https://www.baltimoresun.com/news/environment/bs-md-wheelabrator-impact-20190213-story.html.

2020a   "Baltimore Appeals Federal Ruling That Invalidated Law to Reduce Trash Incinerator Air Pollution." *Baltimore Sun*, March 24. https://www.baltimoresun.com/news/environment/bs-md-incinerator-lawsuit-appeal-20200424-ruqpdwbunfey3bjo33chkrxgju-story.html.

2020b   "Baltimore Launches a Plan to Get to Zero Waste, Starting with the Closure of City Trash Incinerator." *Baltimore Sun*, February 24. https://www.baltimoresun.com/news/environment/bs-md-zero-waste-plan-launch-20200223-i3st3tmrprdsxa5pkshqsm6ixy-story.html.

Daniels, Jessie

2013 "Interview: Brett Stoudt and Maria Torre about the Morris Justice Project." JustPublics@365, November 6, https://justpublics365 .commons.gc.cuny.edu/11/2013/interview-morris-justice-project/.

Davis, John Emmeus

2010 *The Community Land Trust Reader.* Cambridge, MA: Lincoln Institute of Land Policy.

deMause, Neil

2015 "An Industry City Promises a New Sunset Park, Some Residents Fight to Maintain the Old One." *City Limits,* October 27. https:// citylimits.org/2015/10/27/as-industry-city-promises-a-new-sunset -park-some-residents-fight-to-maintain-the-old-one/.

Demczuk, Gabriella

2015 "In Baltimore, Fighting an Incinerator." *New York Times,* January 10. Video, 4:40. https://www.nytimes.com/video/us/10000000 3333133/in-baltimore-a-fight-for-clean-air.html.

Diamond, Phillip

1998 *An Environmental History of Fairfield/Wagner's Point.* Baltimore: University of Maryland School of Law. https://digitalcommons.law .umaryland.edu/cgi/viewcontent.cgi?article=1030&context=mlh _pubs.

Dillon, Lindsey, and Julie Sze

2016 "Police Power and Particulate Matters: Environmental Justice and the Spatialities of In/Securities in U.S. Cities." *English Language Notes* 54(2): 13–23.

Durr, Kenneth

2003 *Behind the Backlash: White Working-Class Politics in Baltimore, 1940–1980.* Chapel Hill: University of North Carolina Press.

Elliot, Debbie

2019 "5 Decades Later, New Communities Land Trust Still Helps Black Farmers." *Morning Edition,* NPR, October 3. https://www .npr.org/2019/10/03/766706906/5-decades-later-communities -land-trust-still-helps-black-farmers.

El Morabet, Rachida

2019 "Effects of Outdoor Air Pollution on Human Health." In *Encyclopedia of Environmental Health,* 2nd edition, 278–86. doi:10.1016 /B978-0-12-409548-9.11509-X.

Environmental Integrity Project

2012   "Air Quality Profile of Curtis Bay, Brooklyn and Hawkins Point, Maryland." https://www.environmentalintegrity.org/wp-content /uploads/2016/11/2012-06_Final_Curtis_Bay.pdf.

Environmental Protection Agency

2021   "Particulate Matter (PM) Basics." Last modified on May 26. https:// www.epa.gov/pm-pollution/particulate-matter-pm-basics.

Fabricant, Nicole

2019   "Over-Burdened Bodies and Lands: Industrial Development and Environmental Injustice in South Baltimore." In *Baltimore Revisited: Stories of Inequality and Resistance in a US City.* New Brunswick, NJ: Rutgers University Press.

2022   "Opinion: CSX Explosion in Curtis Bay Should Alarm Baltimore City and Accelerate Real Change." *Real News.* https:// therealnews.com/opinion-csx-explosion-in-curtis-bay-should -alarm-baltimore-city-and-accelerate-real-change.

Fabricant, Nicole, and Heather Hax

2020   "The Nation's First Fair Development Zero Waste Plan." *Next System Project,* July 9. https://thenextsystem.org/learn/stories /nations-first-fair-development-zero-waste-plan.

Fair Development Roundtable

2019   *Fair Development, Race Equity and Baltimore's Affordable Housing Trust Fund: Rise, Reclaim, and Rebuild.* The Fair Development Roundtable, July 23. https://d3n8a8pro7vhmx.cloudfront.net/unitedworkers /pages/239/attachments/original/1563753707/2019_AHTF _Position_Paper_FINAL.pdf?1563753707.

2020   *Baltimore's Fair Development Plan for Zero Waste.* Fair Development Roundtable, February 2020. https://ilsr.org/wp-content/uploads /2020/02/BaltimoreZeroWastePlan2020.pdf.

Ferber, Dan

2013   "Research Finds Additional Harm from Coal Dust Exposure." *Energy News Network,* February 20. https://energynews.us/2013/02 /20/research-finds-additional-harm-from-coal-dust-exposure/.

Fernández-Kelly, Patricia

2015   *The Hero's Fight: African Americans in West Baltimore and the Shadow of the State.* Princeton, NJ: Princeton University Press.

Fesperman, Dan

1998   "A Man's Claim to Guano Knee-Deep in Bureaucracy Island Fortune in Fertilizer Has Baltimore Connection." *Baltimore Sun*, July 19. https://www.baltimoresun.com/news/bs-xpm-1998-07-19 -1998200032-story.html.

1999   "A Place Apart Fairfield: Money for Improvements Is Finally on Its Way but Most of the People Are Gone." *Baltimore Sun*, March 9. https://www.baltimoresun.com/news/bs-xpm-1997-03 -09-1997068034-story.html.

Fine, Michelle, et al.

2003   "Participatory Action Research: From within and beyond Prison Bars." In *Qualitative Research in Psychology: Expanding Perspectives in Methodology and Design*, edited by Paul M. Camic, Jean E Rhodes, and Lucy Yardley, 173–98. Washington, DC: American Psychological Association. https://doi.org/10.1037/10595-010.

Flin, Briana, et al.

2021   "Baltimore Is Burning Trash, so We're Starving the Fire." *The Guardian*, March 12. Video, 6:52. https://www.theguardian.com /us-news/video/2021/apr/12/inside-south-baltimores-fight-against -burning-trash-video.

Forgo, Rik

2020   "Wagner's Point: The Great Oil Fire of 1920." *Medium*, June 4. https://medium.com/time-passages/wagners-point-the-great-oil -fire-of-1920-f6de1ef03235

Freire, Paolo

[1970] 2018 *Pedagogy of the Oppressed*. 4th edition. New York: Bloomsbury Academic.

Fritts, Rachel

2020   "How Maryland's Preference for Burning Trash Galvanized Environmental Activists in Baltimore." *Inside Climate News*, August 24. https://insideclimatenews.org/news/24082020/baltimore -maryland-waste-to-energy/.

Fullilove, Mindy Thompson

2016   *Root Shock: How Tearing Up City Neighborhoods Hurts America, and What We Can Do about It*. New York: New Village Press.

Gantz, Sarah

2015   "What's under the Hood at Sagamore Ventures' City Garage." *Baltimore Business Journal*, October 5. https://www.bizjournals.com

/baltimore/blog/cyberbizblog/2015/10/heres-whats-under-the
-hood-at-sagamore-ventures.html.

Gaventa, John

2006   "Finding the Spaces for Change: A Power Analysis." *IDS Bulletin*
37(6): 23–33. doi:10.1111/j.1759-5436.2006.tb00320.x

Geertz, Clifford

1973   "Thick Description: Toward an Interpretive Theory of Culture."
In *The Interpretation of Cultures: Selected Essays*. New York: Basic Books.

Geiling, Natasha

2018   "'This Is a Matter of Life and Death': A Virginia Community
Choking on Coal Dust Pleads for Help." *Think Progress*, March 15.
https://archive.thinkprogress.org/lamberts-point-coal-dust
-pollution-6dbec60d1e9e/.

Gilmore, Ruthie

2008   "Forgotten Place and the Seeds of Grassroots Planning." In *Engaging Contradictions: Theory, Politics, and Methods of Activist Scholarship*,
edited by Charles Hale, 31–61. Berkeley: University of California
Press.

Goldstein, Daniel et al.

2019   *Decolonizing Ethnography: Undocumented Immigrants and New Directions in Social Scientific Research*. Durham, NC: Duke University
Press.

Gonzalez, David

2016   "In Sunset Park, a Call for Innovation Leads to Fears of Gentrification." *New York Times*, March 6. https://www.nytimes.com/2016
/03/07/nyregion/in-sunset-park-a-call-for-innovation-leads-to
-fears-of-gentrification.html.

Goodwin, Jeff, and James Jasper

2006   "Emotions and Social Movements." In *Handbook of the Sociology of
Emotion*, edited by Jan Stets and Jonathan Turner, 611–35. Boston:
Springer. https://doi.org/10.1007/978-0-387-30715-2_27.

Goodwin, Jeff, James Jasper, and Francesca Polletta

2001   *Passionate Politics: Emotions and Social Movements*. Chicago: University of Chicago Press.

Gramsci, Antonio

1971   *Selections from the Prison Notebook*. New York: International Publishers.

Green, Jarrid, and Thomas Hanna

2018   "Community Control of Land and Housing: Exploring Strategies for Combating Displacement and Expanding Ownership and Building Community Wealth." The Democracy Collaborative. https://thenextsystem.org/sites/default/files/2018-08/Community ControlLandHousing.pdf.

Hale, Charles

2001   "What Is Activist Research?" *Social Science Research Council* 2(1–2).

2002   "Does Multiculturalism Menace? Governance, Politics and Cultural Rights and Politics in Guatemala." *Journal of Latin American Studies* 34(3): 485–524. Cambridge: Cambridge University Press.

2008   *Engaging Contradictions: Theory, Politics, and Methods of Activist Scholarship.* Berkeley: University of California Press.

Harvey, David

1989   *The Condition of Postmodernity: An Enquiry into the Origins of Cultural Change.* Cambridge: Blackwell.

2008   "The Right to the City." *New Left Review* 53(2): 23–40.

2012   *Rebel Cities: From the Right to the City to the Urban Revolution.* London: Verso.

Heynen, Nik

2016   "Urban Political Ecology II: The Abolitionist Century." *Progress in Human Geography* 40(6): 839–45. https://doi.org/10.1177/03091325 15617394.

Hillier, Amy

2003   "Redlining and the Homeowners' Loan Corporation." *Journal of Urban History.* 29(4): 394–420. https://doi.org/10.1177/009614420 3029004002.

Jackson, Alex

2018   "South Point to Open at West Covington Park in Port Covington." *Patch,* July 19. https://patch.com/maryland/baltimore/south -point-open-west-covington-park-port-covington.

Jacobson, Joan

2015   "Vacants to Value: Baltimore's Bold Blight-Elimination Effort Is Making Modest Progress Despite Limited Renovation Funds and Questionable Accounting." *The Abell Report,* 28(5) November. https://abell.org/sites/default/files/files/cd-vacants2-value1115.pdf.

James, Jennifer

 2012 "'Buried in Guano': Race, Labor and Sustainability." *American Literary History* 24(1): 115–142. https://doi.org/10.1093/alh/ajr050.

Jasper, James

 2011 "Emotions and Social Movements: Twenty Years of Theory and Research." *Annual Review of Sociology* 37(14): 1–28.

Jobson, Ryan Cecil

 2019 "The Case for Letting Anthropology Burn: Sociocultural Anthropology in 2019." *American Anthropologist* 122(2): 259–71. https://doi.org/10.1111/aman.13398.

Johnson, Marilynn

 1996 *The Second Gold Rush: Oakland and the East Bay in World War II.* Berkeley: University of California Press.

Jones, Ken

 2019 "Fairfield Yards: Home of the Liberty Fleet." *The Baltimore Museum of Industry.* https://www.thebmi.org/the-fairfield-yards/.

Kelly, Jacques

 2019 "The B&O's Baltimore's Empire Left Its Imprint throughout the City." *Baltimore Sun*, November 30. https://www.baltimoresun.com/maryland/baltimore-city/bs-md-kelly-rail-20191130-jbj7vfq5m5dftcbw5oz7cmutj4-story.html.

King, Nicole

 2013 "Wagner's Point Oil Tank Explosion of 1920." Online blog. https://mappingbaybrook.org/2018/03/wagners-point-oil-tank-explosion-of-1920/.

 2014 "Preserving Places, Making Spaces in Baltimore: Seeing the Connections of Research, Teaching, and Service." *Journal of Urban History*, 40(3): 425–49.

 2020 "Strengthening UMBC's Public Humanities Infrastructure: The Baltimore Field School." Submitted as *Mellon Grant Proposal*, University of Maryland Baltimore County.

King, Nicole, Kate Drabinski, and Joshua Clark Davis

 2019 *Baltimore Revisited: Stories of Inequality and Resistance in a US City.* New Brunswick, NJ: Rutgers University Press.

King, Nicole, and Meghan Ashlin Rich

 2021 "Building Together in Baltimore? Corporate Mega Development and Coalitions for Community Power." *Urban Affairs Review* (June 24): 1–37. https://doi.org/10.1177/10780874211021325.

Klein, Allison

    2000   "Final Two Residents Close Book in Wagner's Point." *Baltimore Sun*, December 18. https://www.baltimoresun.com/news/bs-xpm -2000-12-18-0012180217-story.html.

Knezevich, Alison, and Christine Condon

    2020   "Baltimore Extends Trash Incinerator Contract Despite Protests." *Baltimore Sun*, November 5. https://www.baltimoresun.com /politics/bs-md-ci-bresco-contract-20201104-z5rqrc6qmbgg7jloa 565p2fo2y-story.html.

Kotlowitz, Alex

    2009   "All Boarded Up." *New York Times Sunday Magazine*, March 4. https://www.nytimes.com/2009/03/08/magazine/08Foreclosure -t.html.

Kramer, Miraim

    2021   "Recap: Jeff Bezos Heads to Space." *Axios*, July 20. https://www .axios.com/live-updates-jeff-bezos-space-blue-origin-9ecfdc37 -83c3-47bb-9daa-080e13068675.html.

Krauss, Louis

    2020   "BRESCO Protestors Wall Off Trucks, Decry a Renewed Contract." *Baltimore Brew*, July 30. https://baltimorebrew.com/2020 /07/30/bresco-protesters-wall-off-trucks-decry-a-renewed -contract/.

Kravetz, Daniel

    2016   "Who Will Benefit from Port Covington?" Shelter Force, October 21. https://shelterforce.org/2016/10/21/who-will-benefit-from -port-covington/.

Kurtz, Josh

    2021   "Hough Tries New Approach in Bid to End Clean Energy Subsidies for Trash Incinerators." *Maryland Matters*, February 11. https://www.marylandmatters.org/2021/02/11/hough-tries-new -approach-in-bid-to-end-clean-energy-subsidies-for-trash -incinerators/.

Lanahan, Lawrence

    2020   "Port Covington Community Investment Poised to Launch. Promises to Be Fulfilled?" *Baltimore Fishbowl*, September 24. https:// baltimorefishbowl.com/stories/port-covington-community -investment-poised-to-launch-promises-to-be-fulfilled/.

Leaders of a Beautiful Struggle

2020   Letter of Accountability by Leadership Team. June 13. https: /www.lbsbaltimore.com/letter-of-accountability/.

Lefebvre, Henri

1996   "Right to the City." In *Writings on Cities*, edited and translated by Eleonore Kofman and Elizabeth Lebas, 63–184. Cambridge: Blackwell Publishing.

Lesher, Peter

2008   "A Load of Guano: Baltimore and the Fertilizer Trade in the 19th century." *The Northern Mariner*. 18(3–4): 121–28.

Lieb, Emily

2015   "Baltimore Killed Freddie Gray." *Politico Magazine*, May 4. https://www.politico.com/magazine/story/2015/05/baltimore -freddie-gray-117614/.

Lockwood, Alan

2012   *The Silent Epidemic: Coal and the Hidden Threat to Health*. Cambridge, MA: MIT Press.

2017   "Interview with Alan Lockwood." MIT Press. Podcast. August 6. https://mitpress.podbean.com/e/episode-45-sep-12-alan-h -lockwood/.

Loperena, Christopher

2016   "A Divided Community: The Ethics and Politics of Activist Research." *Current Anthropology* 57(3): 332–46. https://doi.org/10 .1086/686301.

2017   "Honduras Is Open for Business: Extractivist Tourism as Sustainable Development in the Wake of Disaster." *Journal of Sustainable Tourism* 25(5): 618–33. https://doi.org/10.1080/09669582.2016.1231808.

Luttrell, Cecilia et al.

2007   "The Power Cube Explained." Poverty-Wellbeing.net https:// www.shareweb.ch/site/Poverty-Wellbeing/addressingpovertyin practice/Documents/The%20Power%20Cube%20Explained%20 -%20Cecilia%20Luttrell%20November%202007.pdf.

Marton, Adam, Natalie Sherman, and Caroline Pate

2018   "Port Covington Redevelopment Examined." *The Baltimore Sun*, August 3. https://data.baltimoresun.com/news/port-covington/.

Massey, Douglas, and Nancy Denton

1998   *American Apartheid: Segregation the Making of the Underclass*. Cambridge, MA: Harvard University Press.

Matthews, Joe

    1999a   "City Quietly Begins Buyout in Fairfield Chemical Companies and Government Make Competing Offers." *Baltimore Sun*, June 23. https://www.baltimoresun.com/news/bs-xpm-1999-06 -23-9906230185-story.html.

    1999b   "Goodbye to Wagner's Point; Departure: Legislation Condemning the Neighborhood Goes into Effect Today." *Baltimore Sun*, April 1. https://www.baltimoresun.com/news/bs-xpm-1999-04-01 -9904010319-story.html.

    1999c   "City says Fairfield buyout offer off table; City can't afford to move residents," Schmoke says. *Baltimore Sun* July 02. https://www .baltimoresun.com/news/bs-xpm-1999-07-02-9907020212-story.html.

Mayo Clinic

    2022a   "Asbestos: Symptoms and Causes." https://www.mayoclinic.org /diseases-conditions/asbestosis/symptoms-causes/syc-20354637.

    2022b   "Lead Poisoning." https://www.mayoclinic.org/diseases-conditions /lead-poisoning/symptoms-causes/syc-20354717.

McCraven, Marilyn

    1997   "City Begins Demolishing Huge Fairfield Homes Public Housing Complex: Workers Clearing Site for Use by Light Industry." *Baltimore Sun*, January 26. https://www.baltimoresun.com/news/bs -xpm-1997-01-26-1997026058-story.html.

Medoff, Peter, and Holly Sklar

    1994   *Streets of Hope: The Fall and Rise of an Urban Neighborhood*. Boston: South End Press.

#MeToo Baltimore

    2018   "Leaders of a Beautiful Struggle Petition Group." Facebook, August 16. https://www.facebook.com/Me-Too-Baltimore-27732 3679743691/posts/.

Mirabella, Lorraine

    2017   "Chemical Company Will Investigate Acid Leak in South Baltimore." *Baltimore Sun*, September 19. https://www.baltimoresun .com/maryland/baltimore-city/bs-bz-solvay-investigates-acid -leak-20170919-story.html.

    2022   "Two High-Profile Developers Join Port Covington Team to Take Over Next Phase of Development." *Baltimore Sun*, May 10. https://www.baltimoresun.com/business/bs-bz-port-covington

-developers-macfarlane-mag-20220510-7jylch33grcrzciwngbcwhd
6cy-story.html.

Morfeld, Peter, et al.

2002 "Dust Exposure, Pneumoconiosis and Lung Cancer: An Epide-
miological Study in the Saar Hard Coal Mining." *International
Journal of Occupational and Environmental Health*, 7: S36.

Moten, Fred, and Stefano Harney

2013 *The Undercommons: Fugitive Planning and Black Study*. New York:
Minor Compositions.

Muñoz, Ulysses

2020 "Baltimore Clean Air Advocates Hold Die in Outside BRESCO
Incinerator." *Baltimore Sun*, April 22. https://www.baltimoresun
.com/4f58a92e-a185-451e-8f83-62a7469cb6bd-132.html.

Murphy, Michelle

2016 *Chemical Exposure and Decolonial Potentials*. Paper presented to the
Gender, Bodies, and Technologies: (In)Visible Futures Conference, Virginia Tech. April 21–23.

Noor, Dharna

2021 "Space Tourism Is a Waste." *Gizmodo*, July 19. https://gizmodo.com
/space-tourism-is-a-waste-1847285820.

Noor, Jaisal

2019 "Fighting Apartheid by Taking Ownership of Land and Time."
Real News Network, October 23. https://therealnews.com/fighting
-apartheid-land-time-collective-baltimore.

Noor, Jaisal, Brandon Soderberg, and Lisa Snowden-McCray.

2021 "Battleground Baltimore: The Fight for Green Spaces." *Real News
Network*, July 2. https://therealnews.com/battleground-baltimore
-the-fight-for-green-spaces.

Olson, Sherry

1997 *Baltimore: The Building of an American City*. Johns Hopkins University Press.

Parshley, Lois

2020 "Deadly Mix of Covid19, Air Pollution, and Inequality,
Explained." *Vox*, April 11. https://www.vox.com/2020/4/11/21217040
/coronavirus-in-us-air-pollution-asthma-black-americans.

Patapsco Land Company

1874 *Curtis Bay: The Deep Water Harbor of Baltimore City*. Baltimore:
J. Murphy & Co.

Pellow, David Naguib

2018   *What Is Critical Environmental Justice?* Cambridge: Polity Press.

Pelton, Tom, and Amy Oakes

1999   "Murphy Homes Falls Victim to Change; Demolition: Building High-Rises for Public Housing Is an Idea Whose Time Is Past." *Baltimore Sun*, July 19. https://www.baltimoresun.com/news/bs -xpm-1999-07-02-9907020118-story.html.

Pietila, Antero

2010   *Not in My Neighborhood: How Bigotry Shaped the Great American City.* Chicago: Ivan R. Dee.

Plumer, Brad, and Nadja Popovich

2020   "How Decades of Racist Neighborhood Policy Left Neighborhoods Sweltering." *New York Times*, August 24. https://www.nytimes.com /interactive/2020/08/24/climate/racism-redlining-cities-global -warming.html.

Pollard, Sam, dir.

2021   *Slavery by Another Name.* PBS documentary. https://www.pbs.org /tpt/slavery-by-another-name/themes/sharecropping/.

Pompey, Kyle

2017   *Perspective: Baltimore.* Baltimore: Nice Shot Media.

Pulido, Laura

2008   FAQs: Frequently (Un)Asked Questions about Being a Scholar Activist. In *Engaging Contradictions: Theory, Politics and Methods of Activist Scholarship*, edited by Charles Hale, 341–46. Berkeley: University of California Press.

2016   "Flint, Environmental Racism, and Racial Capitalism." *Capitalism, Nature and Socialism* 27(3): 1–16. https://doi.org/10.1080/10455752.2016 .1213013.

2018   "Geographies of Race and Ethnicity III: Settler Colonialism and Nonnative People." *Progress in Human Geography* 42(2): 309–318. https://doi.org/10.1177%2F0309132516686011.

Pulido, Laura, and Juan de Lara

2018   "Reimagining the 'Justice' in Environment Justice: Radical Ecologies, Decolonial Thought, and the Black Radical Tradition." *Environment and Planning: Nature and Space* 1(1–2): 76–98. https://doi .org/10.1177%2F2514848618770363.

Purcell, Mark

2013   "Possible Worlds: Henri Lefebvre and the Right to the City." *Journal of Urban Affairs* 36(1): 141–54. https://doi.org/10.1111/juaf.12034.

Rabin, Yale

1990   "Expulsive Zoning: The Inequitable Legacy of Euclid." *Real Property, Probate and Trust Journal* 25(3): 591–595. American Bar Association.

Rakumakoe, Dr. Dulcy

2017   "Silicosis the Silent Killer." *Citizen*, October 16. https://citizen.co.za/news/south-africa/health/1690039/silicosis-the-silent-killer/.

Ramos, Annie

2021   "Filbert Street Garden Composts Food Waste into 'Black Gold' to Grow Produce for Community." *CBS Baltimore*, March 3. Video, 1:46. https://baltimore.cbslocal.com/2021/03/23/filbert-street-garden-turns-food-waste-into-black-gold-to-grow-produce-for-community/.

Rasmussen, Frederick

2010   "Are We Northern? Southern? Yes." *Baltimore Sun*, March 28. https://www.baltimoresun.com/maryland/bs-xpm-2010-03-28-bal-md-backstory28mar28-story.html.

Red Emma's

2021   "Right to the City: Baltimore Activists Talk Back to Anthropology." November 19, 2021. https://www.youtube.com/watch?v=xj1aSgLpgOs.

Rice, Kevin et al.

2014   "Environmental Mercury and Its Toxic Effects". *Journal of Preventive Medicine and Public Health* 47(2): 74–83.

Riofrancos, Thea, and Mark Paul

2021   "Biden Risks Botching a Key Chance to Fight Climate Change." *Washington Post*, June 30. https://www.washingtonpost.com/opinions/2021/06/30/biden-risks-botching-key-chance-fight-climate-change/.

Rodriguez, Akira Drake, et al.

2021   "Transforming Public Education: A Green New Deal for K–12 Public Schools." *Climate + Community Project*, July 15. https://www.climateandcommunity.org/gnd-for-k-12-public-schools.

Rosenthal, Greg

2013   "The United Workers: Toward a New Paradigm of Transformative Community-Labor Organizing." Unpublished MA thesis, University of Maryland Baltimore County.

Rubin, Lester, William Swift, and Herbert Northrup

1974   *Negro Employment in the Maritime Industries: A Study of Racial Policies in the Shipbuilding, Longshore, and Offshore Maritime Industries.* Philadelphia: University of Pennsylvania Press.

Rudacille, Deborah

2010   *Roots of Steel: Boom and Bust in an American Mill Town.* New York: Pantheon Books/Random House.

Ruetter, Marc

2022   "Outsted as Port Covington's Developer, Marc Weller Leaves Behind a $650 Million 'Game Changer' in Search of Occupants." *Baltimore Brew* May 19. https://www.baltimorebrew.com/2022/05/19/ousted-as-port-covingtons-developer-marc-weller-leaves-behind-a-650-million-game-changer-in-search-of-occupants/.

Rugh, Jacob, and Douglas Massey

2010   "Racial Segregation and the American Foreclosure Crisis." *American Sociological Review* 75(5): 629–51. https://doi.org/10.1177/0003122410380868.

Samuels, Barbara, and D'Sean Williams-Brown

2016   "Opposition to Port Covington Tax Increment Development District, Bond Issuance and Special Taxing District." American Civil Liberties Union of Maryland. Letter addressed to Jack Young President of City Council, July 27. https://www.aclu-md.org/sites/default/files/field_documents/port_covington_tif_testimony_citycouncil.pdf.

Sanchez, Chelsey

2019   "Industry City: A Green New Deal vs. Gentrification in Sunset Park." *The Indypendent,* April 1. https://indypendent.org/2019/04/industry-city-a-green-new-deal-vs-gentrification-in-sunset-park/.

Sanford, John

2003   "For Reich, 'Productive Discomfort' in Class Is Key to Socratic Method." *Stanford Report,* May 28. https://news.stanford.edu/news/2003/may28/socratic-528.html.

Santoro, Lais, and Bürge Abiral

2021   "No More Empty Promises: Hopkins Needs to Join Baltimore's Zero-Waste Movement Now." *Johns Hopkins News Letter,* June 6. https://www.jhunewsletter.com/article/2021/12/no-more-empty-promises-hopkins-needs-to-join-baltimores-zero-waste-movement-now.

Schuller, Mark

2010   "From Activist to Applied Anthropologist to Anthropologist? On the Politics of Collaboration." *Practicing Anthropology* 32(1): 43–47. http://www.jstor.org/stable/24781869.

Scott, Amy

2020   "Inequality by Design: How Redlining Continues to Shape Our Economy." *Marketplace*, April 16. https://www.marketplace.org /2020/04/16/inequality-by-design-how-redlining-continues-to -shape-our-economy/.

Shane, Scott

2019   "Prime Mover: How Amazon Wove Itself into the Life of an American City." *New York Times*, November 30. https://www .nytimes.com/2019/11/30/business/amazon-baltimore.html.

Shen, Fern

2010   "Battle Heating Up over South Baltimore Trash-Burning Plant." *Baltimore Brew*, June 29. https://www.baltimorebrew.com/2010/06 /29/14288/.

2012a   "Battle over South Baltimore Trash Incinerator Re-igniting." *Baltimore Brew*, August 30. https://www.baltimorebrew.com/2012/08 /30/battle-over-proposed-south-baltimore-trash-incinerator-re -igniting/.

2012b   "With Incineration Plan Curtis Bay Feels Dumped-On Again." *Baltimore Brew*, August 31. https://www.baltimorebrew.com/2012/08 /31/with-incinerator-plan-curtis-bay-feels-dumped-on-again/.

2015   "Incinerator Opponents, Charged with Trespassing, Are Released Today." *Baltimore Brew*, December 16. https://www.baltimorebrew .com/2015/12/16/incinerator-opponents-charged-with-trespassing -are-released-today/.

2016a   "Key Permit for Fairfield Trash Incinerator Revoked." *Baltimore Brew*, June 14. https://www.baltimorebrew.com/2016/06/14/key -permit-for-fairfield-trash-incinerator-revoked/.

2016b   "Young Leader of Curtis Bay Incinerator Fight Wins International Award." *Baltimore Brew*, April 18. https://www.baltimorebrew.com /2016/04/18/young-leader-of-curtis-bay-incinerator-fight-wins -international-award/.

2020a   "BRESCO Incinerator Is Poisoning Families, Protestors Outside Young's House Say." *Baltimore Brew*, October 11. https://www

.baltimorebrew.com/2020/10/11/bresco-incinerator-is-poisoning
-families-protesters-outside-youngs-house-say/.

2020b   "Wheelabrators' Donations to Filbert Street Garden Sparks Conflict in South Baltimore." *Baltimore Brew*, September 19. https://
baltimorebrew.com/2020/09/19/wheelabrators-donation-to
-filbert-street-garden-sparks-conflict-in-south-baltimore/.

Simmons, Melody

2022   "Two New Developers Take Over Port Covington as Weller Development Exits." *Baltimore Business Journal*, May 10. https://
www.bizjournals.com/baltimore/news/2022/05/10/port-covington
-new-developers-weller-exits.html.

Simpson, Audra

2014   *Mohawk Interruptus: Political Life across the Borders of Settler States.*
Durham, NC: Duke University Press.

Smith, Van

2014   "Trash Talk." *Baltimore Sun.* July 22. https://www.baltimoresun
.com/citypaper/bcp-trash-talk-20140722-story.html.

Speed, Shannon

2006   "At the Crossroads of Human Rights and Anthropology. Toward a Critically Engaged Activist Research." *American Anthropologist*
108(1): 66–76.

Spence, Lester

2015   *Knocking the Hustle: Against the Neoliberal Turn in Black Politics.* Brooklyn, NY: Punctum Books.

2018   "Why Baltimore Doesn't Heat Its Schools." *Jacobin*, January 12.
https://www.jacobinmag.com/2018/01/baltimore-freezing-schools
-children-racism-austerity.

Stack, Carol

1975   "All Our Kin: Strategies for Survival in a Black Community."
Social Service Review 49(1):142–44.

Stayner, Leslie, and Judith Graber

2011   "Does Exposure to Coal Dust Prevent or Cause Lung Cancer?"
Occupational and Environmental Medicine 68(3): 167–68. doi:10.1136
/oem.2009.048223.

Stockett, Letitia

1997   *Baltimore: A Not Too Serious History.* Baltimore: Johns Hopkins University Press.

Stuesse, Angela

2016   *Scratching Out a Living: Latinos, Race, and Work in the Deep South.* Oakland: University of California Press.

Sunrise Movement

2021   "Sunrise Movement Baltimore: Public Reckoning and Reflections on White Supremacy within Our Movement," August 24, 2021. https://sunrisemovementbaltimore-11813.medium.com/sunrise -movement-baltimore-public-reckoning-and-reflections-on-white -supremacy-within-our-3d66270ed509.

Sze, Julie

2007   *Noxious New York: The Racial Politics of Urban Health and Environmental Justice.* Cambridge, MA: MIT Press.

2018a   "Denormalizing Embodied Toxicity: The Case of Kettleman City." In *Racial Ecologies,* edited by Leilani Nishime and Kim D. Hester Williams, 107–22. Seattle: University of Washington Press.

2018b   *Sustainability: Approaches to Environmental Justice and Social Power.* New York: New York University Press.

2020   *Environmental Justice in a Moment of Danger.* Berkeley: University of California Press.

Taylor, Dorceta

2014   *Toxic Communities: Environmental Racism, Industrial Pollution and Residential Mobility.* New York: New York University Press.

Taylor, Keeanga-Yamahtta

2016   *From #BlackLivesMatter to Black Liberation.* Chicago: Haymarket Books.

2019   *Race for Profit: How Banks and Real Estate Industry Undermined Black Homeownership.* Chapel Hill: University of North Carolina Press.

Thurston, George

2017   "Written Report of George D. Thurston Regarding the Public Health Impacts of Air Emissions from the Wheelabrator Facility." Chesapeake Bay Foundation, November 20. https://www.cbf .org/document-library/cbf-reports/thurston-wheelabrator-health -impacts-2017.pdf.

Todd, Zoe

2015   "The Decolonial Turn 2.0: The Reckoning." *Anthroadendum,* June 15. https://anthrodendum.org/2018/06/15/the-decolonial-turn-2-0-the -reckoning/.

2019   Twitter Feeds about the American Anthropological Conference. Twitter, November 22.

Torre, Maria Elena et al.

2012   "Critical Participatory Action Research as Public Science." In *APA Handbook of Research Methods in Psychology* 2:171–84. Washington, DC: American Psychological Association. https://doi.org/10 .1037/13620-011.

Tuck, Eve

2008   "The Problem Tree." Blog. http://www.evetuck.com/problem -tree.

University of California Los Angeles

2020   "The Case for Letting Anthropology Burn: Race, Racism and Its Reckoning in America." Race, Racism, Policing and State Violence Lecture Series. Filmed by UCLA Department of Anthropology. Accessed on YouTube, September 23. https://www .youtube.com/watch?v=ScNbIWCRR4I.

US Department of Health and Human Services

1995   *Coal Mine Dust Exposures and Associated Health Outcomes: A Review of Information Since 1995.* Centers for Disease Control, and National Institute for Occupational Safety and Health. https://www.cdc .gov/niosh/docs/2011-172/pdfs/2011-172.pdf.

Vasudevan, Pavithra

2019   "An Intimate Inventory of Race and Waste." *Antipode* 53(3): 770–90. https://doi.org/10.1111/anti.12501.

Voyles, Traci Brynne

2015   *Wastelanding: Legacies of Uranium Mining in Navajo County.* Minneapolis: University of Minnesota Press.

Watford, Destiny

2015   "Speech on Divestment." Human Rights Dinner. https://d3n8a8 pro7vhmx.cloudfront.net/unitedworkers/pages/129/attachments /original/1432161058/SpeechOnDivestment.pdf?1432161058.

2016   Destiny Watford Profile. Goldman Prize Recipients of North America. https://www.goldmanprize.org/recipient/destiny-watford/

2017   "How One Student Activist Helped Her Community Stop a Polluting Incinerator." Filmed October at TEDxMidAtlantic. Video, 9:54. https://www.ted.com/talks/destiny_watford_how_one_student _activist_helped_her_community_stop_a_polluting_incinerator.

2021   Personal Letter addressed to United Worker and Leadership Council, September 4, 2021.

West, Paige

2016   *Teaching Decolonizing Methodologies.* Online blog, August 17. https:// paige-west.com/2016/08/17/teaching-decolonizing-methodologies/.

Wheeler, Timothy, and *Baltimore Sun*

2013   "Tighter Environmental Controls Sought for the Curtis Bay Terminal." *Baltimore Sun,* July 4. https://www.baltimoresun.com/news /environment/bs-xpm-2013-07-04-bs-gr-csx-coal-pier-20130703 -story.html.

Wiggins, Ryan, and Daniella Einik

2009   "Mayor versus Fairfield Improvement Company: The Public's Apprehension to Accept 19th Century Medical Advancements." *Legal History Publications* 17, June 10. https://digitalcommons.law .umaryland.edu/mlh_pubs/17/.

Williams, Rhonda

2004   *The Politics of Public Housing: Black Women's Struggles against Urban Inequality.* New York: Oxford University Press.

Williams, Timothy

2015   "Garbage Incinerators Make a Comeback, Kindling Both Garbage and Debate." *New York Times,* January 10. https://www.nytimes .com/2015/01/11/us/garbage-incinerators-make-comeback-kindling -both-garbage-and-debate.html.

Winbush, Raymond, et al.

2015   "A Comprehensive Demographic Profile of Cherry Hill Community in Baltimore City." Paper presented by the Institute for Urban Research. Morgan State University. https://www2.morgan .edu/Documents/ADMINISTRATION/CENTERS/IUR /Research/Cherry-Hill-Final-Report-1-1.pdf.

Wu, Xiao et al.

2020   "Air Pollution and COVID-19 Mortality in the United States: Strengths and Limitations of an Ecological Regression Analysis." *Science Advances* 6(45): 1–6. doi:10.1126/sciadv.abd4049.

WYPR

2019a   "Collecting the Steel Stories of Sparrow's Point." *On the Record,* April 16. Audio podcast, 26:36. https://www.wypr.org/show/on

-the-record/2019-04-16/collecting-the-steel-stories-of-sparrows
-point.

2019b   "A Toxic Legacy: Confronting Lead Poisoning in Baltimore."
Future City, WYPR, October 16. Audio podcast, 49:24. https://www
.wypr.org/show/future-city/2019-10-16/a-toxic-legacy-confronting
-lead-poisoning-in-baltimore.

INDEX

CALIFORNIA SERIES IN PUBLIC ANTHROPOLOGY

The California Series in Public Anthropology emphasizes the anthropologist's role as an engaged intellectual. It continues anthropology's commitment to being an ethnographic witness, to describing, in human terms, how life is lived beyond the borders of many readers' experiences. But it also adds a commitment, through ethnography, to reframing the terms of public debate—transforming received, accepted understandings of social issues with new insights, new framings.

Series Editor: Ieva Jusionyte (Harvard University)
Founding Editor: Robert Borofsky (Hawaii Pacific University)
Advisory Board: Catherine Besteman (Colby College),
Philippe Bourgois (UCLA), Jason De León (UCLA),
Laurence Ralph (Princeton University), and
Nancy Scheper-Hughes (UC Berkeley)

1. *Twice Dead: Organ Transplants and the Reinvention of Death,* by Margaret Lock

2. *Birthing the Nation: Strategies of Palestinian Women in Israel,* by Rhoda Ann Kanaaneh (with a foreword by Hanan Ashrawi)

3. *Annihilating Difference: The Anthropology of Genocide,* edited by Alexander Laban Hinton (with a foreword by Kenneth Roth)

4. *Pathologies of Power: Health, Human Rights, and the New War on the Poor,* by Paul Farmer (with a foreword by Amartya Sen)

5. *Buddha Is Hiding: Refugees, Citizenship, the New America,* by Aihwa Ong

6. *Chechnya: Life in a War-Torn Society,* by Valery Tishkov (with a foreword by Mikhail S. Gorbachev)

7. *Total Confinement: Madness and Reason in the Maximum Security Prison,* by Lorna A. Rhodes

8. *Paradise in Ashes: A Guatemalan Journey of Courage, Terror, and Hope,* by Beatriz Manz (with a foreword by Aryeh Neier)

Founded in 1893,
UNIVERSITY OF CALIFORNIA PRESS
publishes bold, progressive books and journals
on topics in the arts, humanities, social sciences,
and natural sciences—with a focus on social
justice issues—that inspire thought and action
among readers worldwide.

The UC PRESS FOUNDATION
raises funds to uphold the press's vital role
as an independent, nonprofit publisher, and
receives philanthropic support from a wide
range of individuals and institutions—and from
committed readers like you. To learn more, visit
ucpress.edu/supportus.

9 780520 379329